Manic depressive illness

Manic depressive illness

GEORGE WINOKUR, A.B., M.D

Professor of Psychiatry, Washington University
School of Medicine, St. Louis, Missouri

PAULA J. CLAYTON, B.S., M.D.

Assistant Professor of Psychiatry,
Washington University School of Medicine,
St. Louis, Missouri

THEODORE REICH, B.Sc., M.D., C.M.

Washington University School of Medicine, St. Louis, Missouri;
presently, Van Amerigen Fellow of the Foundations' Fund
for Research in Psychiatry in Population Genetics at the
University of Edinburgh, Scotland

Saint Louis

The C. V. Mosby Company

1969

Preface

This book is written from the vantage point of a classic position in psychiatry, which is characterized by the view that the more one understands about the patient's disease, as well as the patient as a person, the better will be his ability to offer some kind of therapeutic assistance to the patient. Further, this knowledge may lead to the potential discovery of significant etiologic factors. The classic position has close historical associations with all other fields of medicine. Adherence to it implies that the researcher or clinician is interested in a rigorous definition of an illness, a close perusal of specific symptoms, and knowledge of the course of the disease as a starting point for a specific etiology and treatment.

The classic position in psychiatry has its roots in medicine. Psychiatry at present is in a position similar to that of medicine in 1855, when Thomas Addison described such illnesses as Addison's disease and pernicious anemia. Much has been learned since that time, but subsequent advances have all been built upon the edifice that Addison constructed in his descriptions. Such descriptions of diseases are available in psychiatry today, although to a large extent they are ignored. Emil Kraepelin, the German psychiatrist, differentiated the major psychiatric illnesses, discussed their course and prognosis, and had something to say about their etiology. Findings over the past 60 years, particularly in the European countries, have shown these diagnostic categories to be valid and useful in terms of prognosis. The problems of cause in these illnesses, however, have certainly not been solved as yet.

Those who disagree with the classic viewpoint suggest that diagnosis is generally used for the sake of the record rather than with the idea that it has anything to offer in dealing with the patient. Some psychiatrists perceive as worthless all the countless facts that have been accumulated by systematic observers over the course of the years. We believe that to ignore such systematic material is a great error and makes it impossible to advance research and therapy in the psychiatric illnesses.

Critics of a classic position might say that a psychiatrist who adheres to this position does not take cognizance of the individual patient and his feelings but is interested only in the patient's disease. Such a complaint, however,

v

fails to recognize that using the knowledge of the natural history of the patient's illness is eminently helpful and necessary in dealing with the patient. This point may be illustrated by a homely but common example. A psychiatrist begins to see a young college student with a primary depression. As a symptom of this depression the student cannot concentrate, is failing at school, and feels that he should quit and join the Marines. The psychiatrist can deal with this very directly by pointing out to the patient that this solution is a symptom of his illness and a temporary idea that will change when his depression lifts. He most probably will insist that the patient make no major changes in his life while depressed. The psychiatrist is interested in all this patient's interactions with people as they could be directly related to the expected symptoms of his illness. It is impossible to treat a psychiatric patient and not become involved in his personal problems. The difference is that the classic psychiatrist makes few assumptions about causation of illness except as they are grounded in data.

The other criticism of the classic position is that the psychiatrist with this orientation is interested only in patients with definable diseases. As a result of rather stringent criteria of classification, a large number of patients seen fall into a category of undiagnosed psychiatric illness. These patients are followed very closely to observe the course of the illness. They are then best considered as subjects for clinical research. Treatment is largely empirical and the prognosis unknown. A smaller number of patients fall into what may be called "problems of living." These patients may be dealt with psychotherapeutically or may be referred to a social worker, minister, or family agency. Again no assumption about causation is made.

This book discusses manic depressive illness in terms of data collected over the course of many years. By our review of previous studies and our presentation of our own data, we have attempted to offer a set of clinical and genetic findings that are fundamental to the understanding of this illness. We believe that any subsequent studies, whether they be biologic, psychologic, or sociologic, must take into account these findings and build upon their foundations.

The book is divided into three essential sections. The first section deals with previous studies by many authors on the subject of manic depressive disease. In the second part are the results of our own clinical and genetic study of the entity. The third part encompasses possible etiologies and treatment for the disorder.

At this point we would like to express our gratitude to a number of people who have contributed to the completion of this work. We want to thank Dr. Eli Robins, Chairman of the Department of Psychiatry at Washington University School of Medicine, who has always been helpful and interested in our work and who provided a stimulating atmosphere in which we were able to function in an effective manner.

We are grateful, in particular, to Miss Jacquelyn Farrell, who did the lion's share of preparing the manuscript and also functioned as an editorial assistant for us in our efforts to produce the volume. Mrs. Suzi Kahn made important contributions to the preparation of the book. We also acknowledge the help of Miss Alice Stevenson and Mrs. Rita Rigg, the latter, like Macduff, having been "untimely ript" from us.

This work and the studies involved in it were supported in part by grants from the National Institute of Mental Health: MH 13002, MH 05804, MH 07081, and MH 14635.

George Winokur
Paula J. Clayton
Theodore Reich

Contents

Manic depressive illness

Chapter 1

In the beginning

Only occasionally do we have the good fortune to read a description of an illness recorded by a talented writer. For manic depressive disease this kind of description exists. Elliott Nugent, who coauthored *The Male Animal* with James Thurber and starred in the Broadway play "The Voice of the Turtle," has effectively chronicled the course of his manic depressive illness in his autobiography entitled *Events Leading Up to the Comedy*.[2] In his middle life, after many years of successful acting and writing, Mr. Nugent began to suffer from episodes of mania and depression. During his periods of excitement he felt elated and enthusiastic. He did not sleep much and involved himself in an excessive number of activities. He became involved in controversial issues and set off verbal brawls by public accusations. In the height of this excitement he was awake early in the morning and roamed about. Further, during these periods of mania he drank too much. While taking a Rorschach test, he made numerous choices and at the end of 15 minutes had not even finished the first Rorschach card. He was overactive in his behavior.

In describing one of his manic episodes, Mr. Nugent wrote:

> Without realizing that I was sliding into another period of overactivity like the 1947 one, I began to drink too much and to stay up with my various newfound friends until everything was closed—except a contract.
>
> One of the odd-ball notions that popped into my spinning brain that week was to send a cable to Constantin Simonov in Moscow, for the newspapers were full of frightening stories about a crisis in Iran. War with the Soviets seemed imminent, so I wrote a cable to my erstwhile acquaintance:
>
> "If you had listened to me, your comedy and I might today be on Broadway. Who writes the final curtain now? You consult Tolstoy and I will try Stephen Vincent Benét."
>
> I signed my name and addressed it to Simonov, in care of Joseph Stalin, Moscow.

These episodes of excitement alternated with periods of depression, during which time he worried about his financial status and frequently thought of suicide. He was filled with terror about his previous acts and worried over what he had not accomplished. His mood was extremely blue. On one occasion that he contemplated suicide, he wrote a note to his wife and ascended to the tenth floor of a hotel. He went out the fire escape door and looked down to the alley and floors below. A stranger opened the door and saw him. Mr. Nugent made a casual remark to the stranger. He then descended. His mood had changed and he scoffed "at my foolish terror." He tore up the note and went home.

He described the beginning of his despondency as follows:

> I concealed my depression quite successfully from Norma, the children, and to some extent from my father, but it began to grow that fall and I seldom went to sleep without dark thoughts of suicide. I had a goodly lot of life insurance, and this money together with our investments would amply provide for my family. However, I hated the idea of leaving my wife and daughters the memory of a husband and father who had been a cowardly suicide. I thought over various ways of meeting death that could be made to appear quite accidental. The simplest and most convincing would be a "fall" from the balcony of our penthouse.

After a number of such periods of elation and depression, the alternation ceased to occur. Judging from the book, one gathers that the illness left him with no residual psychiatric defect and he was able to lead an active and productive life.

Of his recovery, Mr. Nugent said:

> For the past four years I have not needed a psychiatrist or a hospital. This seems to indicate that the troubles I began to have almost twenty years ago are well under control—if not actually gone. I am happy, hopeful, but still watchful of myself at times.*

When was this disease first recognized? Perhaps it was not by chance alone that the first descriptions of manic depressive disease sprang from the mercurial temperament of the French. About the same time, the French clinicians Falret (1854) and Baillarger (1853) described recurring attacks of mania and melancholia.[3] For a long time, Falret had been studying depressive episodes accompanied by suicide trends and noted that some of them turned into periods of excitement which in turn reverted to depression. Baillarger, in addition to noting the double form of the disease, also observed that some melancholias became states of stupor.

The crystallization of manic depressive psychosis came with the work of Emil Kraepelin.[1] He separated manic depressive insanity from schizophrenia. Unlike schizophrenia, which he found to go on to chronic mental deterioration, he noted that in manic depressive disease there was a uniform prognosis with the end result being a complete disappearance of all morbid manifestations. Within his definition of manic depressive disease he included periodic and circular insanity manifested by depressions and manias, simple manias, melancholias, and finally some cases of delirious insanity. Within the same illness, he distinguished manic states with symptoms of flight of ideas, exalted mood and the pressure of activity from depressive states with sad or anxious moodiness and sluggishness of thought and action. As support for his view that manic depressive insanity was a uniform disease he pointed out that a hereditary factor was present. Members of the same family frequently showed pronounced periodic or circular cases of mania and depression and occasionally states of confusion and mood fluctuations.

In his 1921 monograph on manic depressive insanity, Kraepelin put a

---

*From Nugent, E.: Events leading up to the comedy, New York, 1965, Trident Press, division of Simon & Schuster, Inc., pp. 135, 161-162, 225.

great deal of effort in the delimitation of the illness. He believed that affective disorders classified under the rubric of *manic depressive disease* should include not only such forms as had alternating episodes of mania and depression but also those forms having only one or more manias or melancholias and no alternation. Further, he included the depressive attacks that have been called involutional melancholia in the category of manic depressive insanity. Under the same diagnosis he added those illnesses that were considered exhaustion stupors and some paranoias, particularly those that were periodic and had a good prognosis. Finally, he thought that some patients who had been described as psychopaths, neurasthenics, or hysterics and who also suffered from cyclic mood fluctuations should be considered as manic depressives. It is clear that a good part of Kraepelin's view in these matters was conditioned by a consideration of the course of the illness. He concluded that almost any illness with a good prognosis and with no deterioration could reasonably be thought of as manic depressive disease.

And yet there was some uncertainty in Kraepelin's mind. He stated, "Although . . . the composition of the clinical picture in all these cases will show certain differences, it is yet up till now often scarcely possible from the psychic state alone to come to a reliable decision." But a decision had to be made, and on the basis of the clinical material and outcome he included all the above clinical pictures as variants of manic depressive disease. Thus the seeds were sown for the controversy concerning the nosology of affective disorders, which has flourished up to the present time.

REFERENCES

1. Kraepelin, E.: Manic-depressive insanity and paranoia, Edinburgh, 1921, E. & S. Livingstone, Ltd.
2. Nugent, E.: Events leading up to the comedy, New York, 1965, Trident Press, division of Simon & Schuster, Inc.
3. Zilboorg, G.: A history of medical psychology, New York, 1941, W. W. Norton & Co., Inc.

Chapter 2

Epidemiologic and diagnostic considerations

By using Kraepelin's broad definition of manic depressive disease, which includes an episodic course of illness, the presence of affective symptoms, and remission without serious personality defect, we can cite some epidemiologic material.

Three kinds of studies are possible in the epidemiology of manic depressive disease. These methods give some estimate of risk or prevalence of a disease in a normal population. The first employs a sampling method in which a group of subjects who do not suffer from psychiatric diseases are evaluated for psychiatric illness in relatives. The second approach is that of the census investigation, in which a survey is made within a circumscribed area for the presence of psychiatric illness. The third type of survey is called the biographic method. In the biographic method a long-term follow-up of a randomly obtained group is used.

Stromgren reviewed the results of 18 studies using the sampling method and computed an expectancy rate for manic depressive disease of 0.21% in the general population.[22] Mayer-Gross, conducting a mental health survey in Scotland, used the census method and found that 0.35% of the people suffered from affective psychoses.[15]

In a recent study by Winokur and Pitts, using the sampling method, parents of 250 nonpsychiatric hospital patients were studied and a prevalence of affective disorder of 2% ± 0.62% was found. In this study a broad definition of affective disorder was used, which was similar to Kraepelin's idea of manic depressive disease. Affective disorders included the usual diagnoses of manic depressive disease, involutional psychosis, and psychotic depressive reaction as well as a socially incapacitating neurotic depressive reaction. A parent who became ill and socially incapacitated with depressive and/or manic symptoms and who recovered without defect whether or not he had been hospitalized was counted as having an affective disorder.[27]

Two very complete studies, using the biographic method, have been performed by Fremming on the Danish island of Bornholm and by Helgason in Iceland.[2,8] In both these biographic studies the disease rates in the population are expressed in terms of morbidity risk. The morbidity risk (or disease expectancy) is defined as an estimate of the probability that a person will develop the disease in question at some time or another during his life if he survives the period of risk (manifestation period) for the disease. Both the Fremming study on Bornholm Island and the Helgason study on Iceland calculate very similar morbidity risks. Both studies used essentially the same criteria for diagnosis. The racial stock of the Icelanders is different from the racial stock of the inhabitants of Bornholm Island. The Iceland study is more recent than the Bornholm study. It is also somewhat larger in numbers and is composed of 5395 probands, in whom relevant health date were obtained in 99.4% of the sample. The probands were born in 1895-1897 and were followed to the year 1957.

For the Helgason study, manic depressive psychosis was characterized by attacks of disturbance of affect with either elation or depression and a psychomotor change to overactivity or retardation. Attacks occurred without any clear-cut precipitant and resulted in an eventual recovery without defect. Involutional depression was included as part of the manic depressive psychoses. Another but separate diagnosis, which was relevant to manic depressive disease, was that of psychogenic psychosis. The most common psychogenic psychoses are those dominated by depressive symptoms. The third group, which could be considered as part of the Kraepelinian definition of manic depressive disease, was that of depressive neurosis. In the Iceland study the morbidity risk for manic depressive psychosis (certain plus uncertain diagnoses) was 2.18% for males and 3.23% for females. The morbidity risk for psychogenic psychoses (the majority of which are depressive in nature) was 0.81% for males and 1.50% for females. For depressive neuroses the morbidity risk for males was 2.25% and for females 4.14%. If one adopts the Kraepelinian viewpoint and assumes that all these affective disorder types are variants of manic depressive disease, it is possible to calculate the risk for the population to develop an affective disorder. One thousand eight hundred thirty-five males are at risk (for the period of risk of manic depressive disease), and 1948 females are at risk. There are 40 males and 63 females who have manic depressive disease, 17 males and 34 females who have psychogenic psychoses, and 42 males and 82 females who have depressive neuroses. For the entire group the risk for an affective disorder is 5.39% for males and 9.19% for females. Even if one eliminates the depressive neuroses, one may compute a rather high figure of 3.11% risk for males and 4.98% for females. Compare this to the risk of schizophrenia (certain and uncertain diagnoses), which is 0.69% for males and 1.02% for females! It is clear that affective disorders are many times more frequent in the population than schizophrenia. Using simply the conservative figures of manic depressive psychoses themselves (leaving out psychogenic psychoses and depressive neuroses), we can see that manic depressive psychoses are three times as frequent in the population as schizophrenia.

This leaves us, however, with a significant problem. Should all the various types of affective disorders be included under one rubric? In other words, are they all variants of manic depressive disease, or does the group of affective disorders contain a number of different diseases? One thing all these illnesses have in common is that they are *primary* and *affective* and that all the symptoms seem to arise from the affective component of the illness. An individual who has another disease that predates the affective component should not be counted as having an affective disorder. Thus, a person who is alcoholic or who had anxiety neurosis or hysteria prior to an affective episode should be counted as a person with a *secondary* affective disorder. Nevertheless, the *primary* affective disorders, in themselves, constitute a large number of people, and it is important to determine whether primary affective disorder might encompass one or several illnesses. The question arises as to how one might separate homogeneous categories of diseases from the large mass of primary affective disorders.

One method would be to compare clinical pictures; another would be to compare the course of illness in groups. These two methods will frequently, but not always, differentiate between homogeneous illnesses. Two other ways of dealing with diagnostic problems are available. Both of these depend on the finding of predisposing factors to disease. If one group of illnesses had a set of precipitating factors, psychologic, metabolic, or infectious, and another illness lacked these precipitating factors, there would be evidence for assuming that the illnesses were different. One other type of predisposing factor might be used in differentiation, that of the genetic background. If one group had a totally different family history as well as a different clinical picture, it would be clear that the two groups were representatives of separate disease entities. Much work has been done in attempting to divide up the affective disorders using these four methods or variations of them.

The obvious way to begin a differentiation of the varieties of affective disorder would be on the basis of the clinical picture. Kiloh and Garside published a careful clinical study of patients with affective disorders.[12] Using a factor analysis method, they studied 35 clinical features obtained from 31 patients with a "reasonably certain" clinical diagnosis of endogenous depression and 61 patients with a "reasonably certain" diagnosis of neurotic depression. An endogenous depression is presumably caused by some biologic dysfunction. A neurotic depression is often considered the same as a reactive depression and presumably is a reflection of some kind of external psychologic stress acting on the individual. Among their clinical features were personal details, personality traits, previous history of attacks of depression, and symptoms of the present illness. Their data enabled them to differentiate between neurotic and endogenous depression. Symptoms such as early morning awakening, retardation, diurnal variation, and weight loss correlated significantly with endogenous depressions. There was statistically significant evidence that more than one symptom picture was present. It seemed clear from the work of Kiloh and Garside that certain symptoms tended to hang together.

McConaghy, Joffe, and Murphy, in Australia, attempted a replication of the Kiloh and Garside work.[16] One hundred outpatient depressives were studied and a factor analysis was carried out on 40 clinical features. Of the 40 clinical features, 32 were the same as those used in the Kiloh and Garside study. Of the two symptom pictures that had been outlined by Kiloh and Garside, McConaghy and his co-workers found that neither differentiated the clinical features which were related to neurotic and endogenous depression. Further, eight clinical symptoms were investigated by the Australian authors. Four of these were considered most likely to be associated with endogenous depression; they were age 40 years or over, diurnal variation, significant weight loss, and early morning awakening. The other four features were presumed to be most likely associated with a neurotic depression; these were responsiveness to environmental changes, precipitating factors being present and causal, the presence of self-pity, and the presence of initial insomnia. With these eight symptoms, it was once again not possible to show a differentiation between patients. The authors concluded that the presence of clinical features of one form of depression in a patient in no way excluded the presence in the same patient of clinical features of the other form.

Other studies have separated out various affective disorders according to the symptomatology.

Grinker and co-workers present data indicating several typical subgroupings of depression.[3] In a study of 96 patients who were clinically depressed, they found five patterns of traits that describe the feelings and concerns of the patients. The first factor is characterized by hopelessness, failure, and guilt, the second by concern over material loss, the third by guilt over wrongdoing and a desire to make restitution, the fourth by "free anxiety," and the last by envy and martyred affliction. For behavior, the authors present ten factors: (1) withdrawal, (2) retardation, (3) retardation but less withdrawn than in (1), (4) complaining behavior, (5) somatic complaints, (6) "organic"-like syndrome, (7) agitation, (8) rigidity and psychomotor retardation, (9) minor somatic symptoms, and (10) ingratiating behavior. Grinker and his associates point out that these factors are not mutually exclusive and a number of them may be seen in any single patient.

Among the other factor analysis studies that separate out specific kinds of depressions is the one by Rosenthal and Gudeman.[20,21] These authors studied 100 acutely depressed female patients between the ages of 25 and 65 years, of whom half were inpatients, the other half being outpatients. The patients were rated on a 48–clinical item protocol. The authors separated out a factor that seemed to be similar to other studies and suggested an endogenous pattern. This factor significantly correlated with an absent precipitant, prior affective episodes, personality traits of an obsessive and depressive kind, and a lack of emotional reactivity. On this factor there was a heavy loading of such symptoms as worthlessness, retardation, guilt, decreased concentration, agitation, and diurnal variation. Going further, they separated out a second factor that was independent of the first factor and contained such symptoms as hypochondriasis, psychic anxiety, demanding behavior, and self-pity. The second factor was considered the "self-pitying constellation" in depression. These authors believe that the two factors may represent common clinical pictures rather than two separate disease entities.

That certain symptoms tend to cluster together seems to be a mathematical certainty, but whether this has any biologic meaning is an entirely different matter. Thus, one patient might present himself because of a number of spinal cord symptoms. These symptoms might include severe "lightening" pains in the legs, girdle pains, paresthesias, numbness and tingling of the trunk or hands or feet, and gastric crises. Ataxia might be a significant symptom, and urinary difficulties might occur in some of these patients. A second person might present confusion, apathy, and impaired judgment. Memory would be significantly poor for recent events. The patient might show delusions of wealth and prowess and, on neurologic examination, present tremors of the facial muscles and tongue. A third patient might present the symptoms of aortitis and aortic insufficiency. Aneurysms might develop and the patient might experience anginal attacks as well as congestive heart failure. In all three of the above cases the site of the lesion would determine the cluster of symptoms. However, because of advances in laboratory medicine and knowledge of a specific microorganism (the *Treponema pallidum*), all three of the cases cited above might be diagnosed as showing late manifestations of the same illness, namely, syphilis. Unfortunately, there are as yet no clear-cut pathologic or laboratory findings for affective disorders, and consequently it is not possible to say whether the presence of separate symptom clusters means that two separate diseases should be considered.

In a study that bridged the methods using clinical clusters to those using precipitating factors, Hamilton and White separated depressive patients into two groups, one reactive and the other endogenous.[4] The separation was done on the basis of precipitating factors, and when such factors were present, the patient was considered to have a reactive depression. The endogenous depressives differed from the reactive depressives in that they had more severe and more numerous symptoms of a retarded depression. Such symptoms were those of a depressed mood, guilt, suicide, insomnia, and retardation. There were no mutually exclusive criteria for the two diagnoses. Hamilton and White concluded that it was possible to differentiate the reactive depression from the endogenous or psychotic depression by both precipitating factors and the presence of certain symptoms. In the Hamilton and White study, no criteria were given for the determination of psychologic factors that might precipitate the illness; however, a few case studies were presented. In three cases Hamilton and White gave such psychologic precipitating factors as being left alone for prolonged periods when a wife went to look after the children, being put in charge of a program that was beyond the patient's capabilities, and learning that pulmonary tuberculosis which the patient had had for 9 years was found to be bilateral. All these cases responded to electroshock treatment, although one of the patients relapsed and ultimately committed suicide. A typical endogenous depression was one in which the content of the illness was such that the patient was anxious over business accounts although his business was thriving. Of importance is the fact that of the 64 patients studied, only 11, or 17 %, were clearly considered to be endogenous and 26, or 41 %, were clearly considered to be reactive. Twenty-seven, 42 %, were considered doubtful. Rose, using the same rating scale as Hamilton and White, studied 50 depressed patients.[19] Once again each of the patients was separated on etiologic grounds as being endogenous or reactive, with two doubtful groups. Unlike Hamilton and White, Rose found no significant differences in the symptoms between the groups. All types of depression were judged to be of equal severity. Rose did report that the group designated endogenous on the basis of absence of precipitating factors responded more favorably to electroconvulsive therapy. In a similar vein, Mendels reported that the symptoms usually seen in endogenous depressions were associated with a good response to electroconvulsive therapy.[17] However, not only is differentiation on the basis of clinical picture of questionable value, but so too is categorization on the basis of response to treatment. This seems particularly true when the treatment is symptomatic rather than being aimed at the etiologic factors involved in the disease. For example, electroshock treatment might be used in patients who have general paresis and are grossly manic or depressed. However electroshock treatment would have no value in treating symptoms of infectious aortitis that might be seen in late syphilis. Digitalis could be used in such patients, if they had congestive failure, but it would not be indicated in patients with tabes dorsalis or general paresis. Thus, the mere fact that a particular treatment modality is useful in treating a particular cluster of symptoms does not indicate that this cluster of symptoms must be considered a separate disease entity.

In all the above studies a diagnosis of reactive rather than endogenous depression could have been made in the presence of a history of a poorly adjusted premorbid personality. This might give poor responses to electroshock treatment due to the chronicity of the illness. Further, a neurotic or reactive depression diagnosis in these cases might even indicate the presence of another psychiatric disorder of a chronic nature, i.e., anxiety neurosis, hysteria, or alcoholism, in which case a depression would be of a *secondary* rather than a *primary* nature. Few of the studies have attempted to deal with differentiation between primary and secondary affective disorder, but it is a matter of great significance. In the one study in which a primary affective disorder picture was compared to the clinical picture of a secondary affective disorder no significant symptomatologic differences emerged. Nevertheless, the secondary affective disorder patients had clear histories of psychiatric illnesses prior to the onset of the affective problems.[29] It would be no surprise to find that such patients with chronic psychiatric illnesses and occasional affective symptoms responded differently to treatment that is usually considered valuable in primary affective disorders.

Because the clinical picture, including the response of the therapy, may not be reliable, one might employ other methods, preferably the methods that involve the use of predisposing factors. Two types of predisposing factors might be of value. One of these is the presence of psychologic events that could precipitate an affective disorder. Hamilton and White attempted to deal with this problem. Psychiatrists in the United States tend to differentiate affective disorders that they regard as reactions to psychologic stress from those that they regard as being manic depressive disease or endogenous in nature. In one study that employed the classification of affective disorders used by a group of practicing psychiatrists who normally separate psychotic depressive reaction, neurotic depressive reaction, and manic depressive reaction, no particular differentiation could be made.[25,26] Winokur and Pitts reported that it would have been possible to diagnose many of the patients with neurotic depressive reactions as having endogenous depression. Further, conditions such as alcoholism, hysteria, or anxiety neurosis might account for other groups of neurotic depressive reactions. In addition, the family histories of affective disorder among probands with psychotic depressive reactions and manic depressive disease, and also between probands with neurotic depressive reactions and endogenous affective disorders, were quite similar. Recently Hudgens and co-workers systematically studied a group of patients with primary affective disorder and compared them to a control group of hospitalized medical patients in order to determine the role of social and psychologic stress on the precipitation of the illness. They found no evidence that such stresses play a role of any importance in the pathogenesis of affective disorder.[10]

We may, then, conclude that by use of clinical picture or predisposing psychologic factors it is not possible to separate out specific diseases from the large mass of primary affective disorders. Under these circumstances we must search for a different method to accomplish such a differentiation.

A logical type of predisposing factor that could be used to differentiate between varieties of affective disorder is a genetic one. Hopkinson, in England, studied 100 affective disorder probands by separating them into an early-onset group (before the age of 50 years) and a late-onset group (after the age of 50 years).[9] Morbidity risks were calculated for affective illness in the first-degree relatives in the two proband groups. Comparing the two groups, he found a significant difference for affective disorder in the relatives of the two groups, with the relatives of the early-onset probands having a higher morbidity risk. This was barely significant and only so if all classes of first-degree relatives were considered together. Woodruff, Pitts, and Winokur approached the same problem from a somewhat different viewpoint.[30] They separated a group of patients age 50 years or more into those with no family history of affective disorder and those with such a family history. No differences between the two groups were found in the average age of admission for first psychiatric illness or in the average number of admissions per patient. No differences were found between the two groups as regards family history of alcoholism, schizophrenia, incidence of a recent death in the proband's family, or number of probands who were medically ill at the time of admission. There was thus no reason to differentiate the "genetically positive" from the "genetically negative" group of probands. In a subsequent study, Winokur and Clayton repeated the Hopkinson study with a larger number of probands.[24] The early-onset group had a higher morbidity risk for mothers and fathers having affective disorder than did the late-onset group. However, both male and female sibs were identical in morbidity risk for affective disorder in both the early-onset and the late-onset group. The difference in the risk for parents of the two groups may well have been the result of poor reporting on the part of the late-onset patients. Because of this, it seemed that there was no evidence in the Winokur and Clayton study that patients with an early- or late-onset affective disorder could be differentiated according to their family histories.

Winokur and Ruangtrakool examined the role of genetic factors in affective illness by studying a group of patients who were hospitalized for affective disorders. On the basis of the number of clinical variables, there were only negligible differences between those patients who had a positive family history of affective disorder and those with a negative family history.[28]

Although these preliminary attempts were not fruitful, the use of genetic factors to differentiate types of affective disorder appears to be a productive approach. This is because considerable evidence supports the importance of genetics as a predisposing factor in affective disorder. Hanna has presented a set of criteria that suggest genetic factors in traits of unknown etiology.[5] The first is a greater frequency of occurrence of the illness in relatives of probands than in the general population. Winokur and Pitts have published relevant data as regards this criterion.[27] The prevalence of affective disorder in mothers of affective disorder patients is 22.9 %. The prevalence for fathers is 13.6 %. For a group of well-matched controls, however, the prevalence is for mothers and fathers 1.1 % and 2.2 % respectively. As noted earlier in this book, the general population figures in the biographic studies of Fremming, in Denmark, and Helgason, in Iceland, show morbidity risks for manic depressive illness in males of 1.02 % to 2.18 % and in females from 2.24 % to 3.23 %.[2,8]

It is clear that all these control figures are significantly less than those presented for the parents of affective disorder patients in the Winokur and Pitts study. A second criterion is that of greater concordance in monozygotic than in dizygotic twins. This has been found in numerous studies. Slater and Kallman show expectancy rates of 100 % for monozygotic manic depressive twins; dizygotic twins have an expectancy rate of between 24 % and 25.5 %.[11] In a population study in Denmark, Harvald and Hauge studied all the twins born in the years 1870 to 1910 and found a 66 % concordance for manic depressive disease in 15 monozygotic pairs, a 9 % concordance in 23 same-sex dizygotic pairs, and a 0 % concordance in 17 opposite-sex dizygotic pairs.[6] A third criterion is that of increased frequency of defects in the same functional system in relatives of ill probands when they are compared to the general population. If one considers the problem of alcoholism, this appears to be true of affective disorder. Winokur and Pitts found that 9.5 % of the fathers of affective disorder patients suffered from alcoholism, as opposed to 2.2 % of the fathers in a group of matched controls.[27] A final relevant criterion is the observance of the onset of a characteristic age without any evidence of a precipitating event. This, of course, has been long disputed in the field of psychiatry, but Hudgens' systematic study of 40 affective disorder patients and 40 matched controls reveals little evidence to support the view that life events are of any great significance in the pathogenesis of affective disorder. In 1934 Aubrey Lewis, in making a clinical survey of depressive states, presented clinical data that would lead to the same conclusion.[14] As regards the age of risk or a characteristic time of onset, it must be noted that few patients with affective disorder become ill before their late teens or after the age of 70 years. This gives a very long period of risk and involves the need of a correction for age in any systematic study.

None of these data provide critical evidence necessary to establish a genetic etiology, but they are suggestive. Therefore, it seems reasonable to start from the assumption that genetic factors are involved in the etiology of affective disorders and to investigate the possibilities of differentiating between types of affective disorder on this basis. Actual proof of a genetic etiology in affective disorder for manic depressive disease awaits observation of (1) a distribution of offspring in families that would be consistent with a particular kind of genetic transmission, (2) a distribution of phenotypes in the population that would be compatible with the genetic model, (3) a disease association with a genetic trait (as in peptic ulcer, secretor status, and type O blood), or (4) chromosomal linkage between a known genetic marker and the disease in question. Although such incontrovertible proofs may be difficult to find, we may still work with some of the aspects of the genetics of an affective disorder population in order to differentiate types.

Accepting the probability that a genetic factor was of importance in affective disorder, Winokur and Clayton studied 426 affective disorder probands that were admitted to the hospital.[24] The purpose of the study was to determine whether certain kinds of genetic constellations could separate homogeneous clinical entities from the large mass of the affective disorders. In their study a number of discoveries were made. It was clear that if one examined the sibs of the 426 affective disorder patients there was an increased frequency of female sibs having affective disorder as compared with male sibs. If one

examined 91 probands with one parent affected, it was found that the morbidity risk of affective disorder for their sibs was 26 %; whereas if the probands
had neither parent affected, the morbidity risk for the sibs of the probands
was 12 %. Since almost a quarter of the probands were members of families
in whom there were two generations of affective disorder (the proband and a
parent), a reasonable assumption might be made that a dominant gene was
involved. Because the bulk of the probands had neither parent affected, this
might indicate that two illnesses were involved or that the gene did not manifest itself in the parents of most of the probands (incomplete penetrance).
If simple incomplete penetrance were the case, one might expect that the
number of sibs who were ill in the two classes of parents (both parents unaffected, 1 parent affected) would be equal. As a matter of fact, they were not,
and this suggests that there may be different types of affective disorder.

Further work by Winokur and Clayton compared two groups of probands,
those with a positive family history of affective disorder in two generations
versus those with a totally negative family history. A positive family history
in two generations contained the following possibilities: parent and proband
affected; parent, proband, and sib affected; proband and child affected; and
proband, sib, and child affected. There were 112 patients who fell into the
"two-generation" category and there were 129 patients who fell into the
category of having absolutely no family history of psychiatric disorder at all.
Depressive symptomatology in the two groups was extremely similar. The
male-female ratio, age of onset, and history of previous psychiatric episodes
did not differentiate the family history–positive group from the family history–negative group; however, there was a clear differentiation on the basis
of mania. Of the 112 two-generation probands, 16 were manic at the time of
admission to the study; only four of the 129 probands in the family history–
negative group were manic. About half the manic probands in the study came
from families that had two generations of affective illness.

A subsequent reevaluation of the records and follow-up of some of the
families indicated that of 110 probands of two generation–affected families
23 % had mania at some time during their lives; in the family history–negative group of 123, only 6 % had mania some time during their lives.[23] This
highly significant finding (p < 0.003) indicates the existence of two types
of affective disorder, with mania only occasionally being seen in those
patients without a family history of affective disorder or some other psychiatric illness. In other words, a clinical factor, namely the presence of mania,
and a genetic factor, namely the presence of the two-generation families,
seem to differentiate one group of affective disorder patients.

Other work supports this finding. Hays examined case summaries of
patients with affective disorders in a hospital and classified the patients
according to the mode of onset of their affective illness. There were four
types of onset depressions: (1) sudden onset, (2) gradual onset, (3) neurotic
onset, and (4) fluctuating onset. In the first group, the sudden-onset depressions, Hays showed more evidence of constitutional predisposition than in
the other groups and also found some evidence of hypomanic episodes or
cyclothymia.[7] Leonhard and co-workers found that manic depressives had
more affective illness in their family histories than did patients with other
types of depression.[13] He separated affective disorders on the basis of attack

picture, calling those with both manias and depressions, bipolar, and those with depressions only, monopolar.

An important confirmation of the fact that there are two kinds of affective disorder—manic depressive disease and depressive disease—may be obtained from the recent work of Perris, in Sweden.[18] Perris studied 138 bipolar (manic depressive) probands and 139 unipolar (recurrent depressive) psychotics. In the bipolar probands, bipolar heredity (definite and probable) occurred in 16 % of cases and unipolar heredity in 0.8 % of cases. Among the unipolar probands, a bipolar heredity was estimated to occur in 0.5 % of cases and a unipolar heredity in 10.6 % of the cases. These results show that the bipolar and unipolar recurrent depressive psychoses are genetically different forms of illness. Similar findings have been published by Angst.[1]

As a result of these recent contributions, it seems clear that a viable differentiation of affective disorders has been accomplished. Because some of the older clinical and genetic studies of manic depressive disease or affective disorder did not take this differentiation into account, it is quite difficult to interpret them. Contamination caused by heterogeneous illnesses being considered in one group leads to a lack of precision in the delineation of any of the illnesses. The remainder of this volume will be concerned with material relevant to a specific diagnosis that has been separated out from the mass of affective disorders, namely manic depressive disease. In order to be accepted as manic depressive disease, all illnesses must have a clear-cut mania at some time in their course. It is quite possible that among the remaining affective disorders there are a number of types of depressive diseases. However, since there seems to be a clean delineation of manic depressive disease, with the cutting point being the presence of mania, it seems reasonable to study this as a specific entity.

REFERENCES

1. Angst, J.: Zur Ätiologie und Nosologie endogener depressiver Psychosen, Monogr. Neurol. Psychiat. **112:**1, 1966.
2. Fremming, K.: The expectation of mental infirmity in a sample of the Danish population. Occasional papers on eugenics, no. 7, London, 1951, Cassell & Company, Ltd.
3. Grinker, R., Miller, J., Sabshin, M., Nunn, R., and Nunnally, J.: The phennomena of depressions, New York, 1961, Paul B. Hoeber, Inc.
4. Hamilton, M., and White, J.: Clinical symptoms in depressive states, J. Ment. Sci. **105:**985, 1959.
5. Hanna, B. L.: Genetic studies of family units. In Neel, J. O., Shaw, M. W., and Schull, W. J., editors: Genetics and the epidemiology of chronic diseases, Washington, 1965, U. S. Department of Health, Education, and Welfare.
6. Harvald, B., and Hauge, M.: Heredity factors elucidated by twin studies. In Neel, J. O., Shaw, M. W., and Schull, W. J., editors: Genetics and the epidemiology of chronic diseases, Washington, 1965, U. S. Department of Health, Education, and Welfare.
7. Hays, P.: Modes of onset of psychotic depression, Brit. Med. J. **2:**779, 1964.
8. Helgason, T.: Epidemiology of mental disorders in Iceland, Acta Psychiat. Scand. **40:**(Supp. 173), 1964.
9. Hopkinson, G.: A genetic study of affective illness in patients over 50, Brit. J. Psychiat. **110:**244, 1964.
10. Hudgens, R., Morrison, J. R., and Barchha, R.: Life events and the onset of

primary affective disorders: a study of 40 hospitalized patients and 40 controls, Arch. Gen. Psychiat. **16**:134, 1967.

11. Kallman, F.: Genetic principles in manic-depressive psychosis. In Zubin, J., and Hoch, P., editors: Depression, Proceedings of the American Psychopathological Association, New York, 1954, Grune & Stratton, Inc.
12. Kiloh, L. G., and Garside, R. F.: The independence of neurotic depression and endogenous depression, Brit. J. Psychiat. **109**:451, 1963.
13. Leonhard, K., Korff, I., and Schulz, H.: Die Temperamente in den Familien der monopolaren und bipolaren phasischen Psychosen, Psychiat. Neurol. **143**:416, 1962.
14. Lewis, A. J.: Melancholia: a clinical survey of depressive states, J. Ment. Sci. **80**:277, 1934.
15. Mayer-Gross, W.: Mental health survey in a rural area, Eugen. Rev. **50**:140, 1948.
16. McConaghy, N., Joffe, A. D., and Murphy, B.: The independence of neurotic and endogenous depression, Brit. J. Psychiat. **113**:479, 1967.
17. Mendels, J.: Electroconvulsive therapy and depression: I. The prognostic significance of clinical factors, Brit. J. Psychiat. **3**:675, 1965.
18. Perris, C., editor: A study of bipolar (manic-depressive) and unipolar recurrent depressive psychoses, Acta Psychiat. Scand. **42**:1 (Supp. 194), 1966.
19. Rose, J. T.: Reactive and endogenous depressions—response to ECT, Brit. J. Psychiat. **109**:213, 1963.
20. Rosenthal, S. H., and Gudeman, J. E.: The endogenous depressive pattern, an empirical investigation, Arch. Gen. Psychiat. **16**:241, 1967.
21. Rosenthal, S. H., and Gudeman, J. E.: The self-pitying constellation in depression, Brit. J. Psychiat. **113**:485, 1967.
22. Stromgren, E.: Statistical and genetical population studies within psychiatry. Methods and principal results, Congres International de Psychiatrie **5**:155, 1950.
23. Winokur, G.: Genetic principles in the clarification of clinical issues in affective disorder. Presented at the annual meeting of the A. A. A. S., New York City, Dec. 29, 1967. In Mandell, A. J., and Mandell, M. P., editors: Methods and theory in human psychochemical research, New York, Academic Press, Inc. (In press.)
24. Winokur, G., and Clayton, P.: Family history studies: I. Two types of affective disorders separated according to genetic and clinical factors. In Wortis, J., editor: Recent advances in biological psychiatry, New York, 1967, Plenum Publishing Corp., vol. 9.
25. Winokur, G., and Pitts, F. N., Jr.: Affective disorder: I. Is reactive depression an entity? J. Nerv. Ment. Dis. **138**:541, 1964.
26. Winokur, G., and Pitts, F. N., Jr.: Affective disorder: V. The diagnostic validity of depressive reactions, Psychiat. Quart. **39**:727, 1965.
27. Winokur, G., and Pitts, F. N., Jr.: Affective disorder: VI. A family history study of prevalences, sex differences and possible genetic factors, J. Psychiat. Res. **3**:113, 1965.
28. Winokur, G., and Ruangtrakool, S.: Genetic vs. nongenetic affective disorder, Amer. J. Psychiat. **123**:703, 1966.
29. Woodruff, R. A., Jr., Murphy, G. E., and Herjanic, M.: The natural history of affective disorder: I. Symptoms of 72 patients at the time of index hospital admission, J. Psychiat. Res. **5**:255, 1967.
30. Woodruff, R., Pitts, F. N., Jr., and Winokur, G.: Affective disorder: II. A comparison of patients with endogenous depressions with and without family history of affective disorder, J. Nerv. Ment. Dis. **139**:49, 1964.

Chapter 3

Clinical picture: symptoms, course, and outcome

Because the rigorous definition of manic depressive disease demands the presence of mania in the illness, very few studies have been done that describe the characteristics of a pure group. Most of the work on manic depressive disease heretofore has been done using patients with one or more depressive episodes or a manic and depressive episode or several manic episodes. From the previous chapter, it has become clear, however, that the differentiation of manic depressive disease is a reliable one from a genetic standpoint and depends on the presence of mania in the proband. Only a few studies are available that conform to this definition.

There has been little improvement in the description of the symptom picture of manic depressive disease since Kraepelin's work.[4] He describes attacks of manic excitement that occasionally run their course within a few weeks or a few days but usually extend over many months. He divides the symptom picture according to severity. *Hypomania* is characterized by an inability to work steadily and logically and an incapacity to carry out a definite series of thoughts. A slight flight of ideas makes a distinct appearance. Recollection of recent events is sometimes not exact and frequently augmented by original additions. The patient has no insight and does not think that he is ill; his mood is predominantly cheerful and frequently humorous; and he is sure of success. His actions are impulsive; he has a heightened capacity to work; and he shows an increased busyness. He is frequently restless and changeable. Sexual interests are increased. His movements are lively as a rule, and the patient is often verbose and bombastic. Hypomanic attacks frequently have a long duration and merge into the second level of illness, that of acute mania.

Acute mania usually has a sudden onset; patients become restless and disconnected in their thoughts and speech. All the symptoms that are seen in hypomania are increased in severity. Frequently, fleeting delusions are present. These are generally of a grandiose nature, and the patient often thinks that he is a genius or has some special ability. His mood is unrestrained and exalted and frequently pompous. He cannot sit or lie still; his motor behavior is markedly increased. He jumps around, hops, dances, and is constantly busy. Occasionally he may be destructive. His movements are excessive and often characterized by such things as making faces, saluting in a military fashion, and making constant jokes.

The third type of mania described by Kraepelin is that of *delusional mania.*

The patient is restless, meddlesome; his mood is cheerful and self-conscious. Frequently, however, he will break down in tears. In delusional mania the patient perceives his surroundings to be changed and sometimes has visual as well as auditory hallucinations. Delusions are frequently in the religious area, and there may also be delusions of royal descent or delusions of being immensely wealthy. In delusional mania, excitement is not usually very severe and the patients may appear to be relatively well ordered; however, they do remain restless and meddlesome, and they sing, preach, and are mischief makers.

Finally, Kraepelin describes *delirious mania,* which is accompanied by a dreamy state with profound clouding of consciousness, confused hallucinations, and delusions. The onset is very sudden. Sleeplessness, restlessness, and anxious moodiness may be conspicuous for 1 or 2 days, and then the consciousness becomes clouded. The mood is very changeable in delirious mania. The patient is distractible, often unrestrainably merry, frequently cries, and often shows erotic or ecstatic moods. He is sometimes irritable and sometimes indifferent. In the beginning the patients display senseless raving and excitement and dance about. They show disconnected talk and senseless rhyming. They frequently pray and are abusive. Some patients, however, display only a slight restlessness and whisper flights of ideas to themselves. This state is subject to many fluctuations. At times the patients are quiet but are still confused, and there is a change between excitement and stupor. Slowly the morbid symptoms disappear and recollection of the delirious state is usually dim. An almost complete amnesia for the episode frequently follows.

Clinicians often observe a mixed type of manic depressive illness. This type contains marked mixtures of manic and depressive symptoms on examination. A circular type of illness is also seen. In the circular type there is a continuous alternation of manias and depressions.

Other descriptions of the manic state exist. Clayton, Pitts, and Winokur describe the symptoms in 31 patients who were admitted to a psychiatric hospital with mania.[2] Almost all of them showed hyperactivity, euphoria, flight of ideas, distractibility, circumstantiality, and push of speech. Frequently they showed increased sexuality, grandiosity and/or religiosity, decreased sleep, delusions, and ideas of reference. Such symptoms as depersonalization, derealization, and passivity were also seen in these manic patients. Wellner and Marstal studied 279 manic episodes.[11] About 30% of the patients were strictly typical and showed the three cardinal symptoms of mania, i.e., elevated mood, flight of ideas, and psychomotor overactivity. About 40% of the patients were atypical. Some presented delusions that were not in harmony with the basic deviation of mood; others showed transient autism, ideas of influence, or thought derailment. Still others showed a mixture of paranoid- and hebephrenic-like symptoms. Very rapid mood swings were associated with the occurrence of the atypical state.

The sexual behavior of manic patients has been described by Allison and Wilson.[1] They studied 24 manic patients, of whom 12 were male and 12 were female. Women were far more active in their display of sexuality and seductiveness than the men. Of the women, 83% seemed to have an increase of sexual drive as compared to 58% of the men. There was little change in masturbatory activities among either the men or the women. The kinds of sexual display that were increased were frequent mentions of sexual matters and flirtations, constant talk of sex, and being openly seductive with sexual overtures both physical and verbal. Homosexual oral genital activity was rare in these patients during their illnesses.

One of the major questions about the manic attack is how frequently subsequent attacks change their coloring and become depressive. Lundquist, in a very distinguished study on the prognosis and course of manic depressive disease, followed 95 manic patients who recovered from their first attack.[5] Of these, 43 became ill at least once more. Of these relapses, 11.6 % showed a depressive symptom picture at the time of the second attack. It is clear also from the study of Perris in Sweden that the patients who show pure mania, i.e., no attacks that are other than manic, are relatively unusual. In his study he reported on 138 manic depressives (bipolar), 139 patients who had simply recurrent depressions (unipolar), but only 17 patients who had episodes of mania alone.[7] Lundquist followed 172 depressives who recovered from their first attack. Of these, 67 had at least one relapse. Ten of these relapsing depressives, or 15 %, had a manic episode as their second attack.

The clinical picture of depression poses a considerably different problem. Most studies have not dealt with rigorously defined manic depressive disease. There has been such a large admixture of depressive disease patients (unipolar) in them that it is difficult to tell whether the quality of depression in manic depressive disease is different from the quality of depression in a unipolar psychosis. Kraepelin described the symptoms of depressive states rather well, however; and with the proviso that there may be some difference in the depressive states associated with mania as opposed to those that are simply recurrent depressive states, it is possible to describe the clinical picture. Once more Kraepelin separated his groups according to severity.

The first of these is *melancholia simplex*, in which the mood is dominated by a profound inward dejection. The patient is hopeless; he is indescribably unhappy, skeptical. Everything is disagreeable; he sees only the dark side of life; the world appears to him aimless, and he feels superfluous. Phobias may occur in simple melancholia and the patient is tormented with guilt feelings. Energy is virtually absent; the patient has depressive concomitants such as decreased sexual interest, anorexia and weight loss, sleep disturbance with early morning awakening, and psychomotor retardation. Not all these symptoms are always present in each depressive episode.

The second type of depression is *stupor*. The patient is apathetic and has difficulty perceiving his surroundings and assimilating them. Sometimes he will make occasional detached utterances with confused ideas. He speaks infrequently and may lie mute in bed. *Melancholia gravis* is the third type, in which a patient experiences hallucinations and may see figures and spirits of relatives. Ideas of sin are frequently seen and the person feels that he has led a horrible life and is an abomination on the face of the earth. Sometimes the patient has ideas of persecution, and these are closely related to sinful delusions. The patient may also have somatic delusions with the idea that various parts of his body are rotting away or not functioning in a proper fashion.

Another type of depressive state is a *paranoid melancholia*, where ideas of persecution and hallucinations of hearing voices are frequently present. The patients feel themselves watched and spied upon. Their mood is gloomy and despondent. There is a volitional inhibition and a strong tendency to suicide.

Fantastic melancholia is accompanied by a greater development of delusions and abundant hallucinations of such things as evil spirits, crowds of monsters, a gray head with sharp teeth, angels, Satan, and the Virgin Mary. There is an extraordinary number of delusions and much feeling of guilt, and there are many hypochondriacal delusions with peculiar ideas about bodily deterioration. Consciousness in this form is somewhat clouded at times; mood is characterized by a dull despondency. The patients lie in bed with vacant, restrained expressions on their faces. At other times the patient may scream and throw himself on the floor and beat his head against the wall.

Finally, Kraepelin describes *delirious melancholia,* which has a profound clouding of consciousness. The patient experiences numerous and terrifying hallucinations; he may be mute and inaccessible and feel forsaken. It is clear from the above descriptions that we cannot clearly differentiate one of these clinical pictures from another.

Various degrees of severity of the above states of mania and depression are commonly seen in any hospital that admits acutely ill psychiatric patients. In one study, approximately 40% of patients consecutively admitted to a psychiatric section of a general hospital had some kind of primary affective disorder.[2] Of this group of primary affective disorders, 14% of the patients (5% of the total admissions) had at some time in their lives experienced a mania. In this same American hospital the ratio of manic to depressed at the time of admission was estimated to be 1:11.[2] These figures lend credence to the idea that affective disorders, in general, and manic depressive disease, in particular, constitute a significant portion of the acutely ill psychiatric population.

Although most studies have not separated manic depressive disease from the great mass of affective disorders, some data are available concerning the age of onset of manic depressive disease. In one study, 28 manics were matched with 28 depressive probands on the variables of age, sex, and socioeconomic status. The age of onset in the manic patients was 28 years, and in the depressive patients 35 years. This difference was significant at the 0.05 level of reliability. Of 31 manics in this study, the first type of illness was mania in eight probands and depression in 12. A miscellaneous group of first illnesses was noted in the remainder of the patients.[2] Reich, Clayton, and Winokur studied 59 manics and 353 cases of depression.[10] The age of onset of illness was 34.6 years in the manics and 39 years in the depressives. Once again it appeared that illness in manic depressives starts earlier than illness in patients who simply have depressive disease. Lundquist studied 103 manics at time of first admission to a psychiatric hospital and noted that the modal age for first admission in these patients was under 30 years.[5] Fifty-four percent of the manic patients were first admitted at less than 30 years of age. On the other hand, in 219 depressives the modal age of first admission was between 30 and 39 years, with 69.1% of the group fitting into this category. In a study of 2000 first admissions for manic attacks, Wertham found a modal age between 20 and 25 years.[12] Although cases are rare in which mania develops for the first time before 15 years of age, such cases do occur; and a first manic attack was noted by Wertham to occur as late as the interval between 70 and 75 years of age.

Perris, after separating his bipolar and unipolar patients, found a mean age of onset of 33 years in bipolar males and 30 years in bipolar females.[8] This was considerably lower than the figures for unipolar males (49 years) and unipolar females (39 years). In the bipolar patients, if the first episode was a mania, male patients had their onset at a significantly younger age (25.5 years) than female patients (35.2 years). If the first episode was a depression, bipolar females had their onset at a significantly younger age (27.9 years) than bipolar males (37.0 years). Very few (7%) of the bipolar patients showed relapses of the same kind as the first episode (depressive or manic) before they had an episode of the opposite polarity. This last finding is somewhat in conflict with the findings of Lundquist on changes in polarity that have been noted above.

In summary, it does appear that the onset of manic depressive disease is more frequently associated with an onset at a younger age than depressive disease.

In his large study of 2000 cases, Wertham found that the modal duration of the first manic attack was between 60 and 180 days. Over 50% of the patients had an illness that lasted less than 6 months. About 15% of the 2000 patients had a duration of more than 18 months and a few had durations that lasted more than 5 years. Lundquist, in his 319 cases of first admissions of manic depressive patients (103 manics, 216 depressives), found a variable duration of the first illness. Half of both the manics and depressives who were under 30 years of age at the time they became first ill had an illness that lasted up to 6 months and 75% were well by 10 months. However, of both manics and depressives who were more than 30 years old at the time of the first illness, half the patients remained ill up to 9 months and 75% of the patients were well by 15 months. In those patients who had second attacks of both manias and depressions the duration of the second attacks was not significantly different from the duration of the first attacks. Some clinicians have thought that in cases of repeated attacks the duration of the episodes tends to become longer and longer. Lundquist's studies have indicated that this is not true. In the group of manics who became ill at the younger ages the duration of the attacks tended to be about the same as for the first attacks. However, in the group of older manics, Lundquist found significant differences between the first and subsequent attacks, with the subsequent attacks becoming considerably shorter. This appeared to be related to the fact that in a number of cases the older manics had very long first attacks. In general, assurance can be given to a patient and to his family that subsequent episodes of illness after a first mania (or even a first depression) will not tend toward a more chronic course.

Some data are available concerning the problem of recurrence of attacks. Pollack studied several thousand patients who had statistical files in the New York State Department of Mental Hygiene.[9] He found a statistical record of over 8000 manic depressive cases and followed these cases from 1909 to 1920. In this period of time over half the patients admitted for the first attack of mania had not had a subsequent attack. Twenty percent of the manics had had three attacks or more. Over half the patients admitted first for depression had not had a subsequent attack either, and 17 % had had three attacks or more. Patients who had their first attack prior to the age of 20 or after the age of 40 years tended to have more recurrences of attacks than did those patients who had their first episode between 20 and 40 years of age. Lundquist, in his careful study, also took up the problem of recurrence at some length. His study involves a 20-year follow-up of first admissions. He noted that about half the manics have only a single attack and that about 60 % to 70 % of the depressives have only single depressions. In manics who first become ill prior to the age of 30 years the risk for a recurrence after a first attack was greater than in the older manics. About 33 % of these patients had a relapse within 3 years. On the other hand, manics who were older than 30 years had only about a one-in-ten probability of a relapse within 3 years. The young depressive, in contradistinction to the young manic, had only about a 12 % relapse rate in the course of 3 years. The Lundquist data are particularly noteworthy in reference to the young manics. Most of these patients were very young, with an average age of about 21 years; and of 13 patients, eight had four attacks or more within 3 years. Thus the risk for multiple attacks was greatest for manics and particularly great for those who developed their illness very early in life. Symptom-free intervals between attacks varied in length in the young patients, but in older patients the interval between first and second attack was longer than between subsequent attacks.

Perris noted that 31 % of bipolar patients suffered eight or more episodes of illness, as compared with 4 % of the unipolar patients.[8] He also reports that those bipolar patients in whom the first episode is a mania will be more likely to have a preponderance of manias in their subsequent illnesses; and those bipolar patients in whom the first episode is a depression will have a preponderance of depressions in their subsequent illnesses.

In general, it would appear that manic depressive disease is more likely to be associated with relapses than depressive disease. However, a considerable number of patients will experience only one attack.

The outcome of the illness has been described at some length in the literature. Lundquist noted that of his 103 patients who were manic at first admission, nine had been misdiagnosed and were found later to be schizophrenics. Of his 216 patients initially diagnosed as depressives, schizophrenia was diagnosed later in 13 patients. This is a rather small number (for the combined groups about 7 %) and seems well within the limits of diagnostic error. Of the original manics, eight developed a chronic mania. If one subtracts the nine schizophrenics from the 103 patients, 94 patients remain; and of these, eight (8.5 %) developed a chronic course. Wertham studied six cases of chronic manic excitement. These excitements were from 5 to 11 years in duration. Four of these patients had either previous or subsequent manic attacks, and in two of them the prolonged excitement was the only attack. Onset of the prolonged attack occurred at a mature age. Four of the chronic manics were 50 or more years old at the time of the onset of their chronic mania. Two others were in their middle to late thirties. Wertham also noted that chronicity in mania sometimes manifested itself as sociopathy and occasionally as a paranoid syndrome. MacDonald also presented evidence supporting the view that mania occurs on a chronic basis more often after 40 years of age than before.[6] It is clear, however, that most patients do not follow a chronic course.

In the past, because of relatively ineffective treatment, there were frequent deaths in manic depressive disease. Derby described a high death rate at a receiving hospital for acute manic depressive cases.[3] The largest number of deaths (40%) seemed to be clinically due to exhaustion and excitement. The majority of the patients who died were of a manic type or were mixed, showing symptoms of both mania and depression. In 20 cases of manic depressive patients who died and were autopsied, eight showed such findings as lobar pneumonia, acute hemorrhagic pancreatitis, gangrenous nephritis, etc. The remaining 12 autopsied cases showed only slight anatomic findings and were considered to be exhaustion deaths. In those cases there was an absence of significant positive findings—excepting an expression of terminal toxic condition represented by a subacute nephritic reaction, general dehydration, evidence of insufficient feeding, and a dilated heart with thin walls, which was an expression of the manner of death. In recent years, with more effective treatment, such exhaustion deaths are not usually reported.

It appears that the outcome of manic depressive disease is characterized by (1) not eventuating in a diagnosis of schizophrenia and (2) usually not becoming chronic. Kraepelin was insistent that manic depressive disease was characterized by a *restitutio in integrum* after an attack. Lundquist's data on this point are good. Of his original 103 manics, about 85% could be designated as socially recovered from their attacks. These patients had one or more attacks, with symptom-free intervals. When the patients recovered, there was no difficulty resuming their usual occupations. Lundquist, however, does discuss the mental symptoms of what he calls "insufficiency," which was seen in some of the patients. An occasional patient lacked spontaneity and was unable to manage his work; another patient was considered high strung and unstable; and a third frequently consulted the psychiatric clinic for such things as nervous troubles, insomnia, and occasional hypomania. In general, Lundquist's patients appeared to have a very satisfactory recovery from their manic depressive psychoses. There was no basis to consider that manic depressive psychosis permanently affected those who suffered from it. In this way it is, of course, different from schizophrenia.

At this point it is possible to characterize manic depressive disease as an episodic illness usually with good social functioning between episodes. For the diagnosis of manic depressive disease, there must always be one episode of mania or excitement. Subsequent episodes may be manic or depressive; rarely are all the episodes manic. Specific symptoms are seen in the depressions and manias. In a significant number of patients, only one episode of illness occurs. Each episode is usually a few months in duration, but an episode may go on to chronicity in the unusual case. Only rarely does an important personality defect follow an episode of the illness.

REFERENCES

1. Allison, J. B., and Wilson, W. P.: Sexual behavior of manic patients: a preliminary report, Southern Med. J. **53**:870, 1960.
2. Clayton, P. J., Pitts, F. N., Jr., and Winokur, G.: Affective disorder: IV. Mania, Compr. Psychiat. **6**:313, 1965.
3. Derby, I. M.: Manic-depressive "exhaustion" deaths, Psychiat. Quart. **7**:436, 1933.

4. Kraepelin, E.: Manic-depressive insanity and paranoia, Edinburgh, 1921, E. & S. Livingstone, Ltd.
5. Lundquist, G.: Prognosis and course in manic-depressive psychoses, Acta Psychiat. Neurol. (Supp. 35), 1945.
6. MacDonald, J. B.: Prognosis in manic-depressive insanity, J. Nerv. Ment. Dis. 47:20, 1918.
7. Perris, C., editor: A study of bipolar (manic-depressive) and unipolar recurrent depressive psychoses, Acta Psychiat. Scand. 42:(Supp. 194), 1966.
8. Perris, C.: The course of depressive psychoses, Acta Psychiat. Scand. 44:238, 1968.
9. Pollack, H.: Recurrence of attacks in manic depressive psychoses, Amer. J. Psychiat. 11:567, 1931.
10. Reich, T., Clayton, P., and Winokur, G.: Family history studies: V. The genetics of mania. Amer. J. Psychiat. 125:1358, 1969.
11. Wellner, J., and Marstal, H. B.: Symptoms in mania, an analysis of 279 attacks of manic depressive elation (summary), Acta Psychiat. Scand. 40:(Supp. 180), 175, 1964.
12. Wertham, F.: A group of benign chronic psychoses: prolonged manic excitements, Amer. J. Psychiat. 9:17, 1929.

Chapter 4

Special aspects

There are many interesting clinical facets of manic depressive disease that must be taken up separately. These aspects bear little relationship to each other and are characterized by a paucity of viable data. Nevertheless, they are significant and in the future may open up important vistas of study.

MANIC DEPRESSIVE DISEASE IN CHILDHOOD

It is clear that manic depressive disease may begin in adolescence; however, there is some question as to whether it may begin prior to the onset of puberty. Kraepelin considered the age period 15 to 20 years as the time of the greatest frequency of occurrence of the first attack of manic depressive psychosis. In over 900 cases of this disease he reported only 0.4 % as beginning before the age of 10 years.[16]

Anthony and Scott reviewed the literature on manic depressive psychosis in childhood and presented a well-documented case of a boy who suffered the onset of his first manic episode at 12 years of age, at which time he was described as "undersized" with a "complete absence of facial, axillary, and pubic hair."[1] Prior to his first hospital admission at age 12 years, this boy had been a timid, nervous child who was quite self-depreciatory. The mother was cyclothymic and the paternal grandfather was a periodic alcoholic. On admission, the boy was irritable, delusional, and grandiose. He was overactive and distractible and showed a flight of ideas. In general, he was cheerful and smiled but would break down in tears for short periods. This patient was followed through four hospital admissions to age 22 years. As he became older, he exhibited periodic drunkenness. Elations alternated with depressions. At 21 years of age, he was admitted to the hospital with symptoms of restlessness, pressure of speech, and boastfulness. At 22 years, he was admitted with elation and expansive ideas and was considered to be hypomanic. At this time he was treated successfully with electroshock therapy.

This case has the advantage of a long follow-up, and there can be no question that the patient was a typical manic depressive. He was, however, 12 years old, and even though there were no signs of puberty, one must question whether early pubertal changes were occurring but as yet not manifesting themselves in external signs. The authors themselves believed that the presence of the clinical picture of manic depressive disease in early childhood had yet to be demonstrated.

Barrett reported five cases of manic depressive psychosis in children.[2] Of particular interest was the case of a girl, F. O., who, when she was 12 years old, was seen in the clinic in a state of hyperactivity, exhilaration, and extreme talkativeness. Menstruation at that time had not yet begun. She had had her first attack of affective disorder at the age of 10 years, which was 15 to 24 months before she was seen in the clinic for the first time at age 12. At 10 years she would not go out of the house and was afraid that people were watching her. She had feelings of derealization and expressed the feeling that she did not belong to the world. There was little in the way of spontaneous talk. This depression (which started at the age of 10 years) continued for 7 months, after which she became excited, talked excessively, sat in peculiar positions, and had flighty thoughts. She then went into a period of 4 months in which phases of depression and excitement alternated every 2 weeks. This, in turn, was followed by a depression that lasted for 3 months. A normal mental state intervened for a month, and her illness recurred. It was then that she was seen in the clinic (age 12 years), showing alternating periods of depression and excitement. Her illness remitted in 9 weeks, and she was well for 2 years, during which time the first menstruation occurred. At 14 years of age she again entered the clinic in a state of excitement that had developed after a period of depression; this time she was exhilarated, distractible, boisterously overactive, and continuously talking. In a period of 3 months she improved and was home until the age of 19 years, when she again became excited and had to be admitted to a state hospital. This excitement disappeared in a few weeks, and she regained her normal health. Eight years later another attack requiring hospital admission occurred. This particular case appears to be one in which affective disorder, showing both mania and depression, started considerably before puberty (17 months to 4 years prior to menstruation). There is an adequate follow-up to indicate that the patient's illness was indeed a rather typical manic depressive psychosis.

The remaining cases reported by Barrett had their onsets at ages 11, 12, 10, and 10 years. All the five patients showed mania or had a family member with mania. In three of the patients manic depressive psychoses had occurred throughout three generations. This familial loading of manic depressive disease was quite striking. In four of the patients the first attack was that of a depression.

McHarg presented a case of a girl who was admitted to the hospital at 11 years of age with a typical mania.[20] Her illness had started some 7 months before admission with depressive symptoms. Menstruation did not start until 15 months after her admission. Thus the onset of her affective symptoms occurred about 22 months prior to her menses.

In summary, then, the data indicate that manic depressive disease can occur in childhood and probably begin before the onset of menstruation or pubertal changes. Whether it may occur in early childhood is still open to question.

PROGNOSIS WITH ONSET IN ADOLESCENCE

An early onset of a psychiatric illness is of particular importance because of its possible effect on the learning of social skills. Adolescence is a period during which an individual may make his first significant attempts to engage in an occupation and develop his first important relationships with members of the opposite sex. Little data have been published on the effect of manic depressive attacks that begin in adolescence on the subsequent behavior of the patient.

Olsen studied 28 patients whose first attack of manic depressive disease occurred before the age of 19 years.[22] In only two cases out of the 28 were the first and subsequent attacks purely depressive. Consequently, it would appear that he did, in fact, study patients who might be diagnosed as having true manic depressive disease. The average observation period for these 28 patients whose first attack occurred before 19 years of age was 25 years, with a range between 1 and 52 years. At follow-up the average age was 41 years with a range between 23 and 69 years. The duration of the first attack was generally between 1 and 5 months. Olsen noted that until the age of 18 years mania was four times as common as depression; but after that age manias and depressions occurred almost equally in this group of patients. The frequency of attacks reached its peak at the age of 17 years and decreased gradually thereafter.

In the follow-up, nine of the patients were described as socially incapacitated. They were unable to carry on in the community in an independent fashion. Three of these, however, seemed on the verge of rehabilitation. Nineteen of the patients were rehabilitated, but 10 of these subsequently became socially disabled. Of the 10 who were rehabilitated and then subsequently socially disabled, the social incapacity occurred around the age of 50 years in the majority of cases. Thus nine patients were never rehabilitated and 10 relapsed after a period of acceptable functioning. It would seem from these data that early-onset manic depressive disease carries with it a grave prognosis.

IMPACT OF THE POSTPARTUM STATE

Endocrine changes and in particular the postpartum state have been implicated in the precipitation of affective disorders in women. Winokur and Ruangtrakool studied 71 women who had suffered from primary affective disorder totally independent of the postpartum state.[36] Among these 71 women were five patients who had had a total of six postpartum psychoses. Sixty-six patients with affective disorder had never suffered a postpartum episode. Ten pregnancies preceded the index postpartum psychosis in the five women, and these were not associated with postpartum illnesses; and for four subsequent pregnancies in these five women one was associated with postpartum illness. The specific morbidity risk for the development of an affective disorder in the postpartum state was 10 % in this group of affectively disordered women, which was not significantly different from the morbidity risk of 6 % for affective disorder at any other time during the lives of these women. The conclusions of the study were that in broadly defined affective disorder, patients had frequent episodes and some of these episodes occurred by chance in the postpartum state. However, as far as a specific diagnosis of manic depressive disease was concerned, the data were not sufficient to decide whether there was an increased effect of the postpartum state on the patients. Such an effect would, of course, have increased the probability that an episode of illness would occur after the delivery of the child.

Bratfos and Haug, in Norway, studied puerperal mental disorders in manic depressive females.[6] They investigated 218 patients who were discharged with a diagnosis of manic depressive psychosis. However, only 11 of these patients had mania at the time of admission to the hospital. Basic material of the study comprised 82 manic depressive women who had given birth to a child. Altogether these women had had 251 deliveries and 155 attacks of mania or depression prior to the menopause. Thirty-four percent of these attacks had occurred in the postpartum state, but all the puerperal disorders had occurred in a minority group of 31 women. In this particular group of 31 women, nearly two thirds of all depressive or manic attacks had occurred postpartum. Of the 31 patients, only 11 had been hospitalized because of their postpartum disorder, but the 20 nonhospitalized had had incapacitating symptoms. Nine of the 31 patients subsequently developed a manic degressive psychosis of a circular type, but no single case of postpartum mania was observed. The authors quote data indicating that only 1% of women admitted to psychiatric clinics in the puerperium were manic.

The results of the two studies cited above seem to be at variance. The first study indicates that in broadly defined affective disorder, the postpartum state is a matter of no great importance. The second study suggests that in broadly defined affective disorder, the postpartum state in a sizable minority of women (31 out of 82) is more frequently associated with an affective illness than one would expect by chance alone. It would appear at the present time that a proper evaluation of the importance of the puerperium will depend on a better separation of groups that constitute the *affective disorders* and the investigation of these groups independently of each other. Any studies in the future should separate the *depressive disease* patients from the *manic depressive disease* patients and attempt to investigate the postpartum impact on each of these two groups.

SOCIOECONOMIC STATUS IN MANIC DEPRESSIVE DISEASE

Studies of the socioeconomic status of schizophrenics have shown that the prevalence of schizophrenia is highest in lower socioeconomic groups. Manic depressive disease does not seem to follow this pattern.[32] Unfortunately, most of the available socioeconomic data concern the broad group of affective disorders rather than the rigorously defined manic depressive disease, but it is still possible to come to some conclusions about the social and economic status of "true" manic depressives.

Helgason, in his population study of Iceland, divided the population into three levels of social classes.[15] Social class 1 included professional and technical workers, teachers, employers, administrative personnel, ship officers on larger vessels, and some farmers. Class 2 comprised most farmers, employed artisans, office workers, skilled workers, unskilled foremen, and ship officers on small vessels. The lowest class, class 3, was composed of unskilled workers from all trades and unemployed persons. These three classes also reflected the educational background of the members, the highest class (class 1) having the most education. The study revealed that the morbidity risk of expectancy for schizophrenia was low in class 1 and high in class 3. Manic depressive psychosis was higher in class 1 than in the two remaining social classes. This was true for both men and women but more striking for men.

Wilson presented some evidence which indicated that manic depressive disease was more frequent in the southern states than in northern or western states. His interpretation of this was that the illness was most frequently found among members of more socially established families with traditions of intellectuality. He further presented some data from a questionnaire which showed that members of families that contained manic depressive psychosis felt more pressure to conform to parental attitudes and had less freedom than members of those families without the disease.[12,33] Other authors have also suggested that manic depressive disease is an illness which affects socially striving and potentially mobile individuals, who exhibit a great need for social approbation and success.[3,4] This type of competitive individual might well rise in the social scheme of things and settle in the higher socioeconomic groups.

Woodruff, Robins, Winokur, and Walbran studied 100 patients with primary affective disorder and compared their occupational and educational achievements with those of their same-sex siblings.[37] The authors used the O.D. Duncan Socioeconomic Index to rate the probands and their siblings.[27] This index transforms all census-classified occupations into a prestige rating based on income and education ranging from 0 to 100. Females were compared to their female siblings on the basis of the occupation of their husbands. The one positive finding was that female probands were found to have a higher socioeconomic index than their female siblings. This finding was not true of the male probands and their male siblings. The finding that female probands had a higher socioeconomic index than their female siblings, however, did not appear to be reliable. When ill female siblings of the female probands were compared to the well female siblings, there was no socioeconomic difference. If primary affective disorder were associated with a social advantage, the ill siblings who had the same illness as the probands should have had a higher socioeconomic index than the well siblings.

A comparison was also made between socioeconomic index of manic probands and their siblings separately from a group of depressed probands and their siblings. In this case manic probands and their affectively ill siblings (N = 20) had a socioeconomic index of 55; the well siblings (N = 16) had an index of 44. There is, then, a 20% difference in scoioeconomic index between patients with manic depressive disease and their well siblings, in favor of the patients. The numbers are, however, small and the difference does not achieve significance. A replication of this aspect of the study with a larger number of manic subjects would seem to be in order.

In general, there were no striking differences between manic depressive patients and their siblings. However, population data such as that of Helgason, which reports manic depressives being found in the highest socioeconomic class, may suggest a familial factor that influences both manic depressives and their siblings. A familial factor could account for the population findings. Another point of some importance is that the study of Woodruff and co-workers clearly showed that primary affective disorder or manic depressive disease was not associated with impaired occupational or educational achievement. This is, of course, in marked contrast to patients who suffer from schizophrenia.

PERSONALITY TRAITS

Specific personality types are often considered in association with psychiatric diseases. In his large study of unipolar (depressive disease) and bipolar (manic depressive disease) patients, Perris reported significant differences in personality types between groups.[23] To evaluate the personalities of these two types of patients, Perris used the multidimensional scale of Sjöbring. Manic depressives were more likely to show active and sociable kinds of personalities; depressive patients were likely to score higher in insecure, obsessional, and sensitive traits.

Rowe and Daggett studied prepsychotic personality traits in 50 patients who suffered from affective disorder.[29] Of these patients, 24 had only depressions, 15 had depressions and manias, and 11 had only manias. The authors studied descriptions in the hospital records and attempted to cull from these descriptions all the adjectives and phrases describing each patient. The three groups were similar in that they were frequently sociable and often religious. Patients who suffered only depressions were described as being shy, conscientious, sensitive, and possessed of good judgment. They were not insecure, unstable, "intelligent," egocentric, or promiscuous. Patients who suffered from depressions and elations were described as being "intelligent," shy, active, and possessed of good judgment. They were not insecure, ambitious, thrifty, or promiscuous. Finally, the patients who suffered only from elations were active, egocentric, "intelligent," rigid, self-reliant, and reliable. They were not conscientious, dependent, or thrifty. When depressives were separated from the two groups that contained elations, it was noteworthy that the depressives were frequently conscientious, usually not particularly active, and rarely considered intelligent or egocentric. The finding of conscientiousness and sensitivity associated with patients who suffered only from depressions is, to some extent, similar to the findings in the Perris study.

In a subsequent study, Perris reported the results of the administration of the Maudsley Personality Inventory to 20 bipolar, 49 unipolar, and 20 neurotic (reactive) depressive patients. During the depressive episode itself no significant intergroup differences were found, but at discharge neuroticism scores differentiated the three groups. The bipolar patients scored the the lowest and the reactive depressive patients scored the highest.[24]

OBSESSIONAL NEUROSIS

The occurrence of significant depressive symptoms in the course of an obsessional neurosis has been discussed by Skoog.[30] It is certainly not an uncommon association. Brown, studying the hereditary of 20 obsessional neurotics, found a significant increase for depressive psychosis in the relatives of these patients.[7] Comparatively little, however, has been written about the association of obsessional neurosis to rigorously defined manic depressive disease. Of some importance in this area is the work of Gittleson, who studied 52 patients with depressive psychoses who had exhibited frank obsessions before the onset of the depressions.[13] They were, therefore, categorized as obsessional neurotics. He compared these 52 obsessional neurotics to 346 other depressives. The two groups did not differ significantly for the incidence of depression, suicide, or alcoholism in either parents or siblings. Obsessional neurotics had a higher incidence of obsessional personalities in their parents as well as in their siblings. However, the most interesting finding, insofar as it concerns manic depressive disease, is that none of the obsessional neurotics had had an attack of mania. This was in contrast to the fact that 25 of the 346 other depressives had at some time in their lives suffered from mania.

Stengel maintained that it was only rarely or never that mania occurred in obsessional neurotics.[31]

Though the data are small, they support the idea that obsessional neurosis and manic depressive disease (the latter defined by the presence of mania in the clinical picture) are not related in any significant fashion.

SCHIZOAFFECTIVE DISORDER

The diagnostic nomenclature of the American Psychiatric Association lists a category entitled *schizophrenia, schizoaffective type*.[11] This category is for patients showing a mixture of schizophrenic and affective symptoms. It is possible to call a patient *schizophrenia, schizoaffective type excited* or *schizophrenia, schizoaffective type depressed*. Since schizoaffective disorder is considered under the schizophrenias rather than under the affective disorders, one might presume that it is thought to be basically related to the former illnesses.

Clayton, Rodin, and Winokur studied 39 patients with schizoaffective psychosis and followed up these patients 1 to 2 years after the index admission for their illness.[9] Eighty-five percent of the patients were either well or, if they were ill, were not suffering from schizophrenia. The family history in these 39 schizoaffective patients indicated a high prevalence of affective disorder and a considerably lower prevalence of schizophrenia. In the group of schizoaffective patients 30 % had passivity feelings, 18 % had delusions of depersonalization, 50 % had auditory hallucinations, and 85 % were delusional. Flight of ideas and euphoria were seen in some of the schizoaffective patients. These are, of course, symptoms that are typical of mania. In all but one of the patients who exhibited these manic symptoms (9 out of 10), there was a positive family history for affective disorder. Documented family histories were obtained on nine of the ill first-degree family members in the study, and these records indicated a very strong relationship with ordinary affective disorder rather than with either schizophrenia or a separate schizoaffective psychosis. One case had psychiatric illness in three generations. A maternal grandfather had become ill with a simple depression at the age of 61 years. The schizoaffective patient's mother had developed a mania at 43 years of age, and the patient himself had been admitted at 21 years for the first time with hallucinations, confusion, and symbolic thinking. At subsequent admissions he was euphoric, complained of having his thoughts race, and was overtalkative and overactive.

In general, it would appear that schizoaffective disorder is probably a variant of affective disorder. Many of the patients who are admitted with schizophrenic-type symptoms may well be showing atypical manias or atypical depressions.

REACTIVE MANIA

The diagnosis of reactive depression is made frequently and with confidence by many psychiatrists. This diagnosis carries with it the implication that the depression is a response to significant psychosocial stresses that have occurred in the life of the patient. Also, depressions occur in the course of other illnesses, such as hysteria, anxiety neurosis, sociopathy, and alcoholism. These may be called secondary depressions. Very little has been written about reactive mania, and nothing has been written about secondary mania.

In respect to secondary mania, clinical observation forces one to the conclusion that, if it exists, it is a "rare bird," indeed. The experienced clinician will have difficulty recalling a case of a patient who has been followed for some time with an unquestioned anxiety neurosis, hysteria, sociopathic personality, or alcoholism who develops a mania. Alcoholism, of course, may be seen in mania, but a primary alcoholic does not develop mania.

Reactive mania was handled succinctly by Bleuler.[5] He said it was unknown. Harrowes presented two patients in whom he thought psychologic factors played a role in the precipitation of mania. The first patient had two attacks.[14] In the first attack there was some indication of dissatisfaction with her life situation, a situation that had been going on for years. In the second episode, the patient had difficulty in caring for an invalid mother. In both attacks there was evidence of a toxic factor, the first being associated with fever, albuminuria, and anemia, the second with a head injury, resulting in a wound infection. In the second patient, a death (of an old lady) lessened a burden for the patient and gave the patient more freedom. However, prior to the death, there was already considerable indication that this patient was becoming manic. In view of the toxic factors in patient 1 and the time sequence in patient 2, one must question whether the life stresses were really relevant to the onset of the illness.

Muncie reported four cases of postoperative excitement.[21] The sequence of events in these patients was as follows: (1) fear of operation or postoperative treatment, (2) late onset after operation, (3) mild toxic factors, (4) early fear, mistrust, and depression resulting from the course of postoperative events, (5) a swing to elation and overactivity, with fear much in evidence. One might question whether these cases are simply acute organic brain syndromes.

It would seem questionable from the available data that reactive mania exists at all. Nevertheless, the possibility remains that life stresses might trigger an episode of mania. It is also possible that organic factors (infections, head injuries, metabolic diseases) could be instrumental in precipitating an affective episode. Only a systematic study could answer this question.

DRINKING BEHAVIOR

A relationship to drinking behavior, more particularly alcoholism, in manic depressive disease is suggested by the finding that parents of probands who suffer from affective disorder manifested a higher rate of alcoholism than did the parents of a control group.[26,35] Since affective disorder is seen more frequently in females than males, it seemed possible that the inequality might be accounted for by alcoholism in the males. However, in a study of sex differences and alcoholism in primary affective illness, Winokur and Clayton presented data that discounted this possibility.[34] Nevertheless, the fact remains that within the family constellations of affective disorder patients more alcoholism existed than would be expected from general population figures. Experienced clinicians frequently note that many patients with affective disorder tend to become intoxicated only after periods of depression which have occurred for some time or at the time that they are manic. There are, however, few studies of the relationship between affective disorders and excessive drinking. Cassidy and associates noted that drinking was increased in 36% of men and 25% of women and decreased in 42% and 25% of men and women respectively in conjunction with an episode of affective disorder.[8] However, the data did not specify the type of affective episode involved. Mayfield and Coleman studied a group of 59 patients who suffered from manic and depressive episodes.[19] In this group of 59, 20% had a history of excessive drinking.

Twenty-three of the 59 patients had a change in their drinking pattern. Of these 23 patients, 19 increased their drinking when they suffered from elation and six increased their drinking when they suffered from depression. None of the patients decreased their drinking with elation, but 10 of the patients did so when they were depressed. In general, then, the change in drinking is predominantly one of increase with elation.

In another study, Mayfield and Allen evaluated a change in affect accompanying intravenous alcohol infusion in three groups of male subjects.[18] The first group was admitted to a hospital with acute psychotic depressive reactions. None of these had a history of alcoholism. The second group was composed of 12 primary alcoholics, and the third group was composed of 12 volunteers. The Clyde mood scale was used to measure each subject's affect before and after alcohol infusion. The mood of the depressed patients improved dramatically with the alcohol infusion. The controls showed less but nevertheless definite improvement, and the alcoholics improved least and showed a trend toward deterioration. The affective change in the depressive patients indicated a palliative rather than a euphoriant effect. Of interest was the fact that the depressed patients had not used alcohol even when in a severely depressed state. The study suggests that affects are most profoundly influenced by alcohol when they are disordered and that of all affects, depression is the one that is most likely to be altered.

SUICIDE AND SUICIDE ATTEMPTS

The association of completed suicide with broadly defined affective disorder has been documented by Robins and co-workers, who found that 45% of 134 consecutive suicides in St. Louis in one calendar year suffered from affective disorder.[28] Similarly, Pitts and Winokur reported on the family history of suicide in 748 consecutively admitted psychiatric patients.[25] In this study, 42 first-degree relatives of the probands had committed suicide, and of these, 33 suffered from affective disorder.

Of 365 index patients with affective disorder in the Pitts and Winokur study, 31 deceased mothers had also had affective disorder and 25 deceased fathers had had affective disorder. Of the affectively disordered mothers who died, 6% had died by suicide, and of the 25 affectively disordered fathers who died, 28% had died by suicide. The incidence of suicide in dead parents who had a diagnosis of affective disorder was 16%, which was quite comparable to findings in the literature of probands who were followed up. These findings, however, do not deal with rigorously diagnosed manic depressive disease. It is only in recent years, since the differentiation between unipolar and bipolar psychoses has been made, that such an evaluation is possible.

Leonhard, Korff, and Schulz studied suicides among relatives of monopolar and bipolar phasic psychoses.[17] The bipolar patients had a considerably higher incidence of suicide in their family members than did the patients who had unipolar psychoses (depressive disease).

The most complete studies of suicide and suicide attempts in the two kinds of affective disorder (unipolar and bipolar) have been reported by Perris and d'Elia.[10,23,24] These authors studied 138 bipolar patients and 139 unipolar depressive patients. There was an average follow-up of about 20 years from the date of the first episode. In the bipolar group two females and one male completed suicide. In the unipolar group nine males and three females completed suicide. Thus, although the two groups were about the same size, three of the manic depressive probands had died by suicide as opposed to 12 of the unipolar probands. These findings are difficult to evaluate, however, because the bipolar group contained significantly more female patients than the unipolar group and suicide is more frequently seen in the male population. Further, there are age differences, with the unipolar patients being considerably older at the time they were investigated. As successful suicide rates increase with age, this may account for some of the disparity in rates between the unipolar and bipolar groups. It seems clear that rates for completed suicide in manic depressive patients versus depressive disease patients remains a matter for further study.

The morbidity risk for suicide in first-degree relatives of *manic depressives* and *depressive disease* patients was not significantly different. The presence of suicide or suicide attempts in the proband was not correlated with an increased morbidity risk for suicide in the first-degree relatives.

With respect to suicide attempts, 26% of the bipolar probands attempted suicide and 21% of the unipolar probands did the same. If the probands were divided by sex, it appeared that the male unipolar patients attempted suicide more frequently than did the male bipolar patients. Also, attempted suicide was significantly higher in female than in male bipolar patients, but no difference occurred between male and female unipolar patients. Thus six of 57 male bipolar patients attempted suicide, whereas 30 of 81 female bipolar patients did likewise. Seventeen of 70 male unipolar patients attempted suicide, whereas 12 of 69 female unipolar patients attempted suicide. The striking finding is, of course, that bipolar female patients seem more likely to attempt suicide than any of the other groups, unipolar males and females and bipolar males.

REFERENCES

1. Anthony, J., and Scott, P.: Manic-depressive psychosis in childhood, J. Child Psychol. Psychiat. **1**:53, 1960.
2. Barrett, A. M.: Manic depressive psychosis in childhood, Int. Clin. **3**:205, 1931.
3. Becker, J.: Achievement related to characteristics of manic depressives, J. Abnorm. Soc. Psychol. **60**:334, 1960.
4. Becker, J., Parker, J., and Spielberger, C.: Value achievement and authoritarian attributes in psychiatric patients, J. Clin. Psychol. **19**:57, 1963.
5. Bleuler, E.: Textbook of psychiatry (translated by A. A. Brill), New York, The Macmillan Co. (reissued by Dover Publications, 1951, London).
6. Bratfos, O., and Haug, J.: Puerperal mental disorders in manic depressive females, Acta Psychiat. Scand. **42**:285, 1966.
7. Brown, F.: Heredity in psychoneuroses, Proc. Roy. Soc. Med. **35**:785, 1942.
8. Cassidy, W., Flanagan, N., Spellman, M., and Cohen, M. E.: Clinical observations in manic depressive disease: a quantitative study of 100 manic depressive patients and 50 medically sick controls, J.A.M.A. **164**:1535, 1957.
9. Clayton, P., Rodin, L., and Winokur, G.: Family history studies: III. Schizoaffective disorder, clinical and genetic factors including a one to two year follow-up, Compr. Psychiat. **9**:31, 1968.

10. d'Elia, G., and Perris, C.: Suicidal attempts in bipolar and unipolar depressed psychotics. (Submitted for publication.)
11. Diagnostic and statistical manual of mental disorders, Washington, 1968, American Psychiatric Association.
12. Finley, C. B., and Wilson, D. C.: The relation of the family to manic depressive psychosis, Dis. Nerv. Syst. **12**:39, 1951.
13. Gittleson, N.: Depressive psychosis in the obsessional neurotic, Brit. J. Psychiat. **112**:883, 1966.
14. Harrowes, W.: The reactive manic episode: its implications and scope, J. Ment. Sci. **77**:127, 1931.
15. Helgason, T.: Epidemiology of mental disorders in Iceland, Acta Psychiat. Scand. **40**:(Supp. 173), 1964.
16. Kraepelin, E.: Psychiatrie, ed. 8, Leipzig, 1931, Johann Ambrosius Barth.
17. Leonhard, K., Korff, I., and Schulz, H.: Temperaments in the families of monopolar and bipolar phasic psychoses, Psychiat. Neurol. **143**:416, 1962.
18. Mayfield, D., and Allen, D.: Alcohol and affect: a psychopharmacological study, Amer. J. Psychiat. **123**:1346, 1967.
19. Mayfield, D., and Coleman, L.: Alcohol use and affective disorder, Dis. Nerv. Syst. **29**:467, 1968.
20. McHarg, J. F.: Mania in childhood, Arch. Neurol. Psychiat. **72**:531, 1954.
21. Muncie, W.: Postoperative states of excitement, Arch. Neurol. Psychiat. **32**:681, 1934.
22. Olsen, T.: Follow-up study of manic depressive patients whose first attack occurred before the age of 19, Acta Psychiat. Scand. **45**:(Supp. 162), 1961.
23. Perris, C.: A study of bipolar (manic depressive) and unipolar recurrent depressive psychoses, Acta Psychiat. Scand. **42**:1 (Suppl. 194), 1966.
24. Perris, C.: The separation of bipolar (manic depressive) from unipolar recurrent depressive psychosis. (Submitted for publication.)
25. Pitts, F. N., Jr., and Winokur, G.: Affective disorder: III. Diagnostic correlates and incidence of suicide, J. Nerv. Ment. Dis. **139**:176, 1964.
26. Pitts, F. N., Jr., and Winokur, G.: Affective disorder: VII. Alcoholism and affective disorder, J. Psychiat. Res. **4**:37, 1966.
27. Reiss, A. J.: Occupations and social status, Glencoe, Ill., 1961, The Free Press.
28. Robins, E., Murphy, G., Wilkinson, R., Gassner, S., and Kayes, J.: Some clinical considerations in the prevention of suicide based on a study of 134 successful suicides, Amer. J. Public Health **49**:888, 1959.
29. Rowe, C., and Daggett, D.: Prepsychotic personality traits in manic depressive disease, J. Nerv. Ment. Dis. **119**:412, 1954.
30. Skoog, G.: The Anancastic syndrome and its relationship to personality attitudes, Acta Psychiat. Neurol. Scand. (Supp. 134), 1959.
31. Stengel, E.: A study on some clinical aspects of the relationship between obsessional neurosis and psychotic reaction types, J. Ment. Sci. **91**:166, 1945.
32. Tietze, C., Lemkau, P., and Cooper, M.: Schizophrenia, manic depressive psychosis and socioeconomic status, Amer. J. Sociol. **47**:167, 1941.
33. Wilson, D. C.: Families of manic depressives, Dis. Nerv. Syst. **12**:362, 1951.
34. Winokur, G., and Clayton, P.: Family history studies: II. Sex differences and alcoholism in primary affective illness, Brit. J. Psychiat. **113**:973, 1967.
35. Winokur, G., and Pitts, F. N., Jr.: Affective disorder: VI. A family history study of prevalences, sex differences and possible genetic factors, J. Psychiat. Res. **3**:113, 1965.
36. Winokur, G., and Ruangtrakool, S.: Postpartum impact on patients with independently diagnosed affective disorder, J.A.M.A. **197**:242, 1966.
37. Woodruff, R., Robins, L., Winokur, G., and Walbran, B.: Educational and occupational achievement in primary affective disorder, Amer. J. Psychiat. **124**:57 (Supp.), 1968.

Chapter 5

Previous genetic studies in
manic depressive disease

There are few stable and easily reproducible findings in the field of psychiatry. One of these is that the group of primary affective disorders (those disorders of affect that occur in the absence of other psychiatric illnesses) are familial and may be traced through several generations in many families. All studies, even the most cursory, have found this to be so, and there are no negative investigations. It is, therefore, remarkable that many theorists have ignored the family history and that many psychiatrists investigate the psychologic history of a patient without reference to illness in the parents or siblings.

Several mechanisms might be responsible for the familial nature of the illness and one that has been studied intensively is a possible genetic factor. Many of these studies are European and not well known in the United States. We have shown (Chapter 2) that affective disorders fulfill four criteria presented by Hanna, which indicate a genetic factor in the etiology of an illness, namely, that the illness has (1) higher prevalence in relatives than in the general population, (2) an increased frequency of defects in the same functional system among relatives of patients, (3) greater concordance in monozygotic than dizygotic twins, and (4) an onset at a characteristic age without a precipitating event.[5]

Recent work by Winokur and Tanna and by Reich, Clayton, and Winokur has shown that linkage between "true" manic depressive disease (bipolar psychoses) and well-known genetic markers occurs, further strengthening the hypothesis that a genetic etiologic factor is present.[16,28] These last findings are the logical extensions of an old tradition of interest in heredity in psychiatry.

The early French authors were aware of the role that heredity played in the pathogenesis of "mania." Esquirol, in his text, defined mania as an episodic psychosis with euphoric and depressive elements, which often remitted if the patient did not die of exhaustion or some of the barbaric therapies then in vogue.[4] Its onset was swift and the patient was normal after remission, yet liable to another attack. Drawing upon his own data and the data of the Sâlpetrière he wrote: "The table of causes presents hereditary predisposition as a remote cause, doubtless, but as the most frequent."

EMIL KRAEPELIN

Kraepelin, in his 1921 monograph, considered heredity first among the etiologic factors which he discussed and reported that about 80 % of his cases had a hereditary taint.[8]

Quoting the literature of his day, Kraepelin reports that Walker found a familial taint in 73.4 % of manic depressive cases, Saiz in 84.7 %, Weygandt in 90 %, and Albrecht in 80.6 %. Albrecht noted that 45 % of patients with "numerous attacks" had parents affected with the disorder. Vogt reported that in his manic depressive cases, "mental disease" existed in 22.2 % of the parents and 35.2 % of the siblings; and he showed that this was higher than in other forms of "insanity." To strengthen his point, Kraepelin presents a pedigree of Kölpin in which seven out of 10 children of parents who "probably were both manic depressive by predisposition" were affected. In the grandchildren of these parents, four of the five "had already fallen ill."

Rehm found among 44 children of 19 families signs of "psychic degeneration" in 52 %, particularly in 29 %; and these latter were "mostly depressed." Bergamasco established that among 159 patients in 59 families, 109 belonged to "manic depressive insanity." Kraepelin felt that epilepsy, arteriosclerosis, and dementia praecox did not play any part worth mentioning in the heredity of manic depressive disease.

These authors did not consider the hereditary data in the light of mendelian genetic ratios and reported no opinion as to the kind of transmission that might have been possible.

EARLY GENETIC INVESTIGATIONS AND THEORIES

Ernst Rüdin, in 1923, believed that transmission of a simple dominant or recessive gene, either sex-linked or autosomal, definitely could be ruled out.[19] He suggested a trifactorial mode of inheritance with one dominant and two recessive factors. He added that this held true only without reference to sex and failed to account for the higher incidence figures in women.

Rosanoff, Handy, and Plesset, in 1935, proposed a two-factor genetic theory.[18] One factor, the cyclothymic factor, was autosomal; the other factor, an activating factor, was sex-linked. These authors drew heavily on 59 twin pairs, which they had collected, as well as those of Luxenburger.[10] Concordance of their monoxygotic twins was almost complete.

Eliot Slater, in 1936, simplified matters by proposing a single autosomal dominant gene with reduced penetrance as the mode of transmission of manic depressive psychosis.[20] The illness was *dominant* because it often occurred in successive generations and *autosomal* because fathers of affectively disordered sons could have had the illness. Incomplete penetrance or the absence of the illness in a person who carried the gene was a necessary construct because less than 50 % of the sibs were ill, not all monozygotic twins were concordant, and not all patients had ill parents.

In 1938, Slater wrote on the inheritance factor in manic depressive disease and concluded that no simple mendelian ratio could be found.[21] He used his own extensive data and those of Röll and Entres (on probability of disease in nieces and nephews of manic depressives as well as first-degree relatives.[17] Slater believed that a sex-lined factor was unlikely for it appeared that the excess of women over men in some studies of manic depressive disease was the result of artifacts in the data.

Slater's study group is of particular importance.[21] In order to obtain a large enough sample to study, he took two types of patients. One type had one clear manic and one clear depressive phase. The other type had had three manic or three depressive attacks, all separated from each other and all completely cured. In light of the separation of manic depressive disease (bipolar psychosis) from depressive disease (unipolar psychosis), which was discussed in Chapter 2 of this book, even such distinguished studies as those of Slater must be reinterpreted. This codicil is equally applicable to the well-known and respected work of Kallmann.

Franz Kallmann, in 1954, reviewed his twin data as well as the family histories of the twin probands.[7] He found that by correcting for age his own (27 monozygotic and 55 dizygotic) pairs and those of Slater, the concordance for monozygotic twins was 100% and that for dizygotic twins was 24% to 25.5%. By adding *cycloid* cases to the ill sibs of the families of twins, he found the ratio of affected to unaffected sibs to be 0.9 : 1. Kallmann believed that these findings (100% concordance in monozygotic twins and equal numbers of ill and well siblings), which would support a dominant gene hypothesis, were spurious because of ascertainment problems. He felt the observed higher prevalence in women was "more likely due to differences in the degree of penetrance and clinical certifiability than to the effect of sex-linked dominance." Kallmann's data support an autosomal dominant gene with some reduced penetrance as the genetic mode of transmission.

MODIFICATION IN KRAEPELIN'S CONCEPT OF MANIC-DEPRESSIVE PSYCHOSIS

Any genetic investigation must begin with a single homogeneous entity, and all the studies and theories referred to previously have accepted the Kraepelin diagnostic schema.

Evidence collected recently, however, has shown that Kraepelin's entity *manic depressive* psychosis contains at least two separate illnesses (see Chapter 2); and, therefore, these studies all have a built-in error of considerable and varying proportions.

Leonhard, in Berlin, subdivided manic depressives into bipolar (mania and depression) and monopolar (depression only) forms. In an investigation of the families of monopolar and bipolar phasic psychoses, Leonhard, Korff, and Schulz reported that bipolar patients tended to have bipolar relatives and unipolar patients, unipolar relatives.[9] They found that cyclothymic personalities with *high and low* mood swings occurred in the *bipolar* families and depressive personalities occurred more often in the *monopolar* families. They also found a higher morbidity risk for endogenous psychosis among the first-degree relatives of the bipolar patients. Table 5-1 summarizes these findings as well as other relevant data that support a separation of manic depressive disease (bipolar) and depressive disease (unipolar). The figures are expressed in terms of morbidity risk, which is an estimate of the probability that the relative will develop the disease in question if he survives the period of risk for the disease.

Perris, in his excellent monograph, found that bipolar index patients had a higher prevalence of affective disorder among their first-degree relatives than did unipolar patients.[14] He further reported that the disorder in the relatives of the bipolar patients was almost entirely bipolar. Among the relatives of the unipolar patients, unipolar illness was much more frequent.

Angst reported similar findings to those of Perris. Their findings have been compared to each other in a joint paper and may be seen in Table 5-1.

Table 5-1. Morbidity risk in first-degree relatives of bipolar and unipolar probands

	Percent endogenous psychosis in first-degree relatives
Leonhard, 1962	
Unipolar probands	27.7
Bipolar probands	39.9
Asano, 1967	
Unipolar probands	34.5
Bipolar probands	39.3

	Percent bipolar psychosis in first-degree relatives	Percent unipolar psychosis in first-degree relatives
Angst (Angst and Perris, 1968)		
Unipolar probands	0.29	9.1
Bipolar probands	3.7	11.2
Perris (Angst and Perris, 1968)		
Unipolar probands	0.35	7.4
Bipolar probands	10.8	0.58

Asano, in Japan, also reported a higher rate of endogenous psychosis in *bipolar* versus *unipolar* families (Table 5-1).[2]

A different way of investigating this phenomenon was devised by Winokur and Clayton.[26] They studied the family histories of consecutively admitted patients with a two-generation history of affective disorder (N = 112) and compared them with the family histories of patients who had no family history of any psychiatric disorder (N = 129). Their findings were striking; manics were significantly overrepresented in the *two-generation* group (p < 0.003). Other symptoms failed to differentiate these two groups of patients.

Winokur, in agreement with other authors referred to in this section, has shown that the first-degree relatives of manic patients, when compared to relatives of patients in whom depression alone is found, (1) have a significantly higher prevalence of affective disorders in their families, (2) manifest mania more frequently, and (3) are members of familial constellations in which two generations of affective disorder are more frequently found.[25]

This evidence clearly indicates that Kraepelin's *manic-depressive* psychosis is composed of at least two entities; and in only one does mania occur. All previous studies (especially the genetic ones) must be reexamined in this light.

There is one point of contention in these recent studies, however; and that is the finding of Perris that depression without mania was extremely rare among the first-degree relatives of manic probands.[14] His report suggests that the bipolar and unipolar forms of the illness breed true, and the syndrome is homogeneous as regards the patient and his family.

A comparison of the Perris finding among the families of manic probands and that of other authors reveals that Perris had, not an excess of manics, but a deficiency of depressives. The difference in these findings is probably methodologic in that Perris required three separate episodes of depressive illness for any patient to be diagnosed as unipolar. A patient might have had one or two depressive episodes and by his criteria would have been classified as *unspecified affective disorder*. Adding the unspecified affective disorders and suicides and unipolar depressives together, we find the morbidity risk for depressive illness among the first-degree relatives of bipolar probands to be 8.4%, which brings Perris' findings close to those of the other investigators.

An analysis of the families that were presented by Slater in his twin study reveals that ill family members of manic depressive twins were equally distributed between those that manifested only depression and those that showed manias as well as depressions.[22]

In a joint effort, Angst and Perris published their data side by side.[1] Angst, in accordance with other investigators, found a higher familial loading in the manic depressive patients than in the *depressed-only* patients. He found a considerably lower frequency of bipolar illness in the families of his bipolar patients than did Perris (3.7% for Angst vs. 10.8% for Perris). However, Angst found a high frequency (11.2%) of familial illness characterized by depression only among the families of bipolar probands. Perris found only 0.5% of relatives showing unipolar psychoses. Like Perris and other authors, Angst showed that the frequency of a bipolar psychosis was extremely rare in the family of a unipolar patient. Differences of methodology and the definition of unipolar (at least three depressive episodes) probably explain the divergent findings.

Reich, Clayton, and Winokur, in a preliminary study of the homogeneity-heterogeneity problem, found that in a group of carefully studied manic probands (N = 30) and their families many relatives manifested only depression and had never shown signs of mania. As a matter of fact, more first-degree relatives showed only depression in this study than manifested manias.[16] Whether the depressive illness of the relatives of bipolar patients is clinically different from the depressive illness in the families of unipolar patients awaits further study.

Not all the family studies have found a significant increase in the prevalence of affective disorder among the relatives of manic depressives as compared to pure depressives.[23] Stenstedt, in analyzing his data, found a trend in the expected direction, but this did not reach significance. Winokur re-evaluated Stenstedt's data and reported that mania tended to cluster in certain families and was totally absent in others. In the entire study group, 20% of the ill patients had a mania. However, in one type of family, all ill relatives had depression only; in the other type, 50% of the ill members had mania and 50% had only depression. Thus, mania clustered only in certain families.[25]

The data cited above force one to the conclusion that affective illness in relatives of manic depressive patients is heterogeneous.

TRANSMISSION

The mode of transmission of manic depressive psychosis must be re-evaluated following the separation of bipolar and unipolar forms of the illness. Perris did not discuss this in his 1966 monograph. Reich, Clayton, and Winokur, in a family study of 59 consecutively admitted manic patients, found that the prevalence of all forms of affective disorder was higher in women than men. This was true both of probands and family members. The preponderance of females has been long reported for the broad group of affective disorders and suggests the possibility of some kind of dominant X-linked transmission. Twenty percent of the fathers and 34% of the mothers were affected; the morbidity risk for affective disorder in the sibs of male manics was 24% for brothers and 21% for sisters. The sibs of female manics had morbidity risks of 0% for brothers and 25% for sisters. The excess of females overall and the deficiency of illness among the brothers of female manics are indicative of sex-linked dominant transmission. This hypothesis was strengthened by the finding that ill fathers rarely had ill sons and frequently had ill daughters, whereas ill mothers had a more equal distribution between ill sons and ill daughters. The results were statistically significant. Reviewing theories of transmission, these authors were able to exclude all but two possibilities, namely, that of a single dominant X-linked gene with incomplete penetrance or two dominant genes one of which is sex-linked.[16]

Considerably different data have been reported by Perris. In his bipolar group, the occurrence of secondary cases did not seem to be influenced by which parent was ill.[15] On the other hand, in the unipolar cases affected fathers had an excess of ill daughters. Perris did not find an excess of females in the bipolar group, which is at variance with the findings of Reich, Clayton, and Winokur. No simple explanation for this important difference is readily at hand.

TWIN STUDIES

Most reports on twin research in the literature deal with affective disorders rather than clearly defined manic depressive disease. Zerbin-Rüdin, however, has surveyed the world literature and has made an effort to separate the clinical data on the twin studies into those cases involving manic depressive psychoses (bipolar) and those cases involving depressive psychoses (unipolar).[29] In order to do this, she has made use of individual case reports that have been published as well as series of twin pairs that are in the literature. One of the most valuable of the published series is that of Slater because it provides both a detailed clinical picture of the twins and a family history.[22]

By analyzing some of the tables in the Zerbin-Rüdin paper, one can find 34 pairs of monozygotic twins at least one partner of whom showed a mania at some time during his life. Concordance for affective disorder was found in 28 (82%) of these pairs. Seven of the 28 concordant pairs (25%) showed dissimilar types of affective illness, with one member manifesting mania and the other member showing only depression.

There are 19 dizygotic pairs of twins at least one partner of whom had had a mania. Concordance for affective disorder in this group was seen in seven pairs (37%). Of these concordant pairs, five of the seven (71%) manifested dissimilar types of affective illness, with one member having shown mania and the other member showing only depression.

One might conclude that the twin data support a genetic factor in manic depressive disease since the concordance rate for monozygotic twins is over twice that for dizygotic pairs. Also the data indicate considerable heterogeneity for affective illness *within* twinships in which at least one member was manic.

CONSANGUINEOUS MARRIAGES

If it is necessary for two dominant genes at separate loci to be present for an illness to manifest itself, then consanguinity should be more prevalent among the parents of the patient affected with the disorder. This is true of two recessive as well as two dominant genes. Herlofsen and Ødegaard, in a little-known study of consanguinity among parents of mental patients, found an excess of cousin marriages in parents of patients who showed excitement and depression.[6] Nixon and Slater found an excess of schizophrenia in patients who were products of consanguineous marriages.[12] These studies are contradictory, and as a result no conclusion may be drawn from them.

SEX DIFFERENCES AND ALCOHOLISM

Alcoholism is found quite frequently in family members of patients with broadly defined affective disorder (see Chapter 4). This raises the question of whether the familial illness might express itself as affective disorder in some members and alcoholism in others, especially males.

Winokur and Clayton studied the problem in 426 patients with affective disorder.[27] In this group there was a marked excess of ill females in the first-degree relatives as well as in the probands. Assuming that all alcoholic male relatives had affective disorder, these workers found that there was an equal number of affectively ill relatives of both sexes. However, they found that ill female probands had a significant deficiency of ill brothers and that the brothers and sisters of male probands and the sisters of female probands were equal in morbidity risk. Alcoholism was found to be equal in brothers of both male and female probands, thus indicating that the sex difference (females more than males) was not accounted for by alcoholism. Likewise, in their study of well-diagnosed manic depressives, Reich, Clayton, and Winokur did not find any support for the idea that the sex differences could be explained by alcoholism in male relatives.[16] Nevertheless, it did appear that the fathers of manic probands (but not the male siblings) were more likely to be alcoholic than would be expected from the general population figures for males.

DISEASE-ASSOCIATION STUDIES

Apart from the classic pedigree and twin studies, genetics offers other techniques for the investigation of the disorder. The association of an illness with a well-known genetic trait establishes that the illness is "genetic."

A model for such a study may be found in the research that has suggested an association between secretor status, type O blood, and peptic ulcer. If one found a clear-cut association between a genetic trait such as a specific blood group and manic depressive disease, it would prove a genetic factor is operative in the illness.

Parker and co-workers found an increased association between type O blood group and well-defined manic depressive psychosis.[13] Masters has confirmed this finding.[11] Tanna and Winokur studied the association of blood groups and broadly defined affective disorder (the affective disorder group containing a large number of manic probands); their data indicated a statistically significant association with type B blood, not with type O.[24] In the control group of Tanna and Winokur, 48% of subjects had type O blood.

In their affective disorder subjects, 43 % had type O blood. In the Parker study, 59 % of manic depressives had type O blood. Thus, the manic depressives of the Parker study are closer to the control group of Tanna and Winokur as regards type O blood than they are to the affective disorder patients. There are significant diagnostic differences as well as differences in the choice of control groups (Tanna and Winokur chose the sibs of the patients as a control group; Parker and co-workers used published figures as a control), which may explain these divergent findings.

LINKAGE STUDIES

There have been a few linkage studies between a genetic marker and affective disorders, in particular manic depressive disease. Finding linkage between a genetic marker and manic depressive disease would (1) establish a genetic factor in the illness, (2) clarify the mode of transmission of the illness, and (3) show that the two genes (the illness and the marker) must be physically close to each other on the chromosome since the degree of association within a family unit is dependent on the chromosomal distance between the two genes. Using the sib-pair method, Tanna and Winokur attempted, unsuccessfully, to show linkage. They found no linkage between manic depressive illness and the ABO blood system.[24]

In another study, Winokur and Tanna examined several blood systems (ABO, Duffy, P, Kidd, Lutheran, Kell, MNS, Rh, Xg) and attempted to show linkage. They investigated a limited number of families and demonstrated that X-linkage occurred. There were suggestive data that the Xg blood group (whose locus is on the short arm of the X-chromosome) was linked with manic depressive illness.[28]

Reich, Clayton, and Winokur studied two large families that were assorting for color blindness of the protan and deutan types and for manic depressive psychosis.[16] The manic depressive disorder was linked to the locus of color blindness ($p < 0.005$). Since both color blindness and the Xg blood group have their locus on the short arm of the X-chromosome and since manic depressive psychosis was linked to the color blindness locus and possibly linked to the Xg locus, they speculated that the X-borne gene for manic depressive psychosis was located on the short arm of the X-chromosome between the genes for Xg blood group and color blindness.

In this study, women who carried the gene but did not manifest the trait of color blindness manifested an affective disorder, so the gene for affective disorder must be dominant. The presence of affective disorder in successive generations in these families is also in favor of dominant transmission. The finding of an X-borne gene clarifies the sex ratio (more females than males) that was observed in the study and proves a genetic factor in manic depressive disease.

CYTOGENETIC STUDIES

Chromosome abnormalities have been described in various forms of mental retardation and recently in some cases of antisocial sociopathy. The search for a chromosome abnormality in affective disorders has been recently undertaken by Ebaugh, Freiman, Woolf, Sherman, and Winokur, who cultured white blood cells of hospitalized manic depressive patients and controls and examined these cells for chromosome abnormalities.[3] No aneuploidy, polyploidy, or mosaicism was found to be associated with affective disorder. No other statistically significant findings were found in the morphology of the chromosomes.

The data in all these studies are not large. Most of the population studies have been done using a family history method. A superior technique would have been to use a family study method in which all available ill and well relatives were interviewed. Extension of the linkage studies is in order. Subsequent chapters of this book describe an investigation in which both probands and family members were interviewed and linkage studies were performed in an attempt to study the clinical picture of true manic depressive psychosis and to clarify its genetic nature.

REFERENCES

1. Angst, J., and Perris, C.: Nosology of endogenous depression, a comparison of the findings of two studies, Arch. Psychiat. Nervenkr. **210**:373, 1968.
2. Asano, N.: Clinico-genetic study of manic-depressive psychoses. In Mitsuda, H., editor: Clinical genetics in psychiatry, Kyoto, Japan, 1967, Banko-sha Co., Ltd.
3. Ebaugh, I., Freiman, M., Woolf, R., Sherman, A., and Winokur, G.: Chromosome studies in patients with affective disorder (manic depressive illness), Arch. Gen. Psychiat. **19**:751, 1968.
4. Esquirol, J. E. D.: Mental maladies, a treatise on insanity (1845), N. Y. Academy of Medicine, New York, 1965, Hafner Publishing Co., Inc.
5. Hanna, B. L.: Genetic studies of family units. In Neel, J. O., Shaw, M. W., and Schull, W. J., editors: Genetics and the epidemiology of chronic diseases, Washington, 1965, U.S. Department of Health, Education, and Welfare.
6. Herlofsen, H. B., and Ødegaard, Ø.: A study of psychotic patients of consanguinous parentage, Acta Genet. **5**:391, 1955.
7. Kallmann, F.: Genetic principles in manic-depressive psychosis. In Zubin, J., and Hoch, P., editors: Depression, Proceedings of the American Psychopathological Association, New York, 1954, Grune & Stratton, Inc.
8. Kraepelin, E.: Manic-depressive insanity and paranoia, Edinburgh, 1921, E. & S. Livingstone, Ltd.
9. Leonhard, K., Korff, I., and Shulz, H.: Die Temperamente in den Familien der monopolaren und bipolaren phasischen Psychosen, Psychiat. Neurol. **143**:416, 1962.
10. Luxenburger, H.: Endogener Schwachsinn und geschlechtsgebundener Erbgang, Z. Ges. Neurol. Psychiat. **140**:320, 1932.
11. Masters, A. B.: The distribution of blood groups in psychiatric illness, Brit. J. Psychiat. **113**:1309, 1967.
12. Nixon, W. L. B., and Slater, E.: A second investigation into the children of cousins, Acta Genet. **7**:513, 1957.
13. Parker, J. B., Theile, A., and Spielberger, C. D.: Frequency of blood types in a homogeneous group of manic depressive patients, J. Ment. Sci. **107**:936, 1961.
14. Perris, C., editor: A study of bipolar (manic-depressive) and unipolar recurrent depressive psychoses, Acta Psychiat. Scand. **42**:1 (Supp. 194), 1966.
15. Perris, C.: Genetic transmission of depressive psychoses. In Retterstøl, N., and Magnussen, F., editors: Acta Psychiat. Scand. (Supp. 203), 1968.
16. Reich, T., Clayton, P., and Winokur, G.: Family history studies: V. The genetics of mania, Amer. J. Psychiat. **125**:1358, 1969.
17. Röll, A., and Entres, J. L.: Zum Problem der Erbprognosebestimmung: die Erkrankungsaussichten der neffen und nichten von Manisch-depressiven, Z. Ges. Neurol. Psychiat. **156**:169, 1936.

18. Rosanoff, A. J., Handy, L. M., and Plesset, I. R.: The etiology of manic depressive syndromes with special reference to their occurrence in twins, Amer. J. Psychiat. **91**:725, 1935.
19. Rüdin, E.: Ueber Vererbung geistiger Störungen, Z. Ges. Neurol. Psychiat. **81**:459, 1923.
20. Slater, E.: The inheritance of manic-depressive insanity, Proc. Roy. Soc. Med. **29**:981, 1936.
21. Slater, E.: The genetics of manic-depressive insanity: the parents and children of manic depressives, Z. Ges. Neurol. Psychiat. **163**:1, 1938.
22. Slater, E.: Psychotic and neurotic illnesses in twins, Med. Res. Counc. Spec. Rep. no. 278, 1953.
23. Stenstedt, A.: A study in manic depressive psychosis, Acta Psychiat. Neurol. Scand. (Supp. 79), 1952.
24. Tanna, V., and Winokur, G.: A study of association and linkage of ABO blood types and primary affective disorder, Brit. J. Psychiat. **114**:1175, 1968.
25. Winokur, G.: Genetic principles in the clarification of clinical issues in affective disorder. Presented at the annual meeting of the A.A.A.S., New York, Dec. 29, 1967. In Mandell, A. J., and Mandell, M. P., editors: Methods and theory in human psychochemical research, New York, Academic Press, Inc. (In press.)
26. Winokur, G., and Clayton, P.: Family history studies: I. Two types of affective disorder separated according to genetic and clinical factors. In Wortis, J., editor: Recent advances in biological psychiatry, New York, 1967, Plenum Publishing Corp., vol. 9.
27. Winokur, G., and Clayton, P.: Family history studies: II. Sex differences and alcoholism in primary affective illness, Brit. J. Psychiat. **113**:973, 1966.
28. Winokur, G., and Tanna, V.: Possible role of X-linked dominant factor in manic depressive disease, Dis. Nerv. Syst. **30**:89, 1969.
29. Zerbin-Rüdin, E.: Zur Genetik der depressiven Erkrankungen. Presented at the Internationalen Arbeitstagung der Psychiatrischen und Neurologischen Klinik of the Free University of Berlin, "Das Depressive Syndrom," Feb. 16-17, 1968.

Chapter 6

Methodology of a clinical and genetic study of rigorously defined manic depressive disease

With the aim of studying clinical and genetic factors in manic depressive disease, we embarked on a study that took as its point of departure a group of patients who entered a psychiatric hospital with a clear diagnosis of mania at the time of admission.

Two groups of probands or index cases were investigated by means of a family history method as well as a family study, which included personal interviews of all available first-degree relatives.

The first group of probands (group A) was selected in the following fashion: Between July of 1964 and June 1965, with the exception of the period of January and February 1965, all patients admitted to Renard Hospital, the psychiatric section of the Washington University School of Medicine, in St. Louis, were examined using a systematic interview. The average stay in the hospital is 21 days. At discharge the structured interview was reexamined, and material obtained during the psychiatric course of hospitalization was appended to it. The patients were diagnosed at that time. Thus, except for a few patients admitted late in the study who had not been discharged in July 1966, the series reflects consecutive admissions. Of the patients admitted to Renard Hospital, about 90% are accompanied by a close relative, and this relative was interviewed at the same time as the patient. Each interview, then, contains information obtained from both the relative and the proband himself. Interviews were conducted by the admitting resident, who was instructed that all patients had to be interviewed and all questions had to be asked and all questions had to be answered.

The interview was short (1 page) and contained material on the age at time of first illness and the kind of the first illness in the proband, material concerning the death of the mother and the father with a specification made about suicide, questions concerning psychiatric illness in the father and mother with material concerning the age of onset, whether the parent was hospitalized, what kind of symptoms the parent had, and what kind of recovery the parent had and the diagnosis if known. The number of siblings were enumerated, with sex and age, and questions were asked concerning psychiatric illness and diagnosis in these siblings, the age of first illness, and matters pertaining to suicide. Other material was obtained on a family history of psychiatric illness in secondary relatives such as grandparents, uncles, aunts, and cousins. Children were inquired about, and psychiatric illness in children was recorded.

Finally, in this structured interview the following symptoms were recorded as plus or minus in regard to present illness of the proband: agitation, retardation, overactivity, flight of ideas, depressed affect, tearfulness, suicidal thoughts, suicidal attempts, weight loss, terminal insomnia, euphoria, diurnal variation, self-depreciation, delusions, disorientation, and memory defect.

In view of the fact that a considerable part of the interview was concerned with diagnosis of first-degree family members (mother, father, and siblings), it was necessary that we evolve some criteria to make such diagnoses. Specific psychiatric symptoms were noted in the first-degree relative and were used. Other criteria also used were the course of the illness and the quality of recovery. For example, any illness sustained by a relative that was characterized by chronic hospitalization in a psychiatric facility was considered schizophrenia if it did not begin after the age of 40 years and was not accompanied by marked affective symptoms. If the relative suffered from an illness with prominent affective symptoms from which he recovered without personality defect, with or without hospitalization, he was considered to have had an affective disorder. Thus, in a family member three major determinants were used in making a diagnosis: course of illness, symptom picture, and quality of recovery. Alcoholism and drug addiction were diagnosed using the criteria of the social and medical consequences of abuse of such substances. A deterioration in relationships at home, at work, or with the law would lead to a diagnosis of alcoholism or addiction if they were a direct result of the abuse of such substances.

The diagnoses on the probands that were recorded at the weekly hospital discharge conference took into account the opinions of all attending psychiatrists and residents who had evaluated the patient. Specifically the symptoms considered important were those of Eitinger, Laane, and Langfeldt, for the schizophrenic reaction; those of Cassidy, Flanagan, Spellman, and Cohen, for manic depressive disease; those of Cohen and White and of Winokur and Holemon, for anxiety reaction; those of Purtell, Robins, and Cohen and of Perley and Guze, for hysteria; and those of Jellinek, for alcoholism.[5,3,4,15,13,12,11] Patients giving unclear clinical pictures were diagnosed as having "undiagnosed psychiatric illness." No effort was made to distinguish cases with precipitating factors or to separate those with more clinically severe features from those with a milder clinical picture.

Consecutively admitted patients (N = 1075) were included in the study. The systematically gleaned material was coded and placed on IBM cards, which were then run. There were 426 Caucasian patients given diagnoses of primary affective disorder, which diagnosis might include cases of manic depressive, psychotic depressive, neurotic depressive, or involutional psychotic reaction. A decision of undiagnosed psychiatric illness was reached in 101 patients. It must be noted that none of the patients with a diagnosis of primary affective disorder had any other illness. If an individual had hysteria or anxiety neurosis or alcoholism accompanied by depressive affect or seemed depressed at the time of admission, the depression was coded out as a secondary diagnosis. If it could not definitely be determined whether the patient had a primary depression in addition to a psychoneurosis or alcoholism, the patient was assigned to the undiagnosed group. Clearly, then, the diagnosis of primary affective disorder was made not only on the basis of the symptomatic picture of depression or mania but also in the absence of another illness which, over the course of time, might have been associated with a secondary affective picture.

Of the 426 primary affective disorder patients, 34 were considered to have mania at the time of admission. We extensively perused all the clinical material and threw out four patients in whom we thought there might be some question of the diagnosis. To these 30 patients we added two Negro patients who had been admitted with a clear diagnosis of mania. Thus the first group that was studied consisted of 32 manic patients. In this group we conducted a follow-up of between 1.5 and 3 years after index admission and interviewed all the first-degree family members available. For the diagnosis of mania in this group the patient had to have been different from his usual self and to have shown a euphoric or frantic mood with at least four of the following symptoms: elation, grandiosity, extreme impatience with restraint, excessive plans, extravagance, overtalkativeness, racing thoughts, flight of ideas, short attention span, increased motor activity and a decreased need for sleep. No other diagnosis could be likely for the patient to be included in this group of 32 manics.

The second group of patients (group B) was composed of manic probands (using the same criteria as in the first group) who were consecutively admitted starting January 9, 1967. We collected in this group 29 new patients. (One of the patients in the first group was readmitted to the hospital, and his follow-up and family study were accomplished during the time we were collecting the second group. In the family study we have counted him as being in the second group; for the follow-up we counted him as being in the first group.) We ceased collecting consecutive manic admissions in May of 1967 but added to the 25 manics collected from January to May 1967 an additional four manic probands in the next few months. The reason for stopping in May was simply a result of the time demands of other duties, and the remaining four cases were quite randomly selected.

For both groups we have a systematically obtained family history, and for both groups we have a family study that includes interviews with all first-degree relatives who were available. The family study (personal interviews with all available family members) in the first group was done at the time of follow-up. The family study in the second group was done at the time the patient was in the hospital.

Diagnoses in the family members who were interviewed followed essentially the same criteria as those in the proband. More specifically, for the diagnosis of depression the patient had to have experienced a rapid or gradual onset of persistent or recurrent feelings of depression and to have had at least three of the following symptoms: loss of energy, loss of interest, sleep disturbance, anorexia, loss of libido, psychomotor retardation, diurnal mood variation, social withdrawal, agitation, obsessional worrying, marked irritability, delusions of poverty, sinfulness or disease, and suicide attempt. The disturbance had to have lasted more than 1 month and no other diagnosis could be likely. In the relative as in the proband, alcoholism was a chronic behavioral disorder manifested by the abuse of alcohol, which manifested itself in difficulties in the patient's health and/or in his social or economic functioning. The same criteria for mania were used in both the proband and the first-degree relatives.

All patients in the first group at follow-up, all patients in the second group at admission, and all interviewed first-degree family members were given a systematic interview, which took between 1 and 3 hours to administer. This interview was a reiteration of the family history. It contained detailed information on the clinical course of the psychosis. It contained 20 questions concerning the symptoms of depression and mania; these questions were similar to the ones that had been recorded at the time of the intake interview in group A. It contained 21 items concerning the symptoms of schizophrenia; these symptoms were taken from the work of Astrup and Fish and included passivity feelings, disturbance of symbolization, delusions of depersonalization, auditory and haptic hallucinations, persecutory delusions, apathy, blunting of affect, abnormal movements, rigidity, and muteness.[2,6] Questions were asked concerning symptoms of disorientation and memory impairment, symptoms of anxiety neurosis such as shortness of breath, palpitations, chest pain, and anxiety attacks, symptoms of hysteria such as amnesia, fits, aphonias, deafness, blindness, and paralysis, and symptoms of excessive alcohol intake and trouble with the law. Also the presence of medical illness was inquired about during this interview.

Two sets of IBM cards were made. The first set was for the probands and contained clinical and family history data. The second set was for each of the interviewed first-degree relatives. A considerable effort was made to obtain information from other medical sources, and this material was coded on the cards. These cards were then sorted in order to obtain the data for the subsequent material in this part of the book.

The frequency of mental disorders in relatives was expressed in terms of morbidity risk (disease expectancy), which is defined as an estimate of the probability that a person will develop the disease in question at some time or another during his life if he survives the period of risk for the disease. The formula used for morbidity risk of alcoholism was that of the Weinberg abridged method. The Weinberg abridged formula is as follows:

$$\text{Morbidity risk} = \frac{a}{b - b_o - \frac{1}{2} b_m}$$

where a is the number of affected individuals, b the total number of individuals examined, b_o the number of individuals who have not passed into the risk period, and b_m the number of individuals who are within the risk period. The denominator in the formula corresponds to the number of people at risk. The formula is discussed in the Stenstedt monograph on manic depressive psychosis.[14]

In order to obtain a more precise estimate of the morbidity risk for affective disorder in the first-degree relatives of the manic probands, we employed a modification of the Weinberg method that was suggested by Strömgren.[14] The following formula is used in the Strömgren method:

$$\text{Morbidity risk} = \frac{a}{\Sigma \ b_i \times c_i}$$

In this formula a equals the number of affected individuals, b_i is the number of persons in the age group i, and c_i is the amount of morbidity risk up to the middle of age group i.

The age of risk has been given by such workers as Stenstedt, Slater, and Helgason.[14,10] In different studies the risk period varies between 20 to 60 years of age and 20 to 80 years of age. In the present study, we used as a period of risk a time span that was gained from the age of onset of affective illness in our own proband group. Thus it will be somewhat different from the previous studies but nevertheless probably relevant to the present data.

In order to obtain the morbidity risk for each 10-year period, we evaluated the 61 probands for age of onset of their affective illness. This is given in Table 6-1.

For alcoholism, the age of risk in men is 20 to 40 years, as given by Åmark.[1]

Standard errors for the morbidity risks were calculated by the following formula:

$$\text{Standard error} = \sqrt{\frac{p\,(1 - p)}{n}}$$

In this formula p equals the morbidity risk expressed as a percent, and n is the number of people at risk. In the morbidity risk formulae given above, n equals the denominator. We would expect the true morbidity risk to lie somewhere within plus or minus two standard errors, and we would be wrong in that expectation one out of 20 times.

The χ^2 (chi-square) method was used in comparing the difference between frequencies of two groups. When appropriate, the Yates correction for small numbers was employed.[9]

Numerous sortings concerning clinical and genetic factors were made, and they are best taken up in subsequent chapters. However, some of the data are relevant to the methodology itself, and they are reported here.

The first group, numbering 32, was composed of 12 males and 20 females. The second group, numbering 29, was composed of 15 females and 14 males. There were two Negroes and 30 Caucasians in the first group, three Negroes and 26 Caucasians in the second group.

The family study (personal interviews with all first-degree family members who were available) in the first group was accomplished at the time of follow-up, 1.5 to 3 years after the index admission, except for one case in

Table 6-1. Age of onset of affective illness

Decade (years)	Number of probands with onset in decade	Percent risk by decade	Percent risk to middle of decade (c_i)
10-19	21	34	17
20-29	18	64	49
30-39	9	79	72
40-49	7	90	85
50-59	5	98	94
60-69	1	100	99
70+	0		

which the family study was done at the time the patient was in the hospital for a subsequent admission. In this first group of 31 (excluding the proband studied at the time of a subsequent admission) there were 121 live first-degree relatives, and of these, 59 (or 49%) were interviewed. In the second group the family study was done at time of index admission. Thus in the 29 of the second group, plus the one patient studied at subsequent admission, the family study was accomplished while the patient was hospitalized. In the 30 cases studied while the proband was in the hospital, there were 131 live relatives; of these, 108 (or 83%) were interviewed. In view of the sizable increase in number of relatives interviewed in the second group, it is clear that the logical time to do a family study is at the time of hospitalization of the proband rather than at some time in the future.

We were interested in obtaining some estimate of the reliability of the family history method when compared with the family study. With the family history method, the assessment of illness in a relative is obtained from material given by the proband and another relative. With the family study, the relative in question is interviewed himself. In the investigation there were 61 probands and 167 first-degree relatives who were personally interviewed. If one assumes that the family-study diagnoses of affective disorder, alcoholism, or schizophrenia are the most reliable and compares these diagnoses to the family history diagnoses in relatives made at the time of admission to a hospital (usually reflecting an interview with the proband and a relative who accompanies him to the hospital), one gets the following comparison:

FH+ = Relative positive for affective disorder by family history
FS+ = Relative positive for affective disorder by interview
FH − and FS − relate to well relatives by same methods

FH+, FS+	21 (13%)
FH+, FS −	3 (2%)
FH −, FS+	42 (25%)
FH −, FS −	101 (60%)
Total relatives interviewed psychiatrically	167 (100%)

If we compare the family history at admission to the family-study data, 73% of the diagnoses of psychiatric disease are correct. The error is 27%.

After the patient has been in the hospital and after more relatives are interviewed, we are able to get more complete family history data. If we compare the more complete family history, i.e., the history of affective disorder in relatives obtained from all the interviewed relatives but not including the diagnosis made by the psychiatric interview itself in the relative himself, we get the following breakdown:

FH+, FS+	27 (16%)
FH+, FS −	3 (2%)
FH −, FS+	36 (22%)
FH −, FS −	101 (60%)
Total relatives interviewed psychiatrically	167 (100%)

Thus, the more relatives interviewed, the more reliable is the family history

Seventy-six percent of the cases were correctly diagnosed from the family history. However, there is still a 24% error if one compares the family history to the family study. In general, the largest part of the error is in the false negative, the person called well by family history but found out to be ill with affective disorder, alcoholism, or schizophrenia by personal interview.

The reason for this becomes obvious if one looks at the hospitalization histories of the relatives. There are 27 relatives in the more complete family history data who were FH+, FS+. Of these, 15 (or 56%) were psychiatrically hospitalized at some time during their lives. There are 36 FH−, FS+. Of these, six (or 17%) were hospitalized (χ^2 between groups is 8.82, df=1, p < 0.01). The simple fact of hospitalization in a relative makes it significantly more likely that a person will be able to give an accurate account of affective illness in that relative.

Affective illness is quite likely not to necessitate hospitalization. Fremming found that 40% of the manic depressives in his population study were never hospitalized for psychiatric reasons.[7] Helgason found that 37% of female and 48% of male manic depressives were never hospitalized for their affective illnesses.[8]

It is clear that the most reliable assessment of illness in relatives comes from the family study rather than the family history. In our work-up of the material, we will give two types of data, those obtained from all sources (family history, records, personally interviewed relatives) and those obtained only from the personally interviewed relatives (family-study data). This latter material, though smaller, is, we believe, more reliable. The all-sources material contains a number of relatives on whom we have only a family history. There is a large error (23%) in such assessments. The personally interviewed relatives, on the other hand, either did or did not meet the criteria for illness; and reason dictates that this kind of personal examination should give the best criteria for evaluating a person's psychiatric status. Family history data provide an acceptable qualitative estimate of illness in relatives, but a family study is an absolute necessity for such quantitative calculations as true morbidity risks in sibs and parents.

REFERENCES

1. Åmark, C.: A study in alcoholism, Acta Psychiat. Neurol. Scand. (Supp. 70), 1951.
2. Astrup, C., Fossum, A., and Holmboe, R.: Prognosis in functional psychoses, Springfield, Ill., 1962, Charles C Thomas, Publisher.
3. Cassidy, W. L., Flanagan, N. B., Spellman, M., and Cohen, M. E.: Clinical observations in manic depressive disease: a quantitative study of 100 manic depressive patients and 50 medically sick controls, J.A.M.A. **164**:1535, 1957.
4. Cohen, M., and White, P.: Life situations, emotions, and neurocirculatory asthenia (anxiety neurosis, neurasthenia, effort syndrome), Ass. Res. Nerv. Ment. Dis. Proc. **29**:832, 1949.
5. Eitinger, L., Laane, C. L., and Langfeldt, G.: The prognostic value of the clinical picture and the therapeutic value of physical treatment in schizophrenia and the schizophreniform states, Acta Psychiat. Scand. **33**:33, 1958.
6. Fish, F.: A guide to the Leonhard classification of chronic schizophrenia, Psychiat. Quart. **38**:438, 1964.
7. Fremming, K.: The expectation of mental infirmity in a sample of the Danish

population. Occasional papers on eugenics, no. 7, London, 1951, Cassell & Co., Ltd.

8. Helgason, T.: Epidemiology of mental disorders in Iceland, Acta Psychiat. Scand. 40:(Supp. 173), 1964.
9. Hill, A. B.: Principles of medical statistics, New York, 1961, Oxford University Press, Inc.
10. Hopkinson, G.: A genetic study of affective illness in patients over 50, Brit. J. Psychiat. 110:244, 1964.
11. Jellinek, E. M.: Phases of alcohol addiction, Quart. J. Stud. Alcohol 13:673, 1952.
12. Perley, M., and Guze, S. B.: Hysteria, the stability and usefulness of clinical criteria, New Eng. J. Med. 226:421, 1962.
13. Purtell, J., Robins, E., and Cohen, M.: Observations on clinical aspects of hysteria, J.A.M.A. 146:902, 1957.
14. Stenstedt, Å.: A study in manic-depressive psychosis, Acta Psychiat. Neurol. Scand. (Supp. 79), 1952.
15. Winokur, G., and Holemon, E.: Chronic anxiety neurosis: clinical and sexual aspects, Acta Psychiat. Scand. 39:384, 1963.

Chapter 7

The study: description of manic and depressive episodes

Over many years there has been a dialogue in psychiatry concerning the necessity and usefulness of diagnosis. One viewpoint suggests that the important variables in therapy are the intrapsychic and interpersonal conflicts and therefore diagnosis is just "pigeonholing people," with little usefulness and possibly great harm. Another point of view holds that a rigorous diagnosis enables one to make a meaningful prognosis of a patient's future by knowledge of the behavior of other persons with similar complaints. Being aware of the natural history of a disorder is in psychiatry, as in the rest of medicine, a central issue as regards management and therapy of patients. It is in this spirit that the present study was undertaken.

There are important limitations to our description of the clinical picture of manic depressive psychosis. First, all the patients were treated during each episode in a hospital or in a clinic; and this must be considered when comparisons are made between our patients and those of earlier authors. Second, studying consecutive hospital admissions of manic probands (to Renard Hospital) for a specified period of time may eliminate many selection artifacts but also tends to include patients who are more frequently ill.

ONSET OF MANIC DEPRESSIVE DISEASE AND SOME CHARACTERISTICS OF THE PATIENTS

Thirty-five females and 26 males comprised the patient sample. All of these were manic at the time of index admission to Renard Hospital and were so diagnosed at discharge. The median age of admission was 42 years for males and 36.5 years for females (Table 7-1).

The earliest onset of illness was in a male patient age 15 years, and the latest in a woman, age 67 years. The median age of onset (first illness) was for males 24 years and for females 24 years.

The age of onset in true manic depressive disease is noteworthy by virtue of the fact that over one third the patients had manifested symptoms of their illness prior to reaching their twentieth birthday. Almost two thirds had fallen ill before age 30 years. Since only one patient first became ill after 60 years of age, it appears that a logical risk period for manic depressive disease is 15 to 60 years. In general, the illness attacks late adolescents and young adults, but it is also first seen up to the age of 60 years and rarely after this age.

In a recent paper, Bratfos and Haug presented data on the course of manic

Table 7-1. Age at index admission and onset of illness

Decade (years)	Age on admission			Age at onset of illness		
	M	F	Total	M	F	Total
10-19	2	4	6	8	13	21
20-29	5	7	12	9	9	18
30-39	4	8	12	2	7	9
40-49	7	6	13	3	4	7
50-59	6	7	13	4	1	5
60-69	2	2	4	0	1	1
70-79	0	1	1	0	0	0
Total	26	35	61	26	35	61

depressive psychosis.[1] They studied 207 patients admitted to the Psychiatric Department of the University of Oslo with this diagnosis and followed these patients for 6 years. Somewhat more than 50% of their patients were first-admission patients. Of their 207 patients, 80% had suffered only from depressions, 18% had manias and depressions, and 2% had only manias. Thus, the vast majority of the patients could be considered as having depressive disease (unipolar) rather than manic depressive disease. The mean age of onset for their total groups was 35 years, and the mean age of the first-admission patients was 49 years. The mean hospital stay for the index admission was 9 weeks, and the mean age at discharge from the hospital for all 207 index admissions was 55 years. Comparing these data from Bratfos and Haug to those of the present study, one might infer that the onset of illness for manic depressive disease is much earlier than the onset for depressive disease.

Perris and d'Elia compared the ages of onset in bipolar and unipolar psychoses.[3] Forty percent of the bipolar probands had an onset between 15 and 25 years of age. Less than 10% of the unipolar probands had an onset in this age range. These authors concluded that there was a significantly earlier onset in bipolar patients.

The early age of onset in the patients of the present study and the great prevalence of affective disorder in the population (see Chapter 3) suggest that serious attention should be given to the possibility that a psychiatrically ill adolescent may be suffering from the first symptoms of manic depressive disease.

Thirty-seven patients were manic when they were first ill and 24 were depressed. Thus, 61% of the probands had had a mania as the first manifestation of their illness. There was no statistical difference between those patients whose first illness was mania or depression as regards number of episodes, age of patient at index admission, or age of onset (see Table 7-2).

Perris evaluated the polarity of the first episode in 131 bipolar patients.[7] He found that 45 patients (34%) were manic at onset. The type of first episode had no significant relationship to sex or number of episodes. Male patients had a significantly earlier onset than did female patients if in both cases the first episode was manic. Female patients had an earlier onset than male patients if the first episode was depressive.

Table 7-2. Type of first illness in manic probands

	First illness mania	First illness depression
Male	18	8
Female	19	16
Total	37	24

Table 7-3. Episodes of illness and age at episodes separated by 6 months

Epoch (years)	Number who have passed through the epoch	Manic episodes	Depressive episodes	Mixed episodes	Mean attacks per 10-yr. epoch for both sexes
10-19					
Male		10	10	0	
Female	61	10	9	0	.62
20-29					
Male		13	6	0	
Female	55	22	23	4	1.2
30-39					
Male		19	16	1	
Female	43	23	18	3	1.2
40-49					
Male		15	4	1	
Female	31	12	19	7	1.3
50-59					
Male		7	4	0	
Female	18	21	5	1	2.1
60-69					
Male		4	2	0	
Female	5	3	0	0	1.8
70-79					
Male		0	0	0	
Female	1	3	1	1	5.0
Total					
Male		69	42	2	
Female		93	75	16	
		161	117	18	

In eight patients (4 male and 4 female) the index admission was the first episode of illness in the present study. The majority of patients had had considerable illness before the index admission. Taking into account all the episodes prior to admission, the index admissions themselves, and the episodes of illness in the subgroup of 32, who were followed up for 1.5 to 3 years (group A, see Chapter 6), one clearly sees that the probands were subject to many attacks.

In the 61 patients there were 2.6 manic attacks per person, 1.9 depressive attacks per person, and 0.30 mixed attacks per person. The mean number of affective episodes (regardless of polarity) was 4.9. The range for individuals in the study is between one and 16. The mode in this group of patients is three episodes (13 patients).

An effort was made to determine the mean number of attacks that occurred in each 10-year epoch, starting at 10 years and ending at 79 years. No striking differences were seen; the mean number of attacks in the epoch 10 to 16 years was 0.62, and this low figure could be accounted for by the fact that up to 19 years of age only 33% of the patients had fallen ill. There is a tendency for an increase in mean number of attacks in the epochs from 40 years of age on when they are compared to the epochs from 20 to 29 years and 30 to 39 years. This increase is not marked (Table 7-3).

In comparing the number of episodes suffered by males to those suffered by females, we find that the 25 males in the study had 4.3 episodes per person and the females 5.3 episodes per person. This is a 20% difference, indicating that the females have an increased number of episodes. The importance of this difference becomes somewhat more striking when one notes that the age of the females at index admission was lower than that for males (36.5 years vs. 42 years), thus giving the group of females less years at risk. The medians were 5.3 and 3.2 for females and males respectively. The group median was 4.3. Chi-square evaluation, comparing the males and females above and below the median, revealed that the difference was not statistically reliable (p > 0.05).

In the bipolar patients reported by Perris, 56 males had a mean number of episodes of 1.5, and 75 females had a mean number of 1.9.[7] The observation time for females was shorter than that for males (18.6 years vs. 21.0 years), again giving the females less years at risk. Thus, the Perris data are similar to the data of the present study, showing some increase in number of episodes in women.

One might conclude that manic depressive disease is associated with many episodes of illness (both manic and depressive) and that females tend to show more episodes than men. The difference between men and women does not, however, reach statistical significance.

Ascertainment of whether a patient was ill depended on the presence of the criteria set forth earlier. We also sought for evidence of objective social or economic dysfunction or of hospitalization and treatment in order to make a retrospective diagnosis of which we could be confident. A change of polarity (from manic to depressive or vice versa) was considered a new episode if the new episode also fulfilled the criteria for diagnosis.

In the descriptions of manic or depressed phases, records obtained from other hospitals were often too scanty to be useful. Consequently, evaluations of the clinical picture were made from the systematic interviews on the probands for the index admissions and the Renard Hospital charts for other admissions. Those patients transferred from one hospital to another were counted as "one" hospitalization. Multiple hospitalizations occurring during a prolonged episode were counted as one episode.

In Table 7-3 are recorded 296 episodes of illness for the 61 patients. During

Table 7-4. Number of hospitalizations

	In Renard Hospital				Other hospitals All types of affective episodes
	Mania	**Depression**	**Mixed**	**Total**	
Male	40	5	1	46	43
Female	68	28	13	109	64
Total	108	33	14	155	107

Table 7-5. Depression prior to onset of mania

	Males (N = 26)	Females (N = 35)	Total
Number of separate manic episodes observed	37	63	100
Number of manias with prior depression	17	34	51
Prior depressions with no treatment	6	11	17
Prior depressions treated with drug therapy	11	23	34*
Prior depressions hospitalized	2	12	14
Prior depressions treated with ECT (electroconvulsive therapy)	2	11	13*
Suicide (thoughts or attempts) with prior depressions	2	3	5

*More than one kind of therapy.

these episodes the patients were hospitalized 262 times. Hospitalization occurred less frequently for depressive than for manic episodes (Table 7-4).

The clinical description of the manic episode is based on the 108 admissions to Renard Hospital. The 108 admissions to Renard represent 100 separate manic episodes.

THE MANIC EPISODE
Depression prior to the onset of mania

A depressive mood swing prior to the onset of a manic episode is frequently observed. The duration of this depression is variable (between 1 and 8 months), but the depression is often severe enough to warrant treatment or hospitalization (Table 7-5).

Since the history of depression in most cases was obtained retrospectively, we consider these figures a minimum. There were no significant trends as regards age and sex. In the various decades from 15 to 69 years manias were preceded by depressions 30% to 74% of the times, with no constant increase or decrease with age. In a number of cases, "successful" treatment of the depressive episode was the onset of mania, and we might speculate that the drugs or electroshock therapy were really the "cause" of the manic episode; this question will be dealt with later. Although many of our patients had evident depressions, others, who were scored negatively, had "minor" depressive mood swings or hints of depressive behavior prior to the onset of mania.

The finding that 51 of 100 manic episodes were preceded by significant depressions whose mean duration was longer than 1 month is an important observation. The clinician who treats the depression in manic depressive psychosis must be aware that frequently the depression is followed by a manic episode, and he should look for signs of mania to prevent in advance the considerable social consequences of being manic outside a hospital setting. Our patients had more frequent manic than depressive episodes (Table 7-3), and the depression that precedes a mania is, therefore, a common occurrence in their lives. The mean duration of the depressive episode, including treatment, was 3.7 months, and this adds considerably to the duration of incapacity that the manic episode represents.

It is intriguing to speculate whether all manic episodes are preceded by a period of depression. As previously stated, many manias that were scored negatively in this regard had minor depressive mood swings; however, many well-observed episodes had no evidence of prior depression, and our clinical impression is that the depression prior to the onset of mania is not invariable.

Onset of the manic episode

The onset of a manic episode may be abrupt, i.e., becoming evident on awakening or developing over a few moments or hours. More often it is gradual, taking a few days or weeks to develop fully. On occasion, the change of personality is startling in its rapidity. The following clinical vignette illustrates this:

> Mrs. A. D., a 43-year-old married female, was visiting her elderly mother in a local hospital. The patient and her family had been quite upset because her mother was to have major G.I. surgery the following day and the outcome was uncertain. In addition, Mrs. A. D. was suffering from a "poison oak" rash and had been receiving steroids by mouth for 1 week. During the visit Mrs. A. D. fainted and was wheeled to the emergency room. She awakened while being examined and knelt prayerfully before the surprised intern, kissing his ring. She believed he was Jesus Christ and that there was a halo around his head and light emanating from his red beard. She was ecstatic and had an evident flight of ideas. When she was admitted to Renard Hospital, her diagnosis was manic depressive reaction, manic type. Mrs. A. D. was oriented at all times and remembers the episode to this day. Her illness ran a typical course. Mrs. A. D. had previous and subsequent manias unrelated to steroids.

In addition to type of onset, another important question in the beginning of the manic episode concerns the possible presence of precipitating factors.

Table 7-6 examines the onset of the manic episode and illustrates some important relationships regarding precipitating factors and abruptness of onset. Thirty episodes of mania (in 27 patients) were preceded by one or more noteworthy physical or psychologic occurrences. These were electroconvulsive therapy (ECT, EST) for depression, antidepressant medication, stopping administration of lithium, stopping phenothiazines, administration of other medication, death in the family, divorce, surgery in a relation, attending a political convention, suicide and murder in the family, or the postpartum state. Thus, in 70 out of 100 episodes no clear stresses were found to precipitate the episode. All but two of the 27 patients who showed precipitating

Table 7-6. Onset of the manic episode

	Number of separate manic episodes observed	Abrupt onset	Gradual onset	Physical precipitants	Psychologic precipitants	Postpartum
Male	37	10	27	8	3	0
Female	63	15	48	14	6	3
Total	100	25	75	22	9	3*

*Five months, 1 month, 1 day postpartum.

factors in some of their episodes had other episodes in which precipitating factors played no role.

There are several questions that a study of stress prior to the onset of a manic episode should answer. First, can stress precipitate a psychosis of this type in an individual who does not already suffer manic depressive illness? Second, are there individuals who develop the psychosis only in response to stress? Last, do individuals who already have a manic depressive diathesis respond to stress by becoming ill?

We accepted as stresses only those events that preceded the onset of the episode by a few hours or days, and only those stresses, psychologic or physical, that were severe, unusual in the patient's life, or "likely" to precipitate a manic psychosis (except for the postpartum state, which had to occur within 6 months). It is obvious that the number of episodes which appear to be precipitated would increase if a greater time lapse were permitted between the stress and the first symptoms or if milder stresses were accepted as sufficient to precipitate the psychosis. Because different authors accept different criteria for ascertaining a precipitant, the results are not readily comparable.

Of the 100 manic episodes observed in the hospital, 30 were immediately preceded by a stressful event. Ten of these episodes occurred in men and 20 in women. Four patients had more than one type of stress so that among the 10 "precipitated" episodes in men there were eight physical and three psychologic events. Among 20 episodes in women, there were 17 physical and six psychologic events. All but two of the patients (1 man and 1 woman) had prior or subsequent manic and depressive episodes, indicating that the psychosis occurred in individuals who had the diathesis. Fifty percent of the "precipitated" episodes occurred in patients who were significantly depressed prior to the onset of mania, which might mean that the manic episode would have occurred without the precipitating stress. Five patients developed mania after a course of ECT for depression, and seven while being treated with antidepressants. The role of these agents is impossible to assess. In six cases, patients who had been manic in the past became manic again when phenothiazines (2 patients) or lithium (4 patients) were stopped. These patients had been well for at least 6 months and so were counted as having "new" episodes. It might be, however, that the patients were continuously manic and that the withdrawal of the therapeutic agent revealed the underlying persistent illness. The reasons the patients gave for stopping medication were varied; however, a majority had been taken off the medication by physicians who felt the patients were well enough to do without.

It appears that only those patients with manic depressive diatheses develop the illness following stress. The two patients whose episodes following stress were the only ones they had ever had were both depressed prior to the onset of mania and prior to the precipitating stress.

The last question we posed concerns whether manic depressive patients respond to stress by developing a mania or a depression. This is difficult to answer satisfactorily. We would have to have data concerning stresses to which no illness developed (which we did not obtain) and a normal and carefully matched control group.

One case in which a psychologically stressful situation preceded the onset of mania is presented below:

> The patient is Mrs. B. D., a 58-year-old rural Missouri matron. She had always been somewhat moody but had never been manic until the index episode. Mrs. B. D. had been depressed for 3 to 4 months prior to the manic episode; her symptoms were apathy, social withdrawal, tearfulness, insomnia, and weight loss; she neglected her home and frequently expressed feelings that she was a burden to the family. Her husband, a politically and financially powerful man in the county, arranged that she be appointed as a delegate to a national political convention, "to snap her out of her depression."
>
> At the convention her mood was different from what it had been at home. She was active, aggressive, and interested in the proceedings; and, to the surprise of her family, she made several speeches before the state delegation. During the last and most hectic nights of the convention she slept only 1 to 2 hours per night and uninhibitedly took part in several demonstrations for her candidate. Her behavior was not considered unusual for a delegate.
>
> On her way home the patient and her husband stopped off to visit with her daughter and son-in-law in St. Louis, and her behavior, which was appropriate at the convention, did not change. She continued to make speeches, place calls, and send telegrams on behalf of the candidate. She refused to sleep, and on the next day, the day prior to admission, she began to notice references in the Bible and on TV to her "man" which indicated that she and the candidate would together save the world.
>
> On admission to the hospital the patient was noted to be a tired-looking woman with a hoarse voice who would not stop pacing or talking. She was constantly buttonholing people, enlisting their support for her candidate, and she became hostile when they would not listen to all she had to say. She had a definite flight of ideas and was extremely distractible. She was oriented to time, place, and person. She was grandiose and had grandiose delusions. Diagnosis on admission was manic depressive reaction, manic type. In the hospital the patient received large doses of phenothiazines and within several weeks reverted to normalcy, with full insight into her behavior. At follow-up 3 years later she was well and had shown no depressive or manic symptoms since her hospitalization.

Certainly in this case a series of psychologic stimuli preceded the mania, but their association may have been no more than a chance encounter.

Clinically, however, one wonders whether stressful events, particularly those that evoke strong affective responses (deaths, tragedy, etc.), might trigger an episode. However, the simple fact that 70 of the 100 manic episodes that were observed in Renard Hospital were not preceded by significant physical or psychologic events makes it appear that precipitating factors cannot be considered very important in the pathogenesis of mania.

In a systematic study of life events and the onset of primary affective disorders Hudgens, Morrison, and Barchha reported on 34 depressions, six manias, and 40 nonpsychiatrically ill controls.[3] In one manic patient of the six, the onset of the index affective episode followed 6 months of objective life stress. Thus, five of the manics in the study did not have a psychologic stress preceding their index illness. In another one of the six manics, the illness was present before a significant event but an exacerbation followed the event. These data are very similar to those of the present study and give little support to the idea that life stresses play a major role in mania.

Those patients with abrupt onsets of their manias (25 out of 100 episodes) tended to arrive at a hospital sooner than did those with gradual onsets. Females enter the hospital after onset sooner than males do, for both gradual and abrupt onsets.

Younger patients tended to have abrupt onsets more frequently than did older patients. Of those episodes that started before the age of 30 years, 11 had an abrupt onset and 15 had a gradual onset. Of those episodes that started after 30 years of age, 14 had an abrupt onset and 60 had a gradual onset. The difference was statistically reliable (χ^2 with Yates correction $= 4.43$, df $= 1$, p < 0.05).

The presence of precipitating factors has no relation to the abruptness or gradualness of the onset. However, the type of onset is relevant to other clinical factors. Abruptly beginning manias tend to be somewhat different clinically from those that begin gradually (see Table 7-7).

Significant differences are seen in the presence of delusions and extreme motor activity (shouting, assaultiveness, constant motion), which occur more frequently in episodes with an abrupt onset.

Most patients in whom an abrupt onset occurred had prior or subsequent manic or depressive episodes that had a gradual onset. Finally, those cases

Table 7-7. Clinical findings related to abrupt and gradual onsets

| | Type of onset | | Differences between onset types | |
	Percent abrupt (N = 25)	Percent gradual (N = 75)	χ^2 (with Yates correction)	Significance
Presence of delusions	68	41	4.32	p < 0.05
Presence of hallucinations	32	17	1.62	p $=$ n.s.
Extreme motor activity	64	31	7.41	p < 0.01
Disorientation	12	7	—	p $=$ n.s.
Precipitating factors	49	31	1.77	p $=$ n.s.
Depression prior to onset of mania	49	52	—	p $=$ n.s.

with an abrupt onset were as frequently depressed prior to the onset of mania as were those with a more gradual onset, indicating that the episode did not necessarily begin de novo from a normal mood state but might occur suddenly during the course of a depressive episode.

Reasons for admission to hospital

The manic psychosis provides an excellent opportunity to observe the interaction between a psychotic individual and his environment. Unlike other functional psychoses, the onset of the illness is rather acute and the patient, who is frequently successful in his work, does not have an opportunity to modify his surroundings to accept his unusual and often bizarre behavior. The reason for admission to the hospital (Table 7-8) is not only a measure of how common a symptom is but also how disturbing it can be. It is rare that a patient is admitted without some sort of coercion. He rarely is able to understand that his activities are upsetting. These patients, however, often are aware that they are ill and agree to hospitalization even though they do not appreciate the extent of their bizarre conduct.

As noted before, men are ill longer than women prior to hospitalization. It is interesting to speculate on reasons why this is so; one would expect that men were more often employed and that inability to function would be more easily evident. However, men are better able financially and physically to control their environment.

From Table 7-8, it appears that men more frequently abuse alcohol than do women (χ^2 with Yates correction = 8.25, df = 1, p < 0.01). In spite of heavy drinking and spending money, which they often did not possess, no patient was ever charged with a felony or misdemeanor and many families had to pay off large debts accumulated during a manic episode. Assaultive or destructive behavior was always in the family and never resulted in severe injury.

Increased sexuality was much more common than it appears from this table. It seemed that disturbing promiscuity, more frequent in women, was not common. Most patients who manifested hypersexuality did so in a socially approved fashion.

Insomnia was the most common complaint, and this complaint was always

Table 7-8. Factors leading to admission to hospital

	Percent episodes in males (N = 37)	Percent episodes in females (N = 63)
Extravagant	30	17
Assaultive or destructive	8	17
Abused alcohol	32	8
Sexual problems	3	8
Insomnia	11	37
Overtalkative, overactive	22	25
Delusional, hallucinating	11	25
Work disability	27	13

received from the family. The patient, although he slept little or not at all, rarely felt tired. He was often aware that the insomnia was unusual and not infrequently attributed his ability to stay awake to some special power he had. Unlike the insomnia of depression, in which the patients may lie in bed quietly or sit and brood, the manic is often pacing, talking, arguing, and keeping others awake, hence its prominence as a symptom resulting in admission. Females suffered from insomnia more frequently than did males (χ^2 with Yates correction = 5.88, df = 1, p < 0.03).

Overactivity and overtalkativeness were frequently given as symptoms, and these had to reach considerable proportions before the family would consider hospitalization, especially against the patient's desires.

The development of hallucinations or delusions, where onset was most often rapid, was considered by the family as an ominous sign. The delusions were frequently dramatic and grandiose and were, as we shall see later, associated with extreme hyperactivity. The manic delusions are of short duration and, unlike those in schizophrenia, are an unusual occurrence in the patient's life. In addition, the manic patient, unlike the schizophrenic, is gregarious, loud, and not generally guarded. His delusions are therefore prominently discussed and described and are, hence, very upsetting to his environment.

Of the factors leading to hospitalization, only alcohol abuse in males and insomnia in females significantly differentiate males and females.

Unlike depression, the manic episode almost always results in hospitalization or treatment on an outpatient basis by a psychiatrist, which, we suppose, is a reflection of its disturbing nature and of its relatively abrupt onset. This is not true of those patients with chronic hypomania, whose elevated mood, hyperactivity, and thought disorder tend to be less severe.

Only one case was observed, among the patients or their families, of a patient with manic episodes who had no medical contact. This man (father of one of the index patients) was periodically shut in his cellar by the family and there, alone, manifested wild, full-blown manic excitement.

SYMPTOMS OF MANIA

The hallmark of mania is a change in affect. The mood in mania is elevated, and this elevation in mood ranges from infectious cheerfulness to ecstasy or exaltation. In our series of patients, the degree of mood elevation varied from patient to patient and from time to time during the same episode. The changes in mood were capricious, responding to internal as well as external stimuli and so very changeable that they defied measurement. Ninety-eight percent of the episodes were characterized at some time by this elevation of mood, and 95% by "lability of mood." In only 5% was the mood unchanging over a period of hours or days.

Eighty-three percent of the manic episodes were characterized by hostility, generally verbal but at times physical, and 14% of the admissions were the result, in part, of assaultive or destructive behavior. In two patients this hostility reached homicidal proportions in that the patients expressed the desire to kill a close relative or friend, but no such attempts were ever made.

Table 7-9. Characteristics of affect in mania

	Episodes in		Total (N = 100)
	Males (N = 37)	Females (N = 63)	
Euphoria	35	63	98
Lability	36	59	95
Hostility	32	51	83
Irritability	32	53	85
Depression	18	50	68
Suicide thoughts	3	4	7
Depressive delusions	4	20	24
Diurnal variation			
More manic in A.M.	12	25	37
More manic in P.M.	9	21	30

Perhaps the most reactive symptom of manic behavior is "irritability," defined here as the patient's negative response to minor stimuli. The manic patient is distractible as well as irritable and unable to concentrate on any one thing for more than a few minutes. He responds to internal and external stimuli in a haphazard fashion. He is impatient and constantly besieged with ideas and impulses. His ability to carry out any form of activity is limited because of this. Not being able to ignore minor stimuli seems often to lead to frustration and anger. Requests, rarely sustained for any length of time, are often inappropriate and are, therefore, refused, which leads again to frustration and anger. Eighty-five percent of the episodes were characterized by this symptom.

All the patients were uninhibited and loud, not able or willing to contain hostile feelings; and not infrequently a patient who was restrained in some fashion became angry or assaultive. The manic patient is typically social, more so than usual and is most insistent on being with and talking to others. No patient was seclusive or guarded in his approach either to his family or to the physician. It is this pressure to relate to others that, as often as any of the other symptoms of mania, alerts people in the patient's surroundings to the fact that he is ill. A most characteristic sight when the patient is brought to the hospital is a frightened and exhausted family, which has frequently been awake for 1 or more nights being lectured to by a bright-eyed and excited patient.

In 68% of the patients who were observed, a depressed mood was seen during the manic episode. Usually this was fleeting tearfulness and sadness, lasting a few minutes or hours. In only four cases did a depressed mood last longer than 1 day, in three cases for 2 days and in one case for 3 days. During the depression all the characteristics of manic depressive reaction, depressed type, were seen. Patients might be apprehensive and frequently agitated, or they might be withdrawn and in one case mute. Psychomotor retardation and increased latency of response could be seen. Suicidal thoughts were never expressed during a period of mood elevation but did occur during seven episodes of mania. No suicide attempts were made during the depressed hours, and usually the depressions were too short for plans of this nature to be made. Of the 68 manias in which depression was observed, 24 (35.4%) were associated with depressive delusions or delusional guilt. These were similar to delusions ordinarily seen in depression; ideas of sin, of a death in the family, of having cancer, of having killed someone, or of deserving death were all expressed. The onset of the melancholy was usually quite abrupt and its disappearance usually as quick.

An important observation which can be made during these brief depressions is that they appear endogenous; and, unlike the irritability or hostility which the patient expresses, these short depressive episodes are not reactions to the environment. These brief depressive thoughts or episodes as well as the cycle of manic depressive disease serve to unify the concept of mania and depression.

The short depressive contaminations in the manic episodes were more frequently seen in females (50 out of 63 episodes) than in males (18 out of 37 episodes). This is a significant difference (χ^2 with Yates correction = 8.745, df = 1, p < 0.005).

A letter from a patient to her doctor is illustrative of a brief depressive episode with delusions, hallucinations, and paranoid feelings that lasted about 12 hours and occurred following EST. This patient has had many prior manic and depressive episodes with complete restitution of all her faculties. Apart from the delusions and hallucinations described below, her manic episode is typical.

Dear Doctor:

I am going to write this so you will understand. Yesterday after my shock treatment I had all sorts of weird ideas that I was being held prisoner here and that you would never let me go, that you were a quack and last night I heard and saw things. Perry Mason was on but I kept hearing and seeing all sorts of strange things on the TV and radio. I'd walk down the hall and each time I looked the nurses had changed from one color uniform to another, had a cap at one glance and at the next look none. I was convinced you had me hypnotized, etc. I know the other patients saw how strangely I acted. I felt like a trapped animal. I can't remember exactly how the TV was but I'd hear the names of some of my family and watching the set the mouths were moving to the same words. All sorts of jumbled things kept coming on the screen and I'd see as well as hear them. You must realize I don't belong here with these patients. When I talk to you it seems I say very little but that is why my condition has not been widely known. I just can't express it because I am too ashamed. I find it difficult to write. These hallucinations I had were the first I ever had in my life but I somehow knew what they were. There just isn't anything to work with doctor. I would not harm anyone physically at least I don't think so but I was very impolite to everyone after that one treatment. I paced the floor all day. Everything is going wrong and it's getting worse, all the time. Please doctor realize what this is and that I have to be sent away. I can talk a few minutes and not sound too bad but try to get to the extent of my knowledge and there isn't any I feel so bad that I won't be able to walk or move much longer.

Sincerely,
M. I. S.

Diurnal variation of mood is a classical symptom of depression. Historically, a worsening of depression in the morning is characteristic of *psychotic* or *endogenous* depressions, and feeling more depressed in the evening is characteristic of *neurotic* depression. Diurnal variation may also be seen in mania and was observed in 67% of the episodes. The differences between worsening in the morning or the evening are not statistically significant, and separate episodes in the same patient were associated with different types of variation. The diurnal variation observed referred to the whole syndrome, not just the affect. Patients were "worse" in the morning or in the evening (i.e., more euphoric, hostile, hyperactive, overtalkative), not just more or less euphoric. This diurnal variation did not correlate with age, sex, type of onset, or presence or absence of precipitating factors.

Textbook descriptions of the manic state paint a picture of unrestrained continued exuberance and frequently infer that the other symptoms are secondary to this affective state. Consider the description by L. Binswanger as quoted by Karl Jaspers[4]:

> His [the manic patient's] world is pliant and variegated, bright and rosy . . .
> There is a specific pattern in this particular world which gives it meaning as a whole. It has grown into a peculiar world of its own conditioned by the spirit which illuminates it from within; this vital experience brings about immense vigor, the melting of boundaries, wholesale intrusions and the crowding together of things, an ineffective busyness, a general flitting, a press of talk and good, eloquent speech, in short, the whole behavior of the manic state.*

The mood our patients experienced was elevated. They generally expressed it in religious terms, such as "saved" and "exalted," or in terms of the effect of alcohol or drugs, i.e., "high." Often they were sexually aroused and felt that they were in "love." Not infrequently a combination of these was experienced. In one drawing, a patient pictured herself as a saint wearing a halo; below she drew a large apple (see figure on following page).

Our patients were labile and frequently angry. Their "world" was not stable and rosy but changing without reason and frustrating. Demands were seldom met, rages were often seen, and social contact was always unsatisfying. The mood was not experienced as foreign to the patient or imposed on him, however. He frequently had insight into the fact that he was ill, often at the same time he was expressing delusional or grandiose ideas. Often he would become depressed and hopeless and then euphoric again. On followup, it was clear that most patients did not enjoy being manic; only one patient had stopped his medication in order to get "high." For the most part, the patients remembered being wound up and unable to stop, not feeling tired but aware that something was wrong, upsetting their families, and not being able to stop. This was especially true of being irritable. As one patient described his mania, "It was like being grouchy in the morning, multiplied by one thousand."

Last, two patients had been manic without euphoria. These episodes had

*From Jaspers, K.: General psychopathology, Chicago, 1963, University of Chicago Press.

Self-portrait of a manic patient.

all the other characteristics of mania, and the patients' histories of episodic mood swings made the diagnosis clear.

One of the cardinal symptoms of mania is overactivity. In every case the patient's motility was increased. This varied from an inability to sit still to wild, assaultive behavior, potentially injurious to the patient or others.

We graded hyperactivity on a three-point scale. "Grade I" was the mildest grade and included agitated hand wringing, inability to sit still, and pacing. "Grade II" included running, dashing, and constant motion. The patient still had some measure of control. "Grade III" included the most severe forms of overactivity. The patient was unable to control himself, running, jumping, throwing things, being assaultive and combative, and on occasion requiring seclusion until sedation could take effect. It must be remembered that the overactivity was quite variable. We graded the patient according to the maximum degree of hyperactivity he demonstrated.

The highest grades of motor activity were associated with the most severe thought disorder and with the presence of delusions.

The mildest type of overactivity, grade I, seemed most reactive to internal and external stimuli, the patient responding to the environment in a manner

Table 7-10. Motility in mania

Episodes	(I) Mild increase	(II) Moderate increase	(III) Severe increase	Posturing
In males (N = 37)	9	5	13	1
In females (N = 63)	15	22	26	6
Total (N = 100)	24	37	39	7

appropriate to his mental state and thought content. These patients also had periods of quiescence, during which ordinary tasks such as sewing or playing cards were possible.

The most severe overactivity, grade III, was more spontaneous and less reactive, the patient acting in concert with delusions or hallucinations. Although these patients were less active when placed by themselves, they still were not able to sit or lie down for more than a short time. Quiet periods, lasting only a few moments, would end with a wild fury of movement. These patients also tended to be the loudest and to have the greatest speed of association. It was obvious that staying in the community was impossible in this state. These were patients who were too preoccupied to eat or drink, who slept the least, and who lost weight. Although they frequently looked tired, in only three cases did they admit to feeling less than "fine," and that only after being asked. In these cases the syndrome of manic exhaustion may be seen; and the most severe overactivity of it, lasting longer than a "few days," represented a medical emergency.

One case of manic exhaustion was seen in our patients. This was an 18-year-old girl who was first ill in the early days of chlorpromazine therapy. She lost much weight and was too active to eat or drink. She had not slept for 2 to 3 days in hospital and 7 days at home. Her vital signs remained stable, but she had several syncopal episodes, which were felt to signal the onset of an exhaustion syndrome. The patient was calmed with wet sheet packs in 48 hours.

The most severe forms of excitement were, as we shall see later, frequently treated with electroshock therapy, often twice during the first day. This was done in the older patient, in whom larger doses of phenothiazines were felt to be dangerous.

No cases of *manic stupor*, referred to earlier (Chapter 3), were observed. Posturing was seen in seven cases and was quite unlike that seen in schizophrenia. In five patients the posturing consisted of many hours of prayer, clearly in association with grandiose delusions of a religious nature. In one case the patient assumed the coital position for several hours and insisted she was having multiple orgasms during intercourse with God. In every case in which posturing occurred, delusions and extreme overactivity were seen. In no patient was waxy flexibility observed, and in no case was posturing inappropriate to the remainder of the mental state.

In retrospect, patients were unable to explain the overactivity entirely in terms of their thought content. The fact that their "thoughts were racing" was important, but they often referred to an "uncontrollable" and often

Table 7-11. Thinking changes in mania

Episodes	Flight of ideas	Pressure of speech	Distractibility	Grandiosity
In males (N = 37)	33	36	37	35
In females (N = 63)	60	63	63	51
Total (N = 100)	93	99	100	86

"uncomfortable" urge to keep moving, the so-called "pressure of activity" of Kraepelin.

In addition to euphoria and overactivity, flight of ideas is usually seen in mania. A brief encounter with the manic patient admitted to the hospital is all that is necessary to confirm that a prominent change in his thinking is present (Table 7-11).

The most characteristic type of change in thinking in mania is the flight of ideas described by Linn in the following way[6]:

> . . . a nearly continuous, high speed, flow of speech. The patient leaps rapidly from one topic to another, each topic being more or less meaningfully related to the preceding topic or to adventitious environmental stimuli, but progression of thought is illogical, and the goal is never reached.*

This type of thinking was observed in 93% of the manic episodes. The flight of ideas was, like other symptoms, quite variable, appearing for part of a day or during part of an interview. Often the patient could answer simple questions but would show a flight of ideas in response to an open-ended topic, becoming less and less coherent as the conversation progressed. It seemed that the more severe this type of disorder the more excitable and gradiose the patient was. Clang associations and puns were often noted with this type of thought, and plays on words were often seen, such as the following in a patient's letter to her doctor: "M = marry = merry = Mary = Marie."

Another symptom of mania seen in 99% of the manic episodes is a pressure of speech. The patient has a desire to speak and communicate and will do so to anyone who will listen. In more extreme cases the patient will just continue speaking even if he is alone or is too hoarse to make any sounds. Some of these latter patients may be seen walking through the ward gesticulating, moving their lips without making a sound. The patients usually speak loudly and at times sing or make up poems when they are not talking. An especially common feature of the pressure of speech was giving a sermon or preaching from the Bible, in keeping with the common religious preoccupation of these patients.

This pressure to communicate also manifests itself in writing, usually

---

*From Linn, L.: Clinical manifestations of psychiatric disorders. In Freedman, A., and Kaplan, H., editors: Comprehensive textbook of psychiatry, Baltimore, 1967, The Williams & Wilkins Co., p. 550.

voluminous letters. During five of our 100 episodes the patients spent many hours working "on a book." In one example, the father of an index patient, himself manic, wrote plays during his mania and edited them afterward. One of his plays has been seen on television.

All the patients during each manic episode were distractible. By this we mean that they were readily responsive to minor external stimuli and evidently unable to concentrate for more than a few moments on any topic.

It may well be that distractibility and inability to screen out extraneous thoughts are basic to the manic thought disorder. They were seen in all patients, even those without flights of ideas, and were the last thinking disturbance to disappear as the patients were getting well. Again it appeared that the most severely disturbed patients, i.e., those with delusions and the most extreme pressure of speech, were also the most distractible.

In discussing the change in thinking with the patients retrospectively, we noted that the most frequent feeling the patients had was of having too many thoughts. Many patients stated that their thoughts were racing and that their "brain was going faster than their mouth." The patients were unanimous in asserting that they had no control over their thoughts and could not refrain from saying what they were thinking. In an embarrassed fashion they referred to insults, curses, and scatologic references which they had made. We considered that this inability to focus one's thoughts, or to screen out meaningless associations, was very important in the thought patterns observed. Many patients felt they had "something to say" or had discovered a great truth and wanted to share it with others. Only rarely were the patients aware that they made little sense or that others could not understand them.

It is important to differentiate the manic thinking from the thought disorder of schizophrenia. In the less ill manic patient, the flight of ideas consists of understandably related statements, which is not so in schizophrenia. In the more disturbed manic, only every second or third thought may be reported and the connection becomes impossible to follow. In these cases the remainder of the clinical picture must serve to differentiate the two disorders. One feature of mania that is not seen in schizophrenia is the reactivity and variability of the thought patterns. The manic patient frequently begins his sentence logically and, as he speaks, becomes less and less coherent; extraneous stimuli get worked into the conversation, and the patient frequently continues to talk until he is interrupted. In most cases the patient is aware that he has strayed far from the original topic.

During 81 of the 100 episodes observed, one or two themes dominated the concern of the manic patient. In spite of jumping from one topic to another, he would always come back to this theme. In 32 of the 81 episodes it was religion (more common in women), and in 31 of the 81 episodes it was business or finance (usually men). These themes clearly reflected the patient's life, his hopes, and his major activities prior to becoming manic; and often the same themes occurred in several manic episodes. The patients were characteristically grandiose about themselves (86%) and generally ruminated about things that had a central place in their lives. This was not true in respect to religious concerns, which seemed to follow no pattern when compared with degree of nonmanic piety. Most of the religious concern was

Table 7-12. Themes of manic episodes

Episodes	Religion	Politics	Business	Sex	Fame	Writing book	Art and music	Variable or none
In males (N = 37)	7	2	20	4	5	2	2	5
In females (N = 63)	25	5	11	11	3	3	1	14
Total (N = 100)	32	7	31	15	8	5	3	19

delusional. Apparently these patients associated the ecstatic or exalted mood with a religious experience. Delusions and hallucinations occurred in reference to these grandiose concerns, and the patient's activity prior to his admission also reflected his preoccupation (see Table 7-12).

The patient's ruminations bore no resemblance to obsessions in that they were ego-syntonic, the patient being wholly taken up with his enterprise. On occasion, patients had acted on these concerns, starting businesses, investing money, or buying items that were inappropriate and costly.

The delusions that are seen in schizophrenia usually last for months or years and are often primary in that they do not explain a real or disordered perception. They fulfill the definition of a delusion as a fixed, false belief. In mania the delusions are quite different. They are often evanescent, appearing or disappearing during the course of a day, or even during an interview. They also vary with the patient's total state, being more frequent when he is more active; and his flights of ideas become more pronounced and fading as he becomes more quiet. Frequently they are extensions of the patient's grandiosity.

At times the patient can be talked out of his delusion, and at other times he gives the impression that he is only being playful rather than really being deluded. In our group the delusions were often secondary to the patient's exalted affect. This was especially true of those patients who felt their mood could be described only as a religious experience.

The most subtle and earliest distortions of reality are manifest in the frequent extravagance and grandiose self-image expressed by the patients. This psychotic optimism frequently led to bad judgment in their daily affairs and was often responsible for the social difficulties they experienced as a result of their illness. Extravagance, occurring during 69% of the manic episodes, never led to legal difficulties but many families had huge bills to pay after the patient was hospitalized.

The patient's grandiose self-image, present in 86% of the episodes, was not interpreted as delusional unless the patient maintained a false belief during one of his interviews (Table 7-13).

Delusions were present during 48% of the manic episodes. They were not related to age. Most of the patients were grandiose, and in order to demonstrate the interplay of grandiosity and delusions, we divided the delusions into grandiose and nongrandiose types.

Religious delusions were most frequent, and these were always grandiose. One example of this is a letter in a bold hand from a 57 year old man.

Table 7-13. Delusions, hallucinations and other symptoms in manic episodes

	Episodes In		Total (N = 100)
	Males (N = 37)	Females (N = 63)	
Delusions			
Present	16	32	48
Absent	21	31	52
Religious	10	19	29
Money	2	5	7
Political	7	2	9
Sexual	5	6	11
Control (passivity)	7	15	22
Persecutory	11	8	19
Other types	4	11	15
Symbolization	5	23	28
Extravagance	29	40	69
Depersonalization feelings	0	2	2
Hallucinations			
Auditory	6	15	21
Visual	3	6	9

Friday, Jan. 13   11:00 a.m.

Awoke refreshed showered shaved and had a good breakfast. I went before a staff of doctors and proved that I am Christ the Saviour of the world. I am going to see a Priest this afternoon and ask for help in the right way to use these powers that I did not ask for. Also some way to convince my wife Mary that I am God Creater of Heaven and Earth.

K. M. F.   (C. T. S.)*   *Christ the Saviour

Six hours later the patient was no longer convinced he was Christ, and several months later he was embarrassed and sheepish about his letter, explaining that he "felt so good he thought he must be someone big." Normally he had no religious affiliation but did "read the Bible every evening."

During 52 episodes, 71 different delusional statements were recorded, usually grandiose, concerning religion, sex, money, politics, and other miscellaneous topics. Ideas of control (passivity) were present in 27 episodes, and these were also usually grandiose, most commonly controlled by God in some delusional fashion.

Delusional symbolization was seen in 28 episodes, and most often the delusion was also grandiose. Most frequently patients found references to themselves in the Bible or on the news. These delusions were often primary in that they did not explain any perception or feeling.

It therefore appears that several of Schneider's first-rank symptoms of schizophrenia, such as primary delusions and disordered symbolization, may occur in manic patients.[9]

Persecutory delusions are well known in depression and have been described since Kraepelin. It is interesting that ideas of persecution also occur in mania. As in the depressed phase, they are not systematized or complex and tend to be vague ideas of being watched or threatened. This type of delusion occurred in 19 episodes and was most frequently not grandiose, unlike all the delusions previously described.

Delusions of mania are not well systematized and, apart from grandiose optimism, tend not to be acted upon. This might be a factor of their brief duration or related to the patient's inability to make any sort of concerted action.

Feelings of depersonalization were seen in only two cases, and in both of these the symptom was fleeting. Neither case was otherwise atypical.

In 21% of the episodes, auditory hallucinations were experienced, and in 9%, visual hallucinations occurred. As with delusions, the hallucinations tended to occur in the most disturbed patients. The hallucinations were brief and seldom persisted. They tended to be grandiose, the patient hearing the voice of God or, as in one case, a choir of angels replete with trumpets. The content of the hallucinated experience was often a part of the delusional idea, most often a command from God. Several examples of this were commands to "love thy brother" or "do unto others . . ." Likewise, the visions were "the face of God" or "Heaven in all its glory" and in every case were grandiose. In the few cases that the auditory hallucinations were not grandiose they were simply "hearing someone call my name" or "hearing a song."

There are important similarities between the delusions of depression and mania. In both instances they are appropriate to the patient's mood; in depression, ideas of sin or guilt predominate, and in mania, grandiose or extravagant ideas predominate. In both instances the delusions tend not to be systematized, and hallucinations, when they occur, are fragmented and fleeting.

Clouding of consciousness was reported by Kraepelin as occurring in only the most severe cases.[5] In 8% of our episodes the patients on admission were disoriented to time, never to place or person. The patients were disoriented for 1 day in six cases and for 3 or 4 days in two cases. Those patients who were disoriented were severely excited, often delusional. In two cases the examiner felt the patient was disoriented but was unable to perform a proper examination because the patient was uncooperative. In a previously published study, Clayton, Pitts, and Winokur reported a higher incidence of confusion (disorientation and memory lapses) in mania (58%).[2]

Insomnia is the hallmark of depression. Likewise, it is an almost universal component of the manic state, and we have seen that some form of insomnia was the most frequent reason given for hospitalization. In order to accurately assess the degree of insomnia, we took an average of the first 5 nights in the hospital. The patients are routinely observed by the nursing staff, and we analyzed their sleep charts for our data. All the patients received hypnotics. Most patients were on large doses of phenothiazines. Any patient who averaged 7 hours per night or longer was considered not to have insomnia.

Ninety percent of the episodes were marked by insomnia, using our criteria. The duration of sleep averaged less than 6 hours per night. The means for the age groups ranged between 4.3 and 5.5 hours per night. No patient, even the most exhausted, spontaneously complained of fatigue or feeling sleepy. Thirty-four percent of the episodes were characterized by initial insomnia, 24% by terminal insomnia; 25% had both types together. Although

Table 7-14. Sleep changes with manic episodes

	Episodes in		
	Males (N = 37)	Females (N = 63)	Total (N = 100)
With sleep changes	32	58	90
Without sleep changes	5	5	10
Initial insomnia	16	18	34
Terminal insomnia	6	18	24
Initial and terminal insomnia	9	16	25
Interval insomnia*	4	15	19

*In 12 of these cases, interval insomnia was combined with other types of insomnia.

terminal insomnia or early morning awakening is a classical feature of manic depressive reaction, depressed type, it has not been previously described as occurring in manic patients. It was manifest in 49% of the patients. Nineteen patients had interval insomnia; i.e., they awakened for at least 1 hour during the night. In seven of these patients this was the only type of insomnia noted.

Insomnia is frequently a useful target symptom as regards treatment, and its disappearance heralds the end of the manic state. One of the earliest manic symptoms seems to be insomnia without fatigue. Many families of patients with frequent manic episodes use insomnia as a sign that the patient is becoming ill again. In many cases, insomnia appears to antedate the damaging extravagance and poor judgment shown by these patients when they are ill. In some cases rapid treatment may enable a patient to stay out of the hospital.

All but three of the manic episodes were marked by the nurses' comments that the patient had a good appetite and often requested more food than the hospital provided. In the three episodes where this was not so, the patient was too preoccupied to eat. Accordingly, these patients should have gained weight were it not for their great expenditure of energy. To examine the weight changes, we used the weekly weights routinely charted on all patients, for the patients' statements on admission were generally unreliable. Thus, the weight changes that are discussed here refer only to the hospital course.

In 40 episodes the weight was stable, changing not more than 2 lb. either way during the hospital stay. Twenty-five episodes were associated with loss of weight; however, in only nine episodes did this weight loss occur *throughout* the hospital course (3 of these patients were ill on discharge). Sixteen of the 25 patients who lost weight began to gain weight while their clinical picture was improving in the hospital. As with other appetites, the manic patient relishes his food, and one characteristic of manic patients enshrined in nurses' lore is that the patient frequently demands a meal at the time of admission whether it be day or night.

Those patients who lost weight tended to be the most active, and the change from weight loss to weight gain was frequently a sign of improvement in the symptom of overactivity.

Heightened sexuality has often been described as an important part of

Table 7-15. Sexual behavior in manic episodes

	Episodes in		Total (N = 100)
	Males (N = 37)	Females (N = 63)	
Increased sexual thoughts	5	5	10
Increased sexual contacts, noncoital	1	11	12
Increased intercourse	13	19	32
Promiscuity	6	5	11
Decreased sexual interest	4	9	13
No sexual change	8	14	22

the manic picture. The patients' behaviors ranged from increased thoughts and statements about sex to increased heterosexual and homosexual behavior.

Manic patients are frequently described as uninhibited, and this certainly appears to be so; however, the question of how much restraint the patient exercises over his behavior can give some measure of the internal control the patient has over his impulses. Accordingly the sexual behavior of the patient, i.e., whether or not he is promiscuous or acts in a socially unapproved fashion, can be considered a measure of this control. Statements made by the patient's family and his behavior in the hospital are used in Table 7-15.

Sixty-five percent of the manic episodes were marked by some sort of increased sexuality. In 10% the increased sexuality was in thoughts and statements only. In 12% unsuccessful attempts were made by the patient to have intercourse, or noncoital sexual behavior was exhibited. In 32% increased sexual activity of a socially approved sort was engaged in. This included intercourse with spouses or affairs beginning near the onset of the episode if the patient was unmarried. In no case did the increased sexual demands seem to upset the marriage, and such demands were usually attributed to the patient's illness. Our data are insufficient to assess what long-range effects the widely fluctuating sexual drive of the manic depressive has on his marriage.

In 13% of the episodes, decreased interest in sex was reported. This usually indicated preoccupation with other things. In 22% no change was observed.

In only 11% of the episodes did the patient's sexuality manifest in a socially disapproved fashion. In every case the patient's sexual life between episodes was not unusual, and the hypersexuality was associated clearly with being ill. In all cases these patients were promiscuous. They were generally discreet but responded in an unguarded fashion to the question of their sexual activity. During four of these episodes (2 in men, 2 in women) promiscuous homosexual as well as heterosexual activity occurred. These patients did not admit to homosexual contacts when they were well.

The impact of promiscuous sexual acts during illness seemed to be stronger in younger patients (those under 20 years of age). In each case their first sexual contact occurred during the manic episode, and even after they were well, all but one continued to engage in sexual activity to a degree not acceptable in their community.

Table 7-16. Alcohol consumption during manic episodes

	Episodes in		Total (N = 100)
	Males (N = 37)	Females (N = 63)	
Admissions in teetotalers	5	6	11
Increased consumption	20	22	42
Decreased consumption	0	0	0
No change in consumption	12	35	47

The most striking feature of the data is that 32% of all patients manifested their hypersexuality in acceptable fashion. Of all patients who showed increased coital activity, three fourths did so with their spouses or with a lover of long standing. The restraint which these patients showed was considerable in that many of the patients thought constantly about sex and complained bitterly about being "sexually frustrated" while in the hospital. One patient expressed her desires in the following article she submitted to the hospital newspaper:

Favorite song = "Stout-Hearted Men"
Favorite pastime = Like to get together with *Ralph*—forever and a day
Favorite song = "I'm in the Mood for Love"

She spent most of the day singing her second "favorite song" to protest being in the hospital.

Spontaneous orgasms were reported by one patient, but information about this was not systematically collected.

It has long been a clinical impression that there is an increased consumption of alcohol among patients who are manic. In order to investigate this question, we sought for evidence of increased alcohol consumption prior to manic admissions to the hospital (Table 7-16).

Of 100 manic admissions, 11% were in patients who had never had a drink. This was especially true of patients under 20 years of age. In 42 admissions, an increase in alcohol consumption was noted, and in no patients was a decrease noted. No change was observed in 47% of the admissions. We attempted to obtain information concerning the amount of alcohol per day consumed. Of the 42 episodes associated with an increased consumption, this information was available on 34. Expressed in ounces of whiskey per day, the increase varied from 6 oz. to 37 oz.

Men were more likely to increase their drinking than women (54% vs. 35%) during a mania. If a woman increased her consumption of alcohol, the range of the means for the age groups was between 6 and 17 oz. per day. The means for the various age groups in men showed a range between 10 and 37 oz. per day.

In only two patients was alcohol considered a problem except during affective episodes, and both of these were considered "heavy social drinkers" rather than alcohol addicts. Both had long periods of sobriety when well.

The degree of social disruption due to alcohol is considerable, and this is attested to by the fact that of the 42 episodes where alcohol consumption was increased, abuse of alcohol was a reason for admission to the hospital in 24. These heavy drinkers were more often men.

In the hospital no patient exhibited withdrawal symptoms, and where information was reliably obtained, the increased consumption of alcohol followed the onset of a definite mood change rather than preceded it.

It has often been considered that patients who consume pathologic quantities of alcohol do so initially in order to obtain relief from anxiety and depression. In our cases this theory gains no support, for anxiety feelings are rare and depressive moods are fleeting. The manic patient drinks in company rather than alone and may be drinking heavily to keep company with other heavy drinkers rather than for the effect the alcohol has on himself. In contrast to the alcoholic or depressed patient, who frequently claims that feeling bad, or being unable to sleep, is the basis of his drinking, no such complaint was ever made by the manic patient. The effect of alcohol on the manic seemed to be to dissolve whatever restraints were left to him.

One patient, an 18-year-old man, used marijuana rather than alcohol when manic. Between manic episodes he was a sober rural Missouri citizen who worked regularly, was able to save money, and made realistic future plans. During his manic attacks he became a hippie, living in St. Louis' hippie quarter, and spent a good part of his time smoking marijuana. He denied other types of drug abuse and, during these periods of time, also drank heavily.

At this point it is clear that our patients were quite ill. One half were deluded. A majority were extravagant and grandiose. They all had some form form of thinking change, and their affect was euphoric and infectious. Since sober reflective conversations with these patients are impossible and since retrospective information is colored by so many internal considerations, we decided to use the *insight* a patient had into his being ill as a measure of his contact with reality. It was obvious that all the patients manifested behavior prior to admission that was inappropriate to some degree; and their ability to understand this may be an important clue in differentiating this episodic affective psychosis from the severe, often chronic, personality disintegration seen in schizophrenia. We sought for evidence of the patient's insight during the 24 hours following admission, most often prior to treatment, or, if he was treated, prior to the large doses of phenothiazines that these patients are frequently given.

By "insight," we mean the patient's ability to understand that he was hospitalized because he was psychologically ill or because his behavior was abnormal.

In 37% of the admissions, insight was present at all times. In 29% it was present on occasion only, and in 34% it was absent at all times. The presence of insight did not tend to segregate for age or sex, but insight did tend to be present in the less severely ill. Nonetheless, it was often present in deluded individuals with the most extreme forms of overactivity and most intense affective states.

In the absence of base rates of this variable in other psychotic conditions, an accurate comparison is impossible; however, it is our impression that these patients, in spite of their psychoses, and without insight into their delusions, understood that they were ill (even if they did not want to be in the hospital) to a greater degree than is expected in schizophrenia. On follow-up, all the patients but one agreed that hospitalization had been necessary and beneficial, and this one patient was still angry at the form of coercion used, admitting that she was ill at the time.

Disappearance of the symptoms and duration of the manic episode

Kraepelin reported that the duration of mania in a few patients was only "days or weeks" but that most patients remained ill for many months or even years.

Our own data are obviously a report on the hospitalized and treated manic episode. The kinds of therapy used are reported later. The duration of the episode may be dependent on the type and quantity of therapy as well as the natural course of the illness. The order in which the symptoms disappear is interesting, for it should enable a practitioner to assess the success of his therapy. This assessment is often difficult because of the shifting and variable nature of the symptoms.

Another and more theoretical point regarding the order of disappearance of symptoms is the emergence of a *profile* of the illness. If symptoms that are present in fewest of the patients tend to disappear first, then we may think of them as being manifestations of severity of the illness occurring at its apex. Conversely, the symptoms that are most frequently present may be considered as the clinical core of the illness. The order of disappearance of symptoms might also say something about possible underlying neural mechanisms and enable correlation between biologic and psychologic phenomena. Finally, psychopathologic mechanisms might be uncovered if some symptoms are necessary to the appearance of others, the *basic* symptoms tending to disappear last (Table 7-17).

We followed the duration of the above symptoms when they were present

Table 7-17. Disappearance of symptoms and duration of episodes

	Number episodes in males	Mean duration in males in days	Number episodes in females	Mean duration in females in days	Mean duration in total group in days
Mean disappearance (when present)					
Delusions	15	6.3	29	8.6	7.9
Flight of ideas	30	20.0	54	13.5	15.8
Push of speech	32	24.2	58	16.6	19.3
Distractibility	34	27.1	57	20.0	22.8
Irritability	29	25.5	48	19.0	21.6
Mean duration of hospitalization	34	37.4	57	27.8	31.4
Mean duration of mania = onset of mania → admission → euthymia	34	73.2	57	42.2	53.7

and able to be evaluated. These specific symptoms were chosen partly because they were easily observable and because of their importance in the clinical picture.

In the evaluation of disappearance, the starting point was admission to the hospital.

The first symptoms to disappear were the delusions and hallucinations. The patient stopped talking about his delusions usually less than 10 days after admission. Hallucinations always disappeared before delusions. It was impossible to arrive at whether the auditory or visual hallucinations disappeared first, due to the small number of cases, but the visual hallucinations were usually associated with the most extreme excitement; and it was our impression that they disappeared sooner. The longest any patient was deluded was 56 days, and the median of the distribution was 4.4 days. On follow-up, no patient was deluded. Most patients remembered this feature of their illness with considerable embarrassment.

The manic thinking change was the most carefully studied feature of the illness in this regard. There seemed to be an orderly disappearance of symptoms; first the flight of ideas disappeared, then the push of speech, and finally the distractibility. Distractibility was present in all episodes, and flight of ideas in 95 of the episodes. In no case did flight of ideas occur without push of speech or distractibility. Distractibility, then, may form the basis of the manic thinking change, the inability to screen out extraneous stimuli, both internal and external, either because they are "coming too fast" or because they are "too many at once."

Irritability did not correlate well with the other measures used and seemed present almost as long as any mood disturbance listed. It is probably the most reactive of symptoms; hence its presence would, to a great extent, depend on the environment.

The mean duration of the manic episode, from onset until euthymia, was 73.2 days for men and 42.2 days for women. The mean duration for the entire group of manics on whom we had information was 53.7 days. If this material is broken down, we find that the mean for the entire group (100 episodes) of onset of mania to hospitalization is 29.8 days (men, 43.9 days; women, 21.5 days). Twenty-four males were below this mean and 13 were above; 50 females were below and 13 were above the mean for onset to hospitalization. Chi-square evaluation of this split showed a nonsignificant difference. The mean (for the entire group of 91 episodes on which we had data) for admission to euthymia was 23.9 days (men, 29.3 days; women, 20.7 days). Nineteen men and 34 women were below the group mean for admission to euthymia; 15 men and 23 women were above the mean. Again the chi-square showed no significant difference. In view of the fact that the major contribution to the difference in duration of mania between men and women was contributed by the period between onset and hospitalization, one must question whether the differential in duration is the result of social factors, the men being able to resist treatment more effectively and prevent themselves from being hospitalized. Once in the hospital and treated, men and women are more alike as regards duration.

Patients were kept in the hospital only a few days longer than the attainment of euthymia or "normal mood." In those cases that resulted in longer hospitalization, depression was frequently seen.

In the Bratfos and Haug study, when the length of manic attacks was compared to the length of depressive attacks, the former appeared shorter than the latter.[1] Thus, 17 of the 28 circular or manic patients had attacks of less than 7 months as compared to 64 of 130 depressive patients. Of 14 circular manic depressive patients discharged as free from symptoms, 10 were well 3 months after discharge. The mean hospital stay in this study was 9 weeks. In our study the mean hospital stay was 31 days and depression was a common sequel to the mania. It is possible that the longer hospital stay in the Bratfos and Haug study covered a postmanic depression.

Depression after mania

In 51% of the episodes, significant depression preceded the onset of mania, and in 68% of the cases, evidence of depression could be found while the patients were in the hospital and still manic. Depression after the manic episode was an equally significant problem. Nine patients were discharged while still manic, and no information could be obtained regarding their mental state following the manic episode. Immediately following the manic episode and during the subsequent month, 52 patients became depressed. In 30 of these the depression was observed in the hospital. The symptoms of this depressive episode were similar to those seen during other depressive episodes. Melancholy, insomnia, and loss of appetite and energy were all prominent symptoms; psychomotor retardation or agitation was often seen. In 20 of these patients, rehospitalization for depressive illness became necessary. The 30 patients who became depressed in the hospital represent those depressive episodes that immediately followed the manic one (Table 7-18).

Twenty-two patients received a course of ECT during this phase of their

Table 7-18. Depression following the manic episode

	Episodes in		
	Males (N = 37)	Females (N = 63)	Total (N = 100)
Depression after mania	13	39	52
No depression after mania or unknown if depression occurred*	24	24	48
Depression observed during index hospitalization	8	22	30
Treatment with antidepressant drugs for postmanic depression	9	18	27
Electroshock therapy for postmanic depression	6	16	22
Suicide thoughts or attempts in postmanic depression†	4	9	13
No treatment for postmanic depression	0	2	2
Rehospitalized for postmanic depression	4	16	20
Outpatient treatment for postmanic depression	10	19	29

*In 9 episodes, it was not possible to determine whether a depression occurred after mania.
†Five suicidal attempts, one successful suicide.

illness, and 26 were treated with antidepressant medication (some with both). Only three patients were treated without medication or ECT.

In 13 patients, prominent suicidal behavior was seen. In eight of these, suicidal drive manifested itself only in thoughts or comments. In five patients, attempts were made, two patients maiming themselves, and one patient successfully committed suicide.

The finding that 57.8% of the manic episodes (52 out of 91 for which there was information) were followed by a depression has great importance for management of the manic phase of the disorder, and this figure is a minimum. Many physicians, unaware of this phenomenon, saw the patients only 6 or 8 weeks after discharge. The duration of the depression was a minimum of 1 week (two cases) and ranged from 1 week to 9 months.

Many patients had low moods or some dysphoria following mania, but these were not counted as being "depressed" because they did not fulfill the criteria set out previously.

In many instances, the manic episode of manic depressive psychosis is triphasic, beginning and ending with significant depressive mood swings. The onset of the mania itself may be gradual or abrupt, and in every case except nine the manic episode was terminated in the hospital. These nine cases were generally sent to other hospitals shortly after admission. In no case did they represent a failure of treatment of the manic episodes. In some cases the triphasic curve of the illness was the only episode. In other cases the triphasic curve was preceded and followed by at least a 6-month period of health. Some patients were chronically ill, and the manic episode was one episode in a fluctuating illness.

Eight patients were discharged and then readmitted before 6 months, generally within 1 month. It is unclear whether they were well and then became ill again or were just quiet, successfully fooling their psychiatrist. In several cases, nurses' notes indicated the patients made extravagant purchases on the day of discharge, and it may be presumed that they were still hypomanic at discharge. In other cases they truly were well. All the patients who fell ill again, requiring rehospitalization, had stopped taking their medication. It is not known whether stopping the medication was a cause or a result of being ill.

As with depression before and during the manic episode, depression occurring after mania serves to unify the concept of bipolar manic depressive psychosis. The frequent presence of depressions before and after the manic episodes justifies the use of the adjective *circular*, which is often employed to describe the illness.

"MIXED" MANIC-DEPRESSIVE EPISODES

There is a spectrum of symptoms manifested by the manic depressive patient that ranges from "pure" mania, with no admixture of depression, to pure depression. The majority of manic patients have at least fleeting depressive feelings. During 14 hospital admissions in 10 patients the diagnosis of *mixed manic-depressive psychosis* was made. By this, it was meant that the symptoms of mania and depression were present simultaneously and the patients fitted the criteria for both mania and depression. These episodes unlike either the manic or depressive ones, are difficult to diagnose and were more frequently labeled "undiagnosed." Some patients had an evident pressure of speech and grandiose ideas with severe and suicidal melancholy; and in others the reverse could be seen, i.e., psychomotor retardation with euphoric or excited statements. Eighteen episodes of a mixed variety occurred among our 61 probands, but only 14 episodes in 10 patients were directly observed in hospital and hence useful for analysis. Two patients each had three episodes. In two cases the mixed picture was the only one observed in hospital although both patients had prior and subsequent manic and depressive episodes. Thirteen of the episodes were seen in nine women; one episode was seen in a man.

Eleven of the episodes had a gradual, and three an abrupt, onset; the patients were ill an average of 30.9 days prior to admission. Four of the episodes had stressful events immediately preceding the onset of the illness. In two cases the stress was psychologic, i.e., death of a spouse, and in two cases it was postpartum. The reasons for admission among these patients reflected the fact that there was a mixture of manic and depressive symptoms: two patients were severely insomniac, two patients had ceased to function, two patients were assaultive and destructive, two patients were deluded, two patients were extravagant, and two patients were severely melancholic (one of these had made a serious suicide attempt). On admission, nine of the patients were fully aware that they were ill and required hospitalization, four of the patients lacked insight completely, and one patient had insight on occasion only. Prior depression of significant clinical proportions was seen in 10 of the 14 episodes and lasted an average of 22.5 weeks. Two of these patients had received a course of EST in hospital during these depressive episodes, and one patient was untreated. The remaining seven received outpatient treatment with a variety of antidepressants.

All the characteristics of affect previously described occurred during these mixed episodes. The most striking feature of the mixed manic depressive episode is the variability of the patient's mood. Within seconds the patient's mood may change from ecstasy to despair. One moment the patient may be grandiose, and the next convinced he is cancerous. As with the manic patients, these episodes were marked by periods of hostility and irritability. It is this panoply of varying and contrasting emotions which makes these patients difficult to diagnose. As with the manic episodes, the mood swings, apart from irritability, were not easily influenced by external stimuli. Diurnal variation was present in nine of the 14 episodes. Two were worse in the morning and two in the evening, the worsening being a manifestation of both manic and depressive symptoms at the time. Five of the patients who had diurnal variation showed a change in the polarity of mood during the day. One patient was manic in the morning and depressed at night, and four patients were depressed in the morning and manic at night (Table 7-19).

Like the manic episodes, the mixed episodes had *themes,* and the content of these themes reflected both the fluctuating optimism and the pessimism of these patients. All patients but one had a "theme" that occupied their concern during the illness. In five episodes the patients expressed morbid preoccupation with death; in two cases the theme was a religious one, both

Table 7-19. Symptoms of mixed manic depressive psychosis

	Episodes in		Total (N = 14)
	Males (N = 1)	Females (N = 13)	
Depression	1	13	14
Suicidal threats or attempts	0	6	6
Euphoria	1	13	14
Lability	1	13	14
Hostility	1	10	11
Irritability	1	13	14
Duration of irritability (days)	5	16.1	13.0
Delusions (nondepressive)	0	3	3
Delusions (depressive)	1	4	5
Duration of delusions (days)	13	13.3	13.3
Auditory hallucinations	0	2	2
Visual hallucinations	0	1	1
Grandiosity	1	7	8
Extravagance	0	2	2
Distractibility	1	13	14
Duration of distractibility (days)	41	20.5	22.3
Pressure of speech	1	12	13
Duration of pressure of speech (days)	21	15.7	16.2
Flight of ideas	1	5	6
Duration of flight of ideas (days)	17	14.8	15.2

patients concluding that they were dead and would be resurrected. Two patients ruminated about cancer. Preoccupation with guilt about sexual matters was seen in two patients. Three patients were grandiose, usually about religion, and all three claimed to be the "Virgin Mary" at some time during their hospital stay. One patient spent her time writing a book, and the one male patient had grandiose ideas about "starting a corporation."

Delusions of a nondepressed and grandiose sort, similar to those seen in mania, occurred in three episodes (all of a religious nature). Depressive delusions (including delusional guilt) could be seen in five episodes. The delusions lasted a mean of 13.3 days. Hallucinations were seen in two patients, and one of these patients had both auditory and visual hallucinations. Whereas the hallucinations of mania were always *grandiose*, in these patients they were morbid. In both patients the voices were "from the grave," and the vision one patient had was of her father's deathbed (he was active and well). Three patients felt controlled by God and three patients had grandiose delusions of symbolization. Persecutory delusions occurred in only one patient.

The type of delusion, whether morbid or exalted, seemed to fluctuate with the patient's mood. At times, however, morbid ideation could occur in a setting of what the patients experienced as euphoria. Only six of the 14 patients were observed to have flights of ideas, and the mean duration of these symptoms was 15.2 days. Thirteen of the 14 episodes had pressure of speech, and the mean duration in this case was 16.2 days. All the patients were *distractible*, and this symptom lasted 22.3 days on the average.

The same progression in the disappearance of symptoms as was evident in the purer cases of mania could be seen here. Flight of ideas was less frequently found in mixed episodes than in the purely manic ones. It was clear in observing these patients that the thinking change varied independently of the mood.

Thirteen of the 14 episodes were marked by insomnia occurring during the first 5 days in the hospital, despite nighttime sedation. The average number of hours the patient slept was 4.7 per night. In six patients this was initial insomnia only, and in six terminal insomnia only. One patient had both types together. Unlike the more pure manic excitement, nine of these patients spontaneously complained of fatigue.

In six of the 14 episodes (all in women) anxiety attacks occurred during their hospital stay. These were characterized by feelings of apprehension along with complaints of dyspnea, palpitations, chest pain, sweating or feeling faint, symptoms more characteristic of depression than mania.

Nine patients had a decreased interest in sex, and five patients an increased interest.

All the patients, save one, were fully oriented; and this patient was disoriented for 1 day only.

All the mixed patients showed an increase in motor activity resembling that of mania rather than depression. However, they tended not to be as active as manic patients.

Six patients made suicidal threats prior to hospitalization, and one of these made a medically serious suicide attempt, resulting in her admission.

Alcohol consumption was increased in six patients and unchanged in eight. The average daily consumption of the patients in whom increased drinking was observed was 14 oz. of whiskey or its equivalent per day. Alcohol abuse was not a feature of these patients' life styles prior to the onset of the illness.

The mean duration from onset to euthymia was 23.8 days, and the duration of hospitalization was 33.0 days. The mean time between a prior admission and the one that was mixed manic depressive illness was 15.2 months in 13 episodes. For one patient this was the first admission. As with the manic episode, the mixed episode was followed by a depressive swing in eight patients. Of these, five patients were depressed in the hospital prior to discharge, seven patients were given antidepressants as an outpatient, four patients were rehospitalized for suicidal behavior, and two were given EST. The mean duration of this depressive syndrome was 17 weeks. In no case was the mixed episode immediately followed by mania.

Mixed episodes of mania and depression are not common. They seem to resemble mania as regards push of speech and hyperactivity. Vegetative symptoms are closer to those of depression. The patient's mood fluctuates greatly and rapidly from one pole to the other and is most often a mixture of the other features previously discussed. Delusions, when they occur, tend to be depressive. The very existence of this symptom picture excludes the possibility that all symptoms of mania are related to the mood disturbance, for many of these patients are "manic, as regards their physical activity and associations," and depressed, often morbidly so, as regards their mood.

THE DEPRESSIVE PHASE

The definition of manic depressive psychosis as that form of affective disorder in which mania occurs requires a reexamination of the depressive syndrome, to see whether it differs in any way from other forms of depression. The question of whether it is possible to predict the emergence of "mania" and the bipolar rather than unipolar course of the illness, by examining the patient during a depressive episode, is an obviously important one as regards therapy; it also has many theoretical implications. If the depression is not different in the true manic depressive compared to the unipolar depressive, this definition of manic depressive illness might represent one part of a continuum from *depressed only* to *manic only*. If the depressive mood swing is identifiable in some other way, the probability that these are two or more distinct entities with some similarities is strengthened.

Of the 61 probands, 21 had depressive episodes that were directly observed in the hospital and will be reported on. In addition, depressive illness in the first-degree relatives will be described. Although these relatives were personally interviewed, their illness was reported retrospectively and hence the information is less reliable (Table 7-20).

The 21 patients ranged in age from 19 to 72 years, and they had 33 separate depressive episodes. The maximum number observed in any one patient was four. One patient had three episodes and six patients had two each. There were five males (5 episodes) and 16 females (28 episodes). The mean age during a depressive episode for men was 41 years, and for women 37.4 years.

The onset was abrupt in five instances and gradual in 28. Precipitants preceded the depressive episodes in nine instances (1 male and 8 females), and these stresses were psychologic in five patients (in every case a family member had died) and physical in four (infectious hepatitis in 2, infectious mononucleosis 1, childbirth 1). The stresses were temporally related to the onset of the depression and occurred immediately before the onset. All the patients who had *precipitated* depressions had unprecipitated manic or depressive episodes prior or subsequent to the one that was precipitated. The pres-

Table 7-20. Some aspects of the depressive phase in manic depressive probands

	Male (N = 5)	Female (N = 16)	Total (N = 21)
Number episodes of hospitalized depressions	5	28	33
Mean age during episode (years)	41	37.4	39.2
Abrupt onset	1	4	5
Gradual onset	4	24	28
Psychologic precipitants	1	4	5
Physical precipitants	0	4	4
Mania prior to onset of depression	3	12	15
Mania following depression	1	7	8
Number episodes with mania before, after, or both	3	16	19
Hospitalized with mania before or after depression	3	10	13

ence of these precipitating factors, therefore, does not seem to be a sufficient cause for illness in these patients. There was no significant difference comparing precipitated and unprecipitated cases with regard to family history, abrupt or gradual onset, age, sex, presence of mania immediately before or after the depression, or suicidal behavior.

One major difference between manic depressive, depressed phase, and other affective disorders seems to be the presence of mania immediately before and immediately after the depressive episode. Of the 33 patients, 15 had significant manic symptoms prior to and 8 following the depression (two patients discharged against medical advice were not followed). There was some overlap, and 19 of the depressive episodes were preceded or followed, or both, by mania. The manic symptoms were quite variable and ranged from milder hypomania to severe manic excitement. In every case, however, these manic episodes fulfilled the criteria set out earlier, and these figures are obviously a minimum. For the 15 manic episodes immediately preceding the depression, six patients (2 males and 4 females) were hospitalized, two were untreated, and seven (all female) were treated as outpatients. Of the eight manic episodes that followed the depression, seven patients (1 male, 6 females) were hospitalized and one was treated as an outpatient. Of the 13 hospitalizations for mania before or after depression, 10 were in Renard Hospital and have already been described as part of the 100 manic episodes. In two depressive episodes (both in the same patient), manic excitement was seen transiently (12 hours) during the depression.

Only 14 of the 33 patients with depression observed in Renard Hospital had no evidence of mania immediately before or after the depression. This observation has considerable therapeutic significance, for the psychiatrist must be prepared to treat both poles of the illness during each episode. That the majority of affective episodes in the manic depressive are circular with manias and depressions suggests some strategies for future research; i.e., does the mania which sometimes follows ECT or antidepressant drug therapy indicate that the patient is a bipolar manic depressive?

Table 7-21. Onset of depression

	Episodes in		Total (N = 33)
	Male (N = 5)	Female (N = 28)	
Reasons for admission			
Suicidal behavior*	2	17	19
Inability to function	1	6	7
Delusions and hallucinations	1	1	2
Insomnia	1	1	2
Alcohol abuse	0	1	1
Other	1	3	4
Duration of illness prior to hospitalization (weeks)	13.5	13.5	13.5
Insight present on admission	4	26	30

*One patient was also homicidal.

Like the *manic* or *mixed* episodes, the reasons for admission reflected the symptoms and complications of the illness. Nineteen patients threatened suicide, and this was the most frequent signal that hospitalization was necessary; five of these patients attempted suicide, and four were critically ill as a result (Table 7-21).

The mean duration of depressive illness prior to the patient's hospitalization for depression was 13.5 weeks; the mode was 3 weeks. Of the 33 admissions for depression, eight were first hospitalizations. The patients most often had good insight into their illness, and in spite of the frequently expressed delusional pessimism, they readily accepted the fact that they were ill and required hospitalization.

Since the patients were managed in the community for a longer time when depressed than when they were manic, it would appear that the ability to function without harming oneself or one's social relationships is much greater during depression than during mania.

Symptoms of depression

Melancholy or a depressed mood is the hallmark of the depressive syndrome. The sadness and pessimism are pervasive and unyielding to outside stimuli. They may fluctuate, but neither the patient nor his family has any control over them. Retrospectively the patients reported that being depressed was intensely uncomfortable and unlike any other experience they had ever had, including grief. Several patients expressed their surprise that "more people didn't commit suicide while depressed." The experience of being depressed was described most often as "a black cloud or shadow coming over me" or "a heavy weight on me," and its influence was intrusive in that the patients could not "think it away" or "think of something else" even though the depressive ruminations were so painful. Several patients awoke feeling fine but would feel the depression return after a few minutes. All 33 episodes were marked by a greater or lesser expression of melancholy, and tearfulness occurred in 31 of these. The patients were often observed to burst into tears uncontrollably and "for no reason except she was sad" (see Table 7-22).

Table 7-22. Symptoms of depression

	Episodes in		Total (N = 33)
	Males (N = 5)	Females (N = 28)	
Melancholy	5	28	33
Tearfulness	3	28	31
Irritability	4	21	25
Poor concentration	5	25	30
Diminished clarity of thought	4	26	30
Diminished speed of thought	5	25	30
Psychomotor retardation and prolonged latency of response	3	22	25
Poor memory	3	14	17

Irritability is another major symptom of this depressed affect, and 25 of the 33 episodes were marked by this behavior. In contrast to melancholy, sudden anger and hostility at being "disturbed" or "annoyed" were *reactive* and could easily be elicited by making demands or frustrating the patient. Since the patients were generally ill about 3 months prior to admission, the irritability they expressed often served to drive away close friends or family and tended to increase the patients' isolation and discomfort. Many patients were retrospectively "disappointed" in their families' negative reactions and "lack of understanding" of their illness, and this disappointment was usually with the way the family handled the patient's hostility rather than his sadness and pessimism.

A majority of patients reported that their ability to "think properly" was diminished during the depressive episode, and 30 patients complained of a diminished ability to concentrate while depressed. These patients referred to concentrating on things other than the depressive ruminations that often seemed to occupy them for long periods of time. This symptom was especially disturbing in students; and among patients attending school, a drop in grades was often an early symptom of the illness.

Thirty patients reported that their thoughts were not as clear as usual, and 30 patients felt that their speed of thinking was slowed. Twenty-two patients appeared distractible and could easily be interrupted from a current task by minor stimuli, often being frustrated and angered by the interference. It was obviously an effort for these patients to concentrate. Seventeen patients reported a subjective worsening of their memory, and this appeared as a consequence of their inability to pay attention. No diminution in memory could be objectively demonstrated. The totality of the depressive thought disorder is observed as psychomotor retardation and an increased latency of response. These patients talked very slowly, often with seconds of silence occurring between words, and they would begin an answer often after a prolonged delay. The patients later reported that they generally were not "choosing their words" but that the slowed rate of speech was a reflection of their speed of thinking. The patients were aware that their rate of thinking was slowed and was not under voluntary control. Twenty-five episodes were characterized by observable psychomotor retardation.

All the patients and their families noted a change in the patient's view of both the world around him and himself. The change was always in concert with the depressed mood, and the patients were all abnormally and inappropriately pessimistic (see Table 7-23).

Thirty-two episodes were marked by self-depreciatory statements, and 30 of these patients were also self-accusatory. These patients often recounted events that "proved" they were "evil" or were the cause of family tragedies. All patients expressed guilt feelings about real or imagined wrongdoings. In three patients, all female, a confession of earlier infidelity was made during their depression. Many patients expressed a desire to "confess" their guilt in the hope that this would diminish their painfully low self-esteem; however, relief was not forthcoming. The persistent ruminative account by a patient of his faults and mistakes made psychotherapy with these patients all but impossible. Excessive concerns with finances and ideas of poverty, which were

Table 7-23. Further symptoms of depression

	Episodes in		
	Male (N = 5)	Female (N = 28)	Total (N = 33)
Self-depreciatory	5	27	32
Self-accusatory	5	25	30
Excessive concern with finances	3	12	15
Fear of losing mind	1	15	16
Fear of death	3	8	11
Absence of delusions	3	19	22
Presence of delusions	2	9	11
Auditory hallucinations	1	1	2
Hopelessness	2	15	17
Suicidal thoughts	4	23	27
Suicide attempts	0	5	5
Obsessions	0	2	2

inappropriate, were observed in 15 cases. Usually the patients were overly concerned about their large hospital bill and, on occasion, took self-injurious steps to protect themselves financially, i.e., selling of one's home.

A "fear of losing one's mind" was expressed during 16 of the depressive episodes. This fear was based on the patient's subjective feeling that his speed and clarity of thoughts were changed and that he was "not in control" of these faculties. During 11 episodes, the patients expressed the fear that they were going to die. This fear was a strong premonition, and no concrete explanation of why they felt this way was ever given. The patients usually reacted to feeling this way with intense anxiety, although several patients accepted their impending death as "just punishment."

The category of delusion was reserved for statements that were "fixed false beliefs" rather than inappropriately pessimistic attitudes. Of the 33 episodes examined, 11 were characterized by delusions of one or more kinds. In seven instances the delusions were of having "sinned," in eight cases the patients felt guilty for having committed a crime, and six patients felt they deserved to die because of retrospectively false circumstances. One patient felt he was dead and was in hell. The content of all these delusions appeared to be guilt over some imagined or misinterpreted event. Two delusions were persecutory ones, and these were the only delusions expressed that were not "melancholy" in character. In both instances the patient felt she was the victim of a conspiracy. Two episodes were marked by auditory hallucinations, both patients hearing "voices of the dead calling me." In one of these cases, the voice was that of an "accuser" reiterating the patient's past sins. The delusional thinking of these patients was transient and was never present on leaving the hospital or on follow-up. The patients' later evaluations of their own delusions were most often an "embarrassed" conclusion that they must have been "crazy to think that way."

Hopelessness characterized the thinking in 17 episodes, and all 17 of these patients had strong suicidal urges as well. They frequently rejected

Table 7-24. Somatic symptoms in the depressive phase

	Episodes in		
	Male (N = 5)	Female (N = 28)	Total (N = 33)
Insomnia	5	28	33
Initial	2	17	19
Terminal	3	6	9
Initial and terminal	0	2	2
Interval	0	3	3
Headache	1	21	22
Anorexia	5	27	32
Decreased libido	4	20	24
Anxiety attacks	1	19	20
Decreased motility	4	20	24
Fatigue	4	21	25
Diurnal variations, worse in morning	4	17	21
Teetotaler	1	2	3
Increase in alcohol intake	1	7	8
Decrease in alcohol intake	0	0	0
No change in alcohol intake	3	19	22

therapy on the basis that it was useless, and those without insight expressed the idea that they were "hopelessly evil" rather than that "they were not ill."

An unexpectedly large proportion of patients expressed suicidal thoughts or urges. In two of these, the suicidal thoughts were classically ego-alien obsessions and were present before and after the depressive episode. Twenty-five episodes were marked by frank suicidal urges, and five of these patients attempted suicide. In four patients the attempts were medically serious, and in one patient the attempt was a gesture. The reasons given by the patient for wanting to die were woven into the fabric of morbid concerns, especially feelings of guilt, worthlessness, and hopelessness.

Insomnia was a universal complaint among our patients. The most usual type of insomnia was difficulty getting to sleep (19). Early-morning waking, long considered characteristic of endogenous depression, was observed in nine patients. Two patients had both types. The type of insomnia and number of hours of sleep per night were measured during hourly checks by the hospital staff and averaged for the first 5 nights of the patient's hospital stays. Sleep averaged 5.5 hours per night. Unlike the insomnia observed during the manic phase, the patients often bitterly complained about it, and during 25 of the 33 episodes, spontaneous complaints of extreme fatigue or weariness were made (Table 7-24).

Twenty-two episodes were associated with headache, and 32 with loss of appetite. In 31 episodes, patients had lost weight during the 4 weeks prior to hospitalization, and this averaged 7.5 lb. per patient who had lost weight. The patients often expressed the fear that the weariness and weight loss were a sign of serious medical illness; yet no patient expressed these feelings in a delusional fashion, and all of them were reassured by negative investigative procedures.

All the patients were worried or apprehensive during their illness, and 20 of these illnesses showed full-blown anxiety attacks, replete with dyspnea, palpitations, chest pain, trembling, and paraesthesia. These anxiety attacks occurred only during their episodes of illness and in two cases heralded the onset of a depression, the bulk of the depressive symptoms occurring later. These two patients were both admitted to the medical wards of the hospital for investigation of chest pain, palpitations, tachycardia. Among those patients who experienced anxiety attacks, the anxiety was given equal weight with depression in terms of the discomfort that it caused.

Nine patients had no change in libido, and these were mild depressions; the remaining 24 all were associated with a diminished sex urge, and in several cases (3) this was a source of considerable guilt.

A definite decrease in overall motility was noted during 24 episodes of illness, and this varied from a slowing down of movements to a cessation of all movement superficially resembling catatonic stupor. Five patients had no change in motility, and during four episodes the patient's motility was increased. These latter four patients were agitated, pacing about or wringing their hands; and especially in the elderly, they presented difficult management problems, the danger of an exhaustion syndrome being present. In no case was the increase in motility an increase in energy as is seen during the manic phase. No posturing or abnormal movements were seen.

Diurnal variation has been described as a classical symptom of depression and was present during 27 of the 33 episodes. The patients generally felt worse in the A.M. (21), and some complained of feeling worse in the evening (6). There was no correlation between the type of diurnal variation and the type of insomnia.

None of our patients decreased their alcohol intake, and eight of 30 patients who were social drinkers recorded an increase. In most, there was no change. The average daily consumption of those patients who increased their intake was about 16 oz. of whiskey or its equivalent, and the families often complained of drunkenness. Unlike the manic episodes, only one patient was admitted because of alcohol abuse. The number of manic episodes (see Table 7-16) in which alcohol consumption was increased was greater than the number of depressed episodes with increased alcohol consumption (48% vs. 27%). The difference was not, however, statistically reliable (p > 0.05).

We have not described the natural history of the depressive phase of the illness, for all patients were treated in some fashion. In 31 of the 33 episodes, the patients were considered euthymic on discharge although, as we have seen, eight patients had a period of mania immediately after discharge. Two patients signed out of the hospital against medical advice and no data could be obtained on the course of their depressive episodes.

In 31 episodes, then, the duration from admission to euthymia averaged 20.6 days. This was irrespective of the form of therapy used, however. Psychotherapy alone was used on the least severe depressions (N = 5), and EST in the most severe (N = 18). Drug therapy was used in the others. Duration of hospitalization did not vary with the type of treatment and averaged 11 days longer (31.9 days) than the duration of symptoms observed. Usually those patients with post-EST confusion or postdepressive mania were in the hospital longest. Whether the patient developed mania following his depression did not depend on which type of treatment was used.

The time between the previous psychiatric hospitalizations and the one under consideration varied from 2 weeks to 12.5 years, and eight episodes described were first hospital admissions. Because of the difficulty in reporting retrospectively on the course of the illness, the duration of time between hospitalizations is perhaps the best way to characterize the course of the illness. The average duration out of hospital (for 33 episodes) prior to the present admission was almost 2 years (23.5 months), and the mode of this distribution was 7.5 months.

Social withdrawal of one sort or another was seen in all 21 patients during all 33 episodes. The first and most common type of withdrawal was a loss of interest in hobbies and social activities. As the patients' anhedonia and anergy progressed and deepened, they became increasingly concerned with themselves, progressively contracting their sphere of human contacts. The increase in social and personal isolation of the patients was frequently incorporated as evidence of the patients' self-proclaimed inadequacy. The most frequent response to intrusion into the patient's concern by his family was an angry and irritable one, serving only to increase his isolation and misery. It must be remembered that these patients also had manic episodes and in almost half the cases mania occurred immediately prior to the depression. This incredible contrast in the patient's behavior and attitudes was often cited by the family as most difficult to understand and deal with, and the family's response was generally one of quiet desperation. As we have seen, the patient's suicidal threat, and his inability to work, were the most frequent behaviors that finally galvanized the family into action, resulting in the patient's hospitalization.

Depression among the first-degree relatives of the manic patient

An attempt was made to personally interview each of the available first-degree relatives of our 61 manic depressive patients. Usually the interviews took place in the family home, most often during the evenings or weekends. The family was first interviewed together and then each member individually. All family members were asked about themselves and also about each other. The information was cross-checked for consistency and validity. Dealing with the family in this fashion enabled us to learn a great deal about the course and treatment of the illness in the proband and gave us excellent insights into the stress that the illness placed on the family and the family's response to it. In a majority of families a second family member had been ill with an affective disorder, and those families were well aware that psychiatric illness "ran in the family"; further, the families were sufficiently aware of mania and depression to make comments about the presence or absence of symptoms in themselves. Criteria used for "diagnosis" in the relatives were the same as those used in the patients; and an attempt was made to objectively evaluate the diagnosis by assessing social incapacity and kinds of treatment that were

Table 7-25. Relation of interviewed relative to proband

	N	Total	Mania only	Depression only	Mania and depression
Mother	35	18	3	15	0
Father	19	3	1	1	1
Brother	37	7	0	5	2
Sister	45	17	1	10	6
Son	15	1	1	0	0
Daughter	16	5	1	3	1
Total	167	51	7	34	10

sought. We consider this information to be more subject to error than the clinical description already given because the majority of relatives who had been ill were currently well and were reporting retrospectively on their own problems. All possible psychiatric information was obtained from hospitals, private psychiatrists, and family physicians.

From Table 7-25, it can be seen that 51 relatives suffered at some time in their lives with an affective disorder. Seven of these had been only manic or were chronically hypomanic, and 44 either had evident bipolar illness (10) or had been depressed without any evidence of mania (34). Some of these subjects had other illnesses as well, such as alcoholism. In describing depression in the family members of our patients, we shall describe these 44 people.

Among the 17 relatives who had shown mania, 12 were female and five were male. The figures for those relatives with depression only (28 females and 6 males) do not significantly differ from this ratio. The preponderance of females appears in hospitalized as well as nonhospitalized cases and in the probands as well as the family members. From the genetic standpoint, the persistence of this ratio is an important finding and makes the possibility that it is a sampling artifact less likely.

The mean age of onset of the illness in the 10 bipolar relatives was 25 years, and in those 34 relatives without mania 35.9 years. The 34 patients who were only depressed might have manifested an incomplete or modified form of the illness. They had fewer episodes; they did not, as a rule, require hospitalization (2.9 episodes, 1.4 hospitalizations per bipolar relative—1.9 episodes, 0.9 hospitalizations per depressed only relative); and most indices of severity, such as presence of delusions, severity of dysfunction, and duration of the episode, would indicate that they were not as "sick" as the probands.

That the relatives were "ill" was evidenced by an almost universally reported social or psychologic incapacity (40 of the 44 bipolar and depressed-only relatives). Precipitating factors were rarely present. The relatives most often were fully recovered. The prevalence of illness in these families was unusually high and often the illness could be traced back several generations.

A period of 15 years (average) elapsed between the onset of the illness in the relative and the date of the interview. Since 55% of the patients had only one episode and 25% had two, most of the information was obtained at least

Table 7-26. Symptoms of depression in 34 first-degree relatives (depression only) of manic probands

Symptoms	Percent relatives with symptom
Depressed mood	100
Psychomotor retardation	56
Weight loss	79
Insomnia	100
Decreased concentration	94
Diurnal variation	38
Suicidal threats and/or ideas	29
Suicidal attempts	6
Guilt feelings	50
Agitation	59
Auditory hallucinations	3
Anxiety attacks	35

10 years after the event; consequently, we tried to elicit those symptoms that the patient and his family could objectively answer. We were surprised at how well the patients were able to remember their symptoms; when compared with their hospital or physician's records and in those cases where records could be obtained, disagreement was rare (Table 7-26).

Depressed mood was present in all cases; and in 55% of cases, psychomotor retardation was recalled. A majority of patients had significant problems concentrating, and this was usually reported in relation to work or school. Diurnal variation was recalled by many, and this report often came from the family members who had to contend with the mood swings. Insomnia was universal and was recalled as a painful experience; as before, initial insomnia was more common than classical descriptions of this syndrome would allow. Weight loss was reported in a majority of patients and, along with insomnia, was frequently a sign that "something was wrong." Suicidal ideas and threats were far less common during the depressions of these patients than during the hospitalized depressions of the manic probands; and in all but two patients they resulted in hospitalization. This tends to confirm the data reported earlier, that suicidal threat was the most common reason for hospitalization. Only two suicide attempts were made during the depressive episodes in the 34 relatives who had only depressions.

Variations in sexuality occurred in a minority of the "depressed-only" group. More depressed-only patients reported increased rather than decreased sexuality while ill.

Fifty percent of the patients reported guilt feelings as being prominent during their illness, and most of the delusions elicited were false ideas of having sinned, or of having wronged someone. The line between those with excess guilt and delusional guilt was too fine to be drawn so far removed from the event; however, that the delusions reported occurred in this context tends to confirm what was observed in hospitals among the probands.

Agitation, when it occurred, seemed to be the most painful memory these patients had. They often referred to the inability to relax, or to stop pacing, and the combination of anxiety and depression as that state which was incompatible with "going on."

Feelings of depersonalization and auditory hallucinations were rare and always had a depressive quality.

Anxiety attacks occurred only during depressive episodes and were recalled by about a third of the patients. They were a signal to seek medical help in almost every case; and in those patients treated by a family physician, medication given was generally for relief of anxiety rather than depression.

Only four of the 44 (bipolar and depressed-only) patients gave no report of social or psychologic incapacity during their illness (all 4 saw physicians). Eighty-two percent of those who had only depression and 70% of those with bipolar illness had both social and psychologic incapacity that was manifest only during the episode diagnosed as depression or mania.

Three patients had chronic social disability associated with being ill in the past, and two patients had chronic illness, which was symptomatic. All these patients had been hospitalized and were under medical care when interviewed. Chronic social problems generally resulted from tragic events during a depression, such as the woman who killed her two children when depressed and failed in a subsequent suicide attempt. Those two patients who were chronically psychologically ill both had severe unrelenting depressions that were resistant to treatment.

Problems with alcohol during a depression were reported by four family members, and all these cases were females who drank to excess when depressed. None of these patients had been manic. The number of family members who reported alcohol abuse during their illness is much less than that observed in the bipolar probands. This might be a "real" phenomenon that would relate alcohol abuse to being hospitalized or be the result of underreporting on the part of the families we interviewed.

In summary, manic depressive disease is an illness that has an early onset and manifests itself by many attacks. There is a possibility of an increase of number of attacks in females. Mania and depression succeed each other in the majority of cases, but a sizable minority of cases may show only a mania or a depression that is succeeded by a period of wellness. The close temporal contiguity of manias and depressions is one of the most striking aspects of the illness.

During a mania, such symptoms as overactivity, overtalkativeness, religiosity, grandiosity, flight of ideas, sleeplessness, extravagance, delusions, and euphoria are prominent; but within the manic period, microepisodes of depression are very common. Manias are usually preceded or followed, or both, by a depressive episode. Depressions, though usually preceded or followed by manias, do not contain micromanias within them. Besides such symptoms as low mood, guilt feelings, suicidal trends, retardation, and hopelessness, typical anxiety attacks were seen as part of the depressive phase. The episodes of mania and depression are not ordinarily precipitated by significant life events. They are usually of a severe enough nature to necessitate medical or institutional care.

In a delusional illness such as paranoid schizophrenia, wellness may be considered in terms of the patient's being able to entertain alternate hypotheses other than the delusional ones to account for various stimuli. In manic depressive disease, wellness may be considered a period of functioning with an absence of the specific symptoms of the disease. To study the phenomenon of wellness in manic depressive disease, we followed up 32 of our manic depressives 1.5 to 3 years after the index admission. This material is presented in the following chapter.

REFERENCES

1. Bratfos, O., and Haug, J. O.: The course of manic-depressive psychosis, Acta Psychiat. Scand. **44:**89, 1968.
2. Clayton, P., Pitts, F. N., Jr., and Winokur, G.: Affective disorder: IV. Mania, Compr. Psychiat. **6:**313, 1965.
3. Hudgens, R., Morrison, J. R., and Barchha, R.: Life events and the onset of primary affective disorders: a study of 40 hospitalized patients and 40 controls, Arch. Gen. Psychiat. **16:**134, 1967.
4. Jaspers, K.: General psychopathology, Chicago, 1963, University of Chicago Press.
5. Kraepelin, E.: Manic-depressive insanity and paranoia, Edinburgh, 1921, E. & S. Livingstone, Ltd.
6. Linn, L.: Clinical manifestations of psychiatric disorders. In Freedman, A., and Kaplan, H., editors: Comprehensive textbook of psychiatry, Baltimore, 1967, The Williams & Wilkins Co.
7. Perris, C.: The course of depressive psychoses, Acta Psychiat. Scand. 44:238, 1968.
8. Perris, C., and d'Elia, G.: Pathoplastic significance of the premorbid situation in depressive psychoses, Acta Psychiat. Scand. **40:**(Supp. 180), 87, 1964.
9. Schneider, K.: Primäre und secondäre Symptomen bei Schizophrenie, Fortschr. Neurol. Psychiat. **25:**487, 1957.

Chapter 8

The study: a prospective short-term follow-up

The follow-up study provides a baseline against which therapy may be evaluated, allowing the physician to set realistic goals. Theoretically, the follow-up has much to offer, for by comparing prognosis with other variables, the physician may discover important etiologic or modifying factors. Ideally the follow-up study should examine the patient in his natural environment at several intervals during the course of his illness; and the patients should be selected as early as possible during the course of the illness.

The present study was designed as an 18- to 36-month follow-up of the first 32 of the 61 patients reported on here. The follow-up interviews were generally done in the patients' homes and took between 1.5 and 3 hours. A structured interview was used. All available first-degree relatives were interviewed and asked about the patient's progress. Whenever possible, physician and hospital records were obtained.

Of the 32 patients, 25 were personally interviewed. One patient who committed suicide and two patients who lived too far away to be interviewed personally were included in the follow-up on the basis of information obtained from the family or from attending physicians. In two cases the patients were too distant for follow-up and information could not be obtained; one patient refused and one patient could not be located. Identifying characteristics of the 28 patients followed up are reported in Table 8-1. Although these 28 patients are characteristic of the group as a whole and are typical of a consecutive series of admissions to a private psychiatric hospital for mania, they are weighted in the direction of repeaters. In only four of the 28 patients was the index admission the first admission.

GLOBAL FOLLOW-UP

At follow-up the patients were placed in five categories:
(1) Chronically ill: Patients had no remission or diminution of symptoms during period of observation.
(2) Partial remission with episodes: Patients remained symptomatic during period of observation and had episodes of illness as well.
(3) Partial remission without episodes: Patients remained symptomatic during period of observation and were well at no time. No episodes were observed during period.
(4) Well with episodes: Patients had periods of complete remission between episodes of illness that occurred during period of observation.
(5) Well in every way: Patients had complete remission of symptoms after index episode and no illness during the period of observation.

Table 8-1. Identifying characteristics of 28 manic patients followed-up 18-36 months after index admission

	Male	Female	Total
Number	10	18	28
Age at index admission (years)	42	38	40
Age of onset	31	27	28
Duration between age of onset and index admission (years)	13	13	13*
Index—first admission	1	3	4
Duration between index and follow-up (months)	22	25	24
Average number of depressive episodes before index admission	1.0	2.6	2.0*
Average number of manic episodes before index admission	1.1	1.7	1.5*
Average number of hospitalizations before index admission	1.7	3.4	2.8*
Depression immediately following index manic episode	4	12	16

*Those patients who have had previous episodes only.

Categories (4) and (5) may be considered as the best categories prognostically. It is clear that we are testing the traditional concept that a great majority of patients with manic depressive psychosis remit completely.

Table 8-2 contains the follow-up data of 27 cases. (That patient who committed suicide did so 10 months after discharge from the hospital and is not included.) From this table, it can be seen that after 18 months only 33% of the patients are "well in every way," 30% are well but have continued to have episodes of illness, and 37% have had persistent symptoms of illness severe enough to interfere with their lives or to warrant continued medical management. In two cases (7%) remission of the illness failed to occur.

Of the original 27 patients, 21 were followed to 24 months. By 24 months the proportion of patients who had remained well in every way had fallen to 24%. The decreased proportion of these patients was due to patients who had been well in every way until 18 months and had had episodes of illness during the following 6 months. No patient who was still symptomatic at 12 months following index admission had a complete remission of symptoms during the remainder of the follow-up period.

Of the seven patients followed to 36 months, only two remained well in every way for the entire period. Three of the five who had been well at 18 months had developed an episode by 36 months. One patient, after 24 months of complete remission, made a suicide attempt following a 6-month period of depression and developed a severe chronic brain syndrome as a consequence of carbon monoxide intoxication. At the 36-month cutoff date we put her in the category of "well with episodes," for it is not possible to consider the chronic brain syndrome specifically associated with the natural history of manic depressive disease.

The outcome of the index episode did not depend on age, sex, or duration

Table 8-2. Global follow-up

N	At 18 months					At 24 months					At 36 months				
	Chronically ill	Partial remission with episodes	Partial remission without episodes	Well with episodes	Well in every way	Chronically ill	Partial remission with episodes	Partial remission without episodes	Well with episodes	Well in every way	Chronically ill	Partial remission with episodes	Partial remission without episodes	Well with episodes	Well in every way
♂ 10	0	1	3	2	4										
♀ 17	2	4	—	6	5										
T 27*	2	5	3	8	9										
♂ 5	0	0	1	1	3	0	0	1	2	2					
♀ 16	2	3	—	6	5	2	3	—	8	3					
T 21	2	3	1	7	8	2	3	1	10	5					
♂ 1	—	—	—	—	1	0	0	—	0	1	0	0	—	0	1
♀ 6	0	0	—	2	4	0	0	—	3	3	0	0	—	5	1
T 7	0	0	—	2	5	0	0	—	3	4	0	0	—	5	2

Note: 27 patients were followed to 18 months; of these, 21 patients were followed to 24 months; of the original 27, only seven patients were followed for 36 months.
*One patient of the 28 who were followed up committed suicide 10 months after index admission.

Table 8-3. Outcome at last contact

	Chronically ill	Partial remission with episodes	Partial remission without episodes	Well with episodes	Well in every way
Male (N = 10)	0	1	3	3	3
Female (N = 18)	3	4	0	10	1
Total (N = 28)	3	5	3	13	4

of illness prior to index episode. Of the four patients whose index episode was their first, one patient had a partial remission (without episodes), two patients had a complete remission of symptoms with subsequent episodes, and one patient remained well for 24 months following the episode.

Table 8-3 illustrates the overall outcome of the follow-up study. Each of the 28 patients is included, and information in each case is based on the last contact with the patient. Average duration between admission and follow-up is 24.0 months.

From this table, it is clear that the frequently accepted hypothesis referred to earlier is not the case, in spite of the availability of modern treatment for this illness. Only 14% are well in every way after an average follow-up of 24 months, and only 61% have been totally without symptoms for any length of time (1 month) during these 2 years. Eleven percent have remained chronically ill (no diminution of symptoms), and 64% have had subsequent episodes of either mania or depression. Eleven of the 28 patients (39%) were either chronically ill or only partially remitted during the entire follow-up period.

From Table 8-1, it is evident that there are 16 patients who had significant depressions following the manic phase of the illness. These depressive episodes are counted as part of the index mania and are not included as "episodes" in the follow-up study.

Several variables were tested to compare those patients who were never well with those who had significant periods of wellness (at least 6 months) during the follow-up period. The first group includes those chronically ill and those with partial remission (N = 11); the second group, those who were "well in every way" and those who were "well with episodes during the follow-up period" (N = 17).

The comparisons show that variables such as age of onset, age at index admission, sex, or number and type of prior episode were not significantly different between the two groups. The presence of postmanic depression was not more frequent among the more chronically ill patients but lasted longer.

The number of patients with new manic or depressed episodes was greater among those who had never had complete remissions, and the duration of these episodes was longer. This is especially true of the depressive episodes (8 of 11 vs. 7 of 17 patients).

The average duration of manias in both groups was similar (3.1 to 4.0 months), but depressions lasted longer in the first group composed of the chronically ill and the partially remitted patients (10 months vs. 3.8 months).

These data indicate that depression rather than chronic mania was the major problem during the follow-up period in those patients who did not remit completely.

The duration between the index and next episode was shorter for those patients who had not remitted completely (6 months vs. 14 months); and if a further episode occurred, i.e., the second during the follow-up period, the duration between these two episodes was shorter as well.

QUALITY OF THE REMISSION IN MANIC DEPRESSIVE PSYCHOSIS

Thirty-nine percent of the patients did not remit completely; and in these, several persistent symptoms confronted the patients and their physicians. Symptoms were counted as present during the follow-up period if they interfered with the patient's life in a significant fashion, if they required medication, or if they were present "much of the time" according to the patient, his family, or the physician (Table 8-4).

Symptoms occurred in both groups of patients. In those with periods of complete remission they were short-lived and caused little disruption of the patient's life. This is in striking contrast to the symptoms observed in those patients characterized as "in partial remission." These symptoms were persistent and troublesome and never responded completely to treatment. They interfered with the patient's functioning; and not infrequently, the capricious changes in mood determined much of the patient's activities and were his major concern. Insomnia, depression, inability to concentrate, and irritability were the major difficulties these patients experienced; and, as we have seen previously, these were also the most common symptoms that patients experienced when they were depressed. It is important to note that no patient was chronically hallucinated or deluded or had a persistent thought

Table 8-4. Symptoms during follow-up

	Chronically ill or partially remitted (N = 11)	Complete remission of symptoms with or without episodes (N = 17)
Insomnia	11	4
Depression	9	0
Inability to concentrate	11	0
Excessive alcohol intake	5	0
Tearful	7	3
Push of speech	5	3
Overactive	5	1
Poor judgment or grandiosity	6	0
Irritability	9	1
Apathy	6	2
Anxiety	5	3
Euphoria	5	2
Extravagant	5	0
Psychomotor retardation	2	0
Weight loss	7	0

disorder. "Poor judgment" was either too optimistic or pessimistic, never delusional. No patient withdrew from close personal contact; indeed, they tended to become more dependent and more involved in family affairs, a frequent complaint of family members.

During the follow-up, all those patients who were never well were considered different from their premorbid self and were characterized as having generally depressed (N = 5), generally hypomanic (N = 4), and generally cyclothymic (N = 2) personalities. In contrast, the personalities of those 17 patients who remitted completely at some point in the follow-up changed in only four cases, three being considered more cyclothymic and one more hypomanic than usual. This last patient and his family felt that the increased energy and decisiveness were a great asset, both interpersonally and socially.

Most patients clearly had a premorbid personality that was unusually "exuberant" or "moody"; however, those patients who failed to remit completely were rarely described as even-tempered or without moods prior to the onset of the illness.

Ten of the 11 patients who were only partially remitted were considered to have had a premorbid cyclothymic or hypomanic personality as opposed to 11 of the 17 patients who completely remitted at some time in the follow-up period. None of the partially remitted had had a euthymic personality, whereas five of the 17 completely remitted patients had euthymic personalities. The patients' families were well aware of the excesses of mood, for a majority had at least one other member of the nuclear family with the illness; and the patients were felt, even in these families, to have unusual mood swings. No patient could be considered to have had a schizoid, paranoid, or antisocial premorbid personality although two patients were considered compulsive.

Very few data are available in the literature that may be compared to the present findings. The Lundquist follow-up referred to in an earlier chapter is long-term and deals only with first-admission patients.[2] The Lundquist findings are considerably more optimistic than those that we have presented above. The recent work by Bratfos and Haug, in Norway, is quite relevant to our own data.[1] These workers studied both first-admission patients (20% of their sample) and those who had been repeaters (80% of their sample). They conducted a mean follow-up of 6 years.

In the Bratfos and Haug article, it is noted that 15 patients who had experienced a mania were discharged from the hospital as totally free of symptoms. Altogether there were 42 patients in the study who had had a mania and who were followed up. Of the 15 who were fully remitted at discharge, only one had relapsed in 3 months after discharge. However, the longer follow-up for the total group of 42 patients was quite different. Nineteen of the 42 patients had a chronic course (continuously ill), 20 of the 42 had one or more relapses in the follow-up period, and only three of the 42 remained well.

SOCIAL PROBLEMS IN MANIC DEPRESSIVE PSYCHOSIS

Manic depressive disease, at least in the form that requires hospitalization, is a severe one which disturbs the interpersonal and social fabric of the patient's life and the life of his family.

Although some episodes may be preceded immediately by severe physical or psychologic stresses, no such stress can be found in the majority of episodes; and patients who experience these stresses do not differ from the larger group with respect to age, sex, family history, and prior or subsequent course of the illness. Accordingly, the social and interpersonal changes that immediately follow the episode may be thought of as epiphenomena, i.e., the result of having a psychologic illness and hospitalization.

The relationship between persistent symptomatology and continued social dysfunction is not so clear as to cause and effect. Very likely there is a reciprocal relationship in which those symptoms that persist cause psychosocial disturbances which, in turn, alter the symptoms that are experienced by the patient.

While assessing the social factors, the reader ought to be aware that 24 of the 28 patients had prior episodes; and the duration between onset and index admission in these patients was approximately 13 years. Patients whose economic resources may have been exhausted or who may have required chronic hospitalization were not likely to have been found in an acute treatment unit of a private hospital.

The average duration of the manic phase of the illness is 54 days, and the average durations of the premanic and postmanic depressions are 111 and 114 days respectively; thus, the total duration of the episode in these patients who remit even incompletely is frequently several months. The postdepressive phase is about 3 months longer in those patients who have only partial remissions, and as a consequence the entire episode in those patients lasts much longer. The episode of illness is, therefore, a major event in the patients' lives and one that cannot be isolated from the subsequent conduct of their lives.

As regards the immediate social consequences of the index episode, it is noteworthy that of the 19 patients who were working just prior to the index episode, 15 lost their jobs during or just after the index episode. Of the nine men who were working, six lost their jobs; and the financial burden imposed by extravagance, prolonged unemployment, and expensive hospitalization was enormous. One patient (not in this study) estimated that the cost of 12 years of therapy of her manic depressive illness was $110,000. Mortgage of homes, loans, and the necessity of the other family members to work could be seen even 2 years after the hospitalization. In many instances the whole family could "just meet the hospital bills" and lived in dread of the "next" hospitalization. The loss of employment was especially painful for two older patients who were forced into early retirement by their illness; they could not get another position because of their age (50+ years old). In both instances the patients' wives had to go to work in order to "make ends meet," and the resulting change in family structure was clearly very disturbing. Both these patients had complete remissions, and one has had a subsequent episode. The families of 17 patients reported severe financial problems in relation to the index episode.

Seven patients were students at the onset of the index mania, and all seven lost at least 1 full year of school. Three of the four students who had periods of wellness (with episodes during the follow-up period) did return to school. None of the three patients who did not remit completely returned to their studies. They complained about the "difficulty concentrating" as the most incapacitating symptom of the illness.

Twenty of the patients (9 men and 11 women) were married at the onset of the episode, and two had been divorced prior to the episode. Separation and divorce followed the index episode in five cases and, according to the family, was related to the episode in various ways. Generally those patients with this most extreme marital difficulty had a long history of persistent discord, and the disaffected spouse complained most often of financial problems, excess dependence, and irritability as those things that led to the breakup of the marriage. The vast changes in mood that these patients experienced made an intimate relationship most trying. In six other cases the patient and spouse felt the "marriage was in jeopardy." This singularly high rate of marital discord is a reflection of the severity of the social disturbance that accompanies a manic episode.

A large proportion of the manic patients had changed their dependency relationships during the index episode. Data on this feature of their lives were sought by comparing where and with whom they lived before and after the illness. Nine of the 28 patients changed the place in which they lived. Three patients left home as a consequence of having been ill, and five patients were no longer able to live independently and returned to their parental home to live. One patient, separated from his wife, took a lesser job at a great distance from the community in which he had lived most of his life. Those patients who left home seemed to do so because their conduct prior to hospitalization had made life at home impossible. Those patients who returned home did so either because they could no longer afford to live independently or because their spouses would no longer tolerate their illness, forcing them to return to their parents' homes.

The period of the follow-up was equally associated with social problems. In a sense this period assesses the social cost of the illness. Thirty-nine percent of the patients never had a period of wellness during the follow-up; and, as might be expected, these patients had the most disturbed life style. The premorbid adjustment of the patient and his family was also related to the social performance during the follow-up period; and long-term marital discord, chaotic finances, or poor job history were all associated with continued social disability. Age and sex were important factors, since older men could seldom obtain comparable employment if they had lost a job. Generally, loss of a job was more "important" in men than in women. The evaluation of the patient's performance following his discharge from the hospital was made by the interviewer and the patient's family. The family's expectations are an important and unmeasured variable in this report. Table 8-5 describes the social costs of the illness.

All but one of the patients who had persistent subjective symptoms of the illness were rated by the family as being chronically disabled socially. Only two of the patients who remitted were felt to be chronically disabled. In terms of employment, eight of the 11 patients who remitted incompletely had held "steady employment at one time" but not during follow-up. This was also true of one fourth those patients who had periods of wellness.

Most of the 19 patients who were employed prior to the index episode

Table 8-5. Social costs of manic depressive psychosis

	Percent who had partial remission or were chronically ill (N = 11)	Percent who had total remission with or without subsequent episodes (N = 17)
Patient "chronically disabled" according to family	91	18‡
Was working steadily at some previous time and not during follow-up	73	18*
Took lesser job during follow-up	73	18*
Not working at all at follow-up	36	18
Chronic financial problems with outside support necessary	64	23
Decreased social circle due to inability to meet people	100	6‡
Disapproved drinking habits	46	0*
Chronic marital problems (including divorce)	73	29
Too dependent according to family	91	18‡
No complaints from anyone regarding social behavior	0	65†

*$p < 0.05$.
†$p < 0.01$.
‡$p < 0.001$ by chi-square test with Yates correction when the two groups are compared.

took lesser employment during the 2 years after hospitalization, and those students who did not return to school also worked at jobs that were below their educational level, i.e., a clinical psychologist with a Ph.D. degree who became a personnel manager. Seven patients, almost all of whom were women, were not working at all. The poor work performance was reflected in the necessity for finding additional sources of income either within or outside the family, and this was necessary in 11 cases. Nine of them drawn from that group remitted incompletely.

Five patients among those who were partially remitted or chronically ill had a continued and socially disapproved increase in their alcohol consumption. This was not seen in those patients who had periods of wellness. None of these patieuts fulfilled the criteria set out in an earlier chapter for alcoholism.

The marital problems appeared to be unresolved (except by divorce) after 2 years. This was as true for those patients who were well at some time as it was for those who were continually symptomatic.

Thirteen of the 28 families complained that the patient was too "dependent," and this referred to economic as well as interpersonal feelings. In response to the question "Is the patient chronically unable to meet people and has his social circle diminished?" 12 patients or their families answered yes; and this factor correlated perfectly with the persistence or absence of symptoms.

No complaints concerning the social behaviors of 11 patients, all of whom had complete remissions following the index episode, were elicited.

Table 8-6. Global social remission (from family and follow-up interview) as related to medical remission during follow-up

	No social remission	Partial social remission	Complete social remission
Chronically ill or partially remitted (N = 11)	5	6	0
Periods of complete medical remission (N = 17)	0	6	11

Table 8-6 explores further the relationship of the social remission as evaluated by both the family and the investigator to the quality of medical remission (the presence of significant symptoms of the illness during the follow-up period).

It seems clear from the data that a considerable interaction occurs between the two types of remission, with the social and medical status being directly dependent on each other.

In 11 patients the onset of the illness occurred in adolescence (under 21 years). At the time of index admission, these 11 patients were as a group 13 to 20 years past the age of onset. One of the 11 patients showed no social remission, seven showed a partial social remission, and three showed a complete social remission during the follow-up period. The patients who had had the onset of their illness during adolescence did not differ from those 17 patients who had their onset in adulthood.

The five patients who were partially remitted with episodes were compared to the 13 patients who were totally well with episodes. The average duration of time between episodes was 10.2 months for the partially remitted group and 21.7 months for the group that was totally well between episodes. Those patients who had periods of complete wellness had more time to recoup socially from the excesses of their illness. This finding appears to favor the idea that the medical status of the illness may be the cause of the social problems.

It is of importance to note that none of the 32 patients in the original group were chronically hospitalized in a psychiatric facility during the follow-up period except for the one woman who attempted suicide by carbon monoxide inhalation and suffered a chronic brain syndrome.

The role of treatment during the follow-up period is a matter of importance. Of the three chronic patients, two received chlorpromazine therapy and one received no drug therapy. In the five patients who showed a partial remission with episodes, two were on chlorpromazine, one received amitriptyline, one chlorpromazine and amitriptyline, and one received no drug treatment. Of 12 who were well with episodes, 10 received no treatment between episodes. One was on lithium and one was on amitriptyline. Both of these became ill while on their medication. All the 12 were treated for their episodes. Of the four who were completely well during the follow-up period, none had any drug therapy. The use of drug therapy in the follow-up period did not produce improved functioning. The numbers are small, however, and a systematic study of treatment might lead to other conclusions.

In general, one may conclude from the short-term follow-up that manic depressive illness is associated with a high degree of psychiatric and social morbidity. The minority of patients have complete and lasting remissions. Depressive rather than manic symptoms were the major problem during the follow-up. The illness retains its character; and the symptoms, though frequently chronic and occasionally severe, continue to be those seen in manias and depressions and not those of a more malignant thought disorder with deterioration such as schizophrenia.

REFERENCES

1. Lundquist, G.: Prognosis and course in manic depressive psychosis, Acta Psychiat. Scand. (Supp. 35), 1945.
2. Bratfos, O., and Haug, J. O.: The course of manic depressive psychosis, Acta Psychiat. Scand. 44:89, 1968.

Chapter 9

The study: diverse clinical findings

Although the present study was mainly concerned with descriptive, follow-up, and genetic material, several other kinds of data were of interest. In some cases these findings were the result of systematic investigation; in others they were chance observations. We present them in this chapter with some note regarding the quality of the material.

PREMORBID PERSONALITY IN MANIC DEPRESSIVE ILLNESS

In all the interviewed first-degree relatives as well as the probands, an effort was made to assess clinically the presence of a premorbid cyclothymic or hypomanic personality. This was attempted in a systematic fashion, but the criteria were essentially impressionistic. A cyclothymic personality was considered present if the subject was prone to marked ups and downs of mood and activity, such changes necessitating no special medical or social intervention. A hypomanic personality was characterized by a high energy level ordinarily with a great number of interests and an excessive amount of participation in various social areas. Other types of personality were noticed, but they were small in number except for the normothymic personality. This last type was defined in reality as the absence of cyclothymia or hypomania.

The findings were as follows: Of 61 probands and 17 bipolar relatives, 62 persons (80%) were considered cyclothymic or hypomanic. Of 34 relatives who suffered only from depression, 12 (29%) were considered cyclothymic or hypomanic. Of 116 relatives who were without affective disorder (N = 86) or who had other psychiatric problems (N = 30), 36 (31%) were considered cyclothymic or hypomanic.

The difference between bipolar subjects and depression-only subjects in the same families on the variable of cyclothymic or hypomanic personality is quite significant (χ^2 with Yates correction = 18.705, d.f. = 1, p < 0.001). However, the depression-only relatives appeared similar to the well relatives on this same variable.

It is noteworthy that the relatives of manic probands who suffered only from depression had a markedly lower incidence of cyclothymic or hypomanic personalities than did the probands themselves and the relatives who had experienced a mania. Thus, both the psychiatric symptomatology and the personality vary in the same direction. In a sense, one may speculate whether two factors are needed for manias and depressions to coexist in the same person, one a propensity for significant mood change and another a tendency for the mood change to vary in a bipolar fashion.

SUICIDE ATTEMPTS AND COMPLETED SUICIDES

Forty-three of the 61 manic probands (16 males, 27 females) had made threats of suicide at some time during their lives. Attempts at suicide had been made 21 times by 15 patients. Of the 35 female probands in the study, 14 had made a suicidal attempt; of the 26 male probands, one had made one attempt. If seems clear that female manic depressives are much more likely to attempt suicide than males with the same illness (χ^2 with Yates correction = 8.6562, d.f. = 1, p < 0.005).

Two of the 21 attempts were by jumping, and the results were medically serious. Thirteen attempts were made by taking excessive medication. Eight of these were medically serious. Two attempts were by cutting; one of these was medically serious. Four were by such means as burning, carbon monoxide inhalation, and poisoning. Three of these were medically serious.

One of the female probands committed suicide 10 months after the index admission while she was in her 30's. Two other females in their 30's made attempts which have totally incapacitated them. One inhaled carbon monoxide and now is permanently hospitalized with a chronic brain syndrome. The other burned herself and has had numerous operations for scarring and keloid formation. But for the grace of God or man, these last two women might have been considered as suicides.

We examined the data on the parents who had died in order to assess the frequency of suicide in them. Thirty fathers were deceased; of these, three were diagnosed as having affective disorder. None of them had died by suicide. Five of the 30 deceased fathers had a diagnosis of alcoholism, and three of these had committed suicide. All three had a documented history of severe and long-standing alcoholism. Of 19 deceased mothers, eight had manifested an affective disorder; one of these had died by suicide.

Our data tend to indicate that suicide behavior (attempts and completed suicides) is a greater problem in female than in male manic depressives, at least in the age ranges of our patients. At the time of admission to the study the males had a median age of 42 years, and the females 37 years. It is, of course, possible that as the patients grow older the males may surpass the females in completed suicides.

COMPULSIVE GAMBLING IN FAMILY MEMBERS

Among the male relatives of three female manic patients, five compulsive gamblers were found. The gamblers were the patients' fathers in three cases, a brother in one case, and a paternal uncle in another. The absence of base rates for "compulsive gambling" makes it difficult to assess whether these persons are overrepresented in our sample, but clinical experience indicates that this syndrome is unusual in the general population. These gamblers were not discovered in a systematic fashion but were diagnosed during the open-ended part of the interview administered to the patients and their families; therefore, the true prevalence, even among our families, is unknown. Three of these gamblers were interviewed personally (2 fathers and 1 brother), and two case histories were obtained from family members. The life history and psychopathology in all of these gamblers were strikingly similar.

The gamblers showed neither unusual permissiveness nor rigidity in their upbringing, and gambling was universally disapproved. They all began gambling for money during late adolescence and quickly became noted for their interest in cards. They tended to associate with other teen-agers with similar interests; however, none of the patients had unusual school or legal difficulties. All gamblers graduated from high school without missing a grade; three attended college; two managed to obtain professional degrees. Throughout their schooling they gambled three to five times weekly, and this pattern continued during their adult life. Most gambling was done in the company of friends, but all five of them had frequently visited illegal casinos. None were ever arrested.

They all married during their early 20's, and it quickly became apparent that gambling was an insurmountable problem to their families. In four of the five cases, their wives were forced to work and maintain separate accounts. One gambler reported winning $300 on his wedding night and a further $800 during his honeymoon.

All the families reported chaotic finances and frequent bankruptcies as a result of the gambling. Three stormy marriages ended in divorce after an average of 12 years (separations were frequent). One gambler, age 35 years, was recently separated from his wife.

In all but the youngest gambler (age 33 years) frequent attempts were made to stop gambling without success. The gambling-free intervals lasted up to 6 months. The families and those gamblers interviewed all referred to a desire to stop gambling and an inability to control their gambling behavior once they started to play (i.e., loss of control). "Binges" of 48 hours or more were common (with catnaps); and the games usually ended due to physical or financial exhaustion.

The most common pattern observed was for the gambler to begin playing in the late afternoon and continue late into the night and next morning. Weekends were often completely spent in gambling.

At the time of the study, two of these gamblers were dead (ages 61 and 64 years) and three were alive (ages 59, 61, and 33 years). Only one gambler (age 59 years) stopped gambling (with "great effort") at age 45 but still had the "urge." He was a teetotaler as regards games of chance even when money was not involved. The two gamblers who died gambled up until their terminal hospitalization.

The families felt the gamblers were good providers and gentle fathers when they were "winning" but hostile and irritable when losing. It seemed that their total existence was bound up with and fluctuated according to their compulsion.

None of the gamblers drank pathologically and all agreed that drinking heavily precluded gambling successfully. All the gamblers interviewed felt they were generous to a fault with their winnings but did not win "too often."

In view of the strong family history of affective disorder, evidence for affective abnormalities was sought in these patients, yet little could be found. They were not hypomanic, unusually cyclothymic, or depressed, and none had ever had a clinical psychiatric illness. One gambler saw a psychiatrist for treatment of his gambling compulsion but was unable to afford more than a few sessions.

Many similarities between compulsive gambling and alcoholism were observed in these patients, including loss of control, binges, lifelong compulsive devotion to their habits, and a chaotic social result of their behavior.

Those gamblers who were interviewed were charming, quick-witted individuals, and all were excellent raconteurs. Their histories agreed in essence with those of their families. They all felt their compulsions had been destructive and uncontrolled, yet they boasted about their winnings. As in alcoholism, pious contrition was a frequent response to the marital difficulties they experienced.

OCCUPATIONAL STATUS AND MANIC DEPRESSIVE ILLNESS

In a previous chapter, a review of studies indicated that manic depressives very likely were found in high socioeconomic segments of the population. This could indicate (1) that manic depressive illness conferred a social advantage on its bearer or (2) that the family of the manic depressive *as well as the ill person* was likely to be found in the more advantaged socioeconomic strata. Only when the manic depressive patient is compared with his well sibling can a properly controlled study be done that may provide an answer to which of the two alternatives listed above is true.

All probands at the time of admission were rated on an 8-point occupational scale. All personally interviewed first-degree relatives were also rated on this rough scale. The items in the scale from highest to lowest were as follows: professional, executive, small business owner, white collar worker or student, foreman, skilled laborer, unskilled laborer, and unemployed.

When married female probands were compared to their married siblings, the comparison was on the basis of the occupations of the husbands. In general, both probands and interviewed relatives were of high socioeconomic status, but this was not surprising since all the probands were obtained from a private hospital situation.

Nine male probands were compared to nine male siblings, and 15 female probands were compared to 15 female siblings. Of these 24 comparisons, four were not relevant because one partner of the female pair was unmarried and the other was married. This left 20 useful comparisons of probands with same-sex siblings. In 10 of these 20 comparisons, proband and sibling were equal in occupational status. In five cases the probands were above the siblings and in five cases the probands were below the siblings.

In general, with these rough data, it is possible to say that there is no support for the theory that manic depressive illness itself confers a social advantage. The evaluations of status refer to the time of index admission and, therefore, do not take into account the rather poor functioning of the follow-up period. However, this is probably only a small factor, since most of the probands were not first-admission cases. The striking thing is that manic depressive illness, though fraught with many social difficulties, does not destroy a patient's capacity to function occupationally in a similar fashion to his well sibling.

POSTPARTUM IMPACT

The data were of value in assessing the impact of the postpartum state in a patient who had a diagnosis of manic depressive disease which was made independently of the postpartum state. This is the first time that an opportunity has presented itself to gauge the postpartum impact in such a rigorously diagnosed group of patients.

Of the 35 females in the study, 20 had delivered 46 children. Eight of these 20 females had had 14 children. The onset of manic depressive illness in these eight women had occurred at least 5 years after the birth of their last child. In this group of eight patients the postpartum state seemed to bear no relation to the precipitation of illness.

The remaining 12 females had had the onset of their illness prior to the birth of their last child. These women had 32 children in all. Four of the 12 women had 12 children and no postpartum episodes. However, the other eight women all had postpartum episodes, and these were frequent. Thus, the eight women had 20 children born alive, and associated with these 20 live births were 14 postpartum episodes, three depressions and 11 manias. The average duration between delivery and hospitalization was 85 days for the depressions and 34 days for the manias. For only three episodes did the hospitalization occur at greater than 3 months after delivery (in all these three episodes, hospitalization occurred before 6 months); in eight of the 14 episodes, hospitalization occurred within 1 week of delivery. Five women had one postpartum episode; one had two episodes; one woman had three episodes; and one woman had four episodes. Two of the probands, then, accounted for seven of the 14 episodes.

Twenty children were born after the diagnosis of manic depressive illness had been established, and postpartum episodes were associated with 10 of these births (50%). In three probands the postpartum affective episode was the first episode in the course of the disease.

In women who had at least one postpartum episode ($N = 3$), six live births without an episode had occurred prior to the first postpartum episode. On the other hand, six children were born to the three women after a first postpartum episode. All six of these births were associated with a postpartum affective episode. Therefore, no woman had a live birth without a postpartum episode after having had such an episode. In eight women, the postpartum episode occurred with the last child.

Altogether the 20 women who had borne children had 118 separate affective episodes, of which 15 were postpartum. The 15 women who were childless had 66 episodes.

The above findings are in support of the following conclusions: Childbirth, in itself, does not lead to the onset of manic depressive illness. However, apparently, once the illness is diagnosed, there is a high probability that delivery of a baby will trigger an episode of the disease. Certainly in women who have manic depressive illness and who are thinking of a pregnancy, the strong possibility of a postpartum episode must be considered by the physician and possibly discussed with the patient. In particular, a manic depressive woman who has had a previous postpartum episode may be considered as having a special risk for a subsequent similar episode.

Chapter 10

The study: genetic findings

Considerable evidence in favor of a significant genetic factor in manic depressive disease has already been presented in Chapters 2 and 4 of this book. In previous studies, the data have been gleaned through mixtures of family history, family study, and record techniques. These sources of data are usually not specified in such a way as to relate how much each method was used. From the data in Chapter 5, it seems clear that the most reliable source of information is the family study. The findings that are a composite of all sources (family history, family study, and documents) are likely to suffer from a considerable error, mostly because cases of affective disorder among the relatives, which could have been found only by a personal interview, are missing. This problem of false negatives raises the question of whether previous studies are quantitatively reliable.

In this study we will present some of the data obtained from all sources side by side with data obtained from the family study. The family study functions as a population study, the population being a high-risk group who are relatives of the manic probands. The family study not only will serve as a check of qualitative relationships found in the "all-sources" data but also will be used for more precise quantitative relationships. The present study will attempt to clarify the homogeneity of the familial syndrome, to ascertain possible kinds of genetic transmission in manic depressive disease, and to determine the nature of sex differences in the frequency of the illness.

HETEROGENEITY-HOMOGENEITY PROBLEM IN RELATIVES OF MANIC PROBANDS

A large proportion of the first-degree relatives of the manic probands suffered from a primary affective disorder. The question arises as to whether these affected relatives suffered from manias and depressions or whether a significant proportion showed only depressions. Table 10-1 shows the kinds of illnesses in parents that were obtained from all sources.

Thirty-six parents had a primary affective disorder, unrelated to alcoholism; of these, 28 (78%) had only depressions; eight (22%) had manifested a mania. Considerable alcoholism was seen among the fathers (9/61, or 15%).

The all-sources data indicated that 33 sibs suffered from an affective disorder. The breakdown as to type is shown in Table 10-2. In the case of both male and female sibs, the majority had never experienced a mania. Five of 12 male sibs with affective disorder experienced a mania, and eight of 21 female sibs had suffered from a mania.

Table 10-1. Illnesses in parents of 61 probands (all-sources data)

	Father	Mother
No illness	33	24
Depression only	3	25
Mania only	2	4
Alcoholism only	9	1
Depression and mania	1	1
Alcoholism and depression	1	1
Other	9	5
Unknown	3	0
Total	61	61

Table 10-2. Quality of affective disorder in sibs of 61 manic probands (all-sources data)

	Brothers	Sisters
Depression only	7	13
Mania only	2	1
Depression and mania	3	7

Turning to the family study data, we may note that of 167 personally interviewed first-degree relatives of the 61 manic probands, 58 suffered from some form of affective disorder and/or alcoholism. Table 10-3 gives these data.

Of the 29 first-degree relatives with depression only, six were male and 23 were female. Twenty had had only one episode of depression, four had had two episodes, and four had had three or more episodes of depression. The median age of onset of the 29 was 52 years. One patient had had a chronic depressive illness. Of the 17 relatives who had experienced mania, five were male and 12 were female. The median age of onset for affective disorder of the 17 was 48 years. Five of the 17 had experienced only one attack of mania. Thus, except for the increased number of attacks, the patients who had manias and those who had depressions only were rather similar.

Of those 29 relatives of probands who suffered from depression only, one third (10 cases) were over 60 years of age (4 were over 70) at the time of interview. Eight of the 10 patients were mothers and two were sisters. Eight of the 10 patients had had only one attack of depression, one had had five attacks, and one was chronically depressed. Nine of the 10 had first become ill after 40 years of age. It would seem unlikely that after the age of 60 years very many of these patients would develop a mania.

Our data clearly indicate heterogeneity in the families of manic probands, with large proportions of affectively ill relatives manifesting only depressions. Alcoholism is seen frequently in these relatives also. One may conclude that manic depressive disease in relatives of manic probands is heterogeneous, with a large proportion showing manias and the majority showing only

Table 10-3. Affective disorder and alcoholism in 167 personally interviewed first-degree relatives

Type of illness	Number
Alcoholism only	7
Depression only	29
Mania only	7
Depression and alcoholism	5
Mania and depression	10
Indeterminate (undiagnosed)	4
Not ill with affective disorder or alcoholism	105

depressions. The family picture of affective illness in manic depressive disease is quite different from that of depressive disease. Perris' data clearly show that unipolar patients (depressive disease) have only a negligible percent of ill relatives who manifest mania.[2] In manic depressive disease (bipolar illness), the present data indicate that the proportion of patients showing mania is considerably higher, with 17 of the 46 affective disorder relatives (those in which alcoholism was not a problem) being a manic at some time during their lives (see Table 10-3). In subsequent sections of this chapter, pathology in the first-degree relatives will relate to affective disorder (mania only, mania and depression, or depression only) rather than to a breakdown of types of affective disorder.

MORBIDITY RISKS FOR FIRST-DEGREE RELATIVES OF MANIC PROBANDS

In 56 of the 61 manic probands, information was available on all the parents and sibs, and it was possible to calculate morbidity risks for these relatives. Morbidity risk (or expectancy rate) is the percentage of the relatives of manic probands who would develop an affective disorder if they passed through the age of risk. In Chapter 5 it was noted that the age of risk for the manic probands started at 15 years and by 60 years all the probands had fallen ill. Table 10-4 gives a breakdown of morbidity risks (Strömgren method) for various classes of relatives and probands, using data obtained from all sources.

From Table 10-4, certain facts should be noted:
1. Of the 31 female probands, approximately twice as many had ill mothers (50%) as had ill fathers (23%).
2. No male proband had a father who was ill with affective disorder; however, 63% of the mothers of the male probands suffered from affective disorder themselves. Females, on the other hand, had ill fathers and ill mothers.
3. There is a tendency for female probands to have had fewer ill brothers (23%) than ill sisters (46%).
4. Thirty-four percent of the parents of the total proband group had an affective illness. An equal number of sibs (35%) had affective disorder.
5. Of 99 male first-degree relatives at risk, 19 had affective disorder. Of 100 female relatives at risk, 50 had affective disorder. In the group of rela-

Table 10-4. Morbidity risks for affective disorder in first-degree relatives of manic probands (all-sources data)

	Number of relatives	Number at risk	Number ill with affective disorder	Percent morbidity risk for affective disorder	Standard error
Female probands (N = 31)					
Fathers	31	30	7	23	± 7.7
Mothers	31	30	15	50	± 9.1
Brothers	33	22	5	23	± 9.0
Sisters	39	28	13	46	± 9.4
Male probands (N = 25)					
Fathers	25	24	0	0	—
Mothers	25	24	15	63	± 9.9
Brothers	29	23	7	30	± 9.5
Sisters	24	18	7	39	±11.5
Male and female probands (N = 56)					
Fathers	56	54	7	13	± 4.6
Mothers	56	54	30	56	± 6.8
Brothers	62	45	12	27	± 6.6
Sisters	63	46	20	44	± 7.3
All parents	112	108	37	34	± 4.6
All sibs	125	91	32	35	± 5.0

tives, females were significantly more likely to be affected ($\chi^2 = 20.846$, d.f. = 1, p < 0.0005).

From the all-sources data, it was possible to get an estimate of alcoholism in first-degree relatives. Alcoholism was negligible in the female relatives, but in the 56 fathers of the manic probands, eight suffered from alcoholism. All fathers had passed through the age of risk for alcoholism (20 to 40 years); and, consequently, the morbidity risk for alcoholism in the fathers was 14%. Seven of the alcoholic fathers were the fathers of male probands, and only one alcoholic father was the father of a female proband. Fifty-four brothers were at risk, and three were alcoholic, giving a morbid risk of 6%. It appears, then, that alcoholism is a significant factor, particularly in the fathers of the male probands.

The most reliable data, of course, come from the interviewed first-degree relatives of the family study. One hundred sixty-seven relatives were interviewed.

In the family study, the affectively ill first-degree relatives were rated according to the type of psychiatric care they received. Thirty-six percent of the relatives who had manifested affective disorder had been hospitalized for their illness; 56% had not been hospitalized but had sought medical help for the symptoms of their affective illness; only 8% had neither been hospitalized nor sought medical care. Table 10-5 presents these relatives and their ages at the time of interview.

Table 10-5. 167 first-degree relatives and their age at time of interview (family-study data)

Age of interview (years)	Mothers	Fathers	Brothers	Sisters	Sons	Daughters
10-19	—	—	3	6	8	8
20-29	—	—	13	8	3	7
30-39	2	—	11	6	3	—
40-49	6	2	7	6	1	1
50-59	7	8	3	12	—	—
60-69	11	7	—	6	—	—
70+	9	2	—	1	—	—
Total number	35	19	37	45	15	16

The morbidity risks for these relatives were calculated by the Strömgren method and are given in Table 10-6. Included in Table 10-6 are the risks for alcoholism in fathers and brothers, which were calculated by using the Weinberg method.

From Table 10-6, certain affective disorder findings are noteworthy:

1. Ill mothers outnumber ill fathers (55% vs. 17%, p < 0.025).
2. Ill sisters outnumber ill brothers (52% vs. 29%, p = N.S.).
3. Forty-one percent of all parents are ill; an almost equal number of sibs are ill (42%).
4. Ill female relatives are significantly in excess of ill male relatives (χ^2 = 11.254, d.f. = 1, p < 0.001).

Alcoholism appears to be an important factor in the fathers.

SEX RELATIONSHIPS IN ILL PARENT–ILL CHILD PAIRS

In order to further explore the nature of the sex differential (females outnumbering males), a search was made in the all-sources data for instances in which a parent and a child both manifested affective disorder. These instances included information from second-degree relatives as well as first-degree relatives. In the all-sources data, 69 such ill parent–ill child pairs were found. These are recorded in Table 10-7.

It is clear that there is a marked and significant deficiency of ill father–ill son pairs (χ^2 with Yates correction = 7.98, d.f. = 1, p < 0.01). Within the present study of manic depressive disease ill fathers do not pass their illness on to their sons but may very likely pass it on to their daughters. A previously reported family history study indicated that if one investigated a mixed group of affective disorder probands (composed mainly of depressive probands) a finding of father-son transmission was common.[4] It is only when one studies manic probands and their families that father-son transmission is absent.

INFLUENCE OF AFFECTED PARENTS ON THE MORBIDITY RISK FOR AFFECTIVE DISORDER IN THE SIBS OF MANIC PROBANDS

The influence of an affected parent on the number of affected sibs may provide information concerning the type of genetic transmission. In two

Table 10-6. Morbidity risks in interviewed first-degree relatives of manic probands (family-study data)

| | For affective disorder | | | | |
Type of relative	Number interviewed	Number at risk	Number ill with affective disorder	Percent morbidity risk for affective disorder	Standard error
Mothers	35	33	18	55	± 8.7
Fathers	19	18	3	17	± 8.8
Sisters	45	33	17	52	± 8.7
Brothers	37	24	7	29	± 9.3
Sons	15	6	1	17	±15.3
Daughters	16	6	5	83	±15.3
All parents	54	51	21	41	± 6.9
All sibs	82	57	24	42	± 6.6
All children	31	12	6	50	±14.4
All male first-degree relatives	71	48	11	23	± 6.1
All female first-degree relatives	96	72	40	56	± 5.8

| | For alcoholism | | | | |
Type of relative	Number Interviewed	Number at risk	Number ill with alcohol	Percent morbidity risk for alcohol	Standard error
Fathers	19	19	4	21	± 9.3
Brothers	37	24	1	4	± 4.0

Table 10-7. Sex relationships in parent-child pairs, both members having affective disorder (all-sources data)

	Number of pairs
Ill mother–ill son	28
Ill mother–ill daughter	29
Ill father–ill son	0
Ill father–ill daughter	12

previous studies, when affective disorder probands (mainly depressive probands) with one parent ill were compared to affective disorder probands with neither parent ill, a highly significant increase in ill siblings was seen in the former group.[3,4] A similar evaluation was made for the sibs of the 61 manic probands, and this is presented in Table 10-8. Because three fathers were unknown among the 61 probands and one set of male sibs was unknown, the analysis was made on the basis of 57 manic probands.

It is clear from Table 10-8 that an ill parent does not increase the likelihood that the sibs of manic probands will be ill. When the rate of affective disorder

Table 10-8. Influence of parents with affective disorder on the morbidity risk of sibs of manic probands (all-sources data)

	Number sibs	Number sibs at risk	Number sibs with affective disorder	Percent morbidity risk for affective disorder	Standard error
Both parents ill (proband, N = 2)	2	2	1	50	±39
One parent ill (probands, N = 33)	73	50	14	28	± 6.3
Neither parent ill (probands, N = 22)	58	46	17	37	± 7.1

was compared between sibs with an ill parent and sibs with no ill parents, a χ^2 of 0.879 was obtained (p = not significant).

TWINS

Five of the manic probands were the products of twin births. Pertinent data concerning them are as follows: It should be noted that none of the twins have passed through the age of risk.

1. Proband is a female, age 50 years. Her twin sister is probably monozygotic and is concordant for affective illness and more specifically for mania.
2. Proband is a male, age 35 years. His twin brother is dizygotic and discordant for affective illness. Another brother is affectively ill, but only with depression.
3. Proband is a male, age 25 years. His twin brother is dizygotic and discordant for affective illness. Another brother is affectively ill, but only with depression.
4. Proband is a male, age 58 years. He was the result of a twin birth, but the twin (sex unknown) was stillborn.
5. Proband is a female, age 24 years. Her twin brother is well.

Normally only one out of 88 births is expected to produce twins. Since five out of 61 probands were twins, it is reasonable to question whether this overrepresentation of twins in the study is a chance phenomenon or associated in some fashion with manic depressive illness.

OTHER PSYCHIATRIC DISEASES IN FIRST-DEGREE RELATIVES OF MANIC PROBANDS

Besides affective disorder and alcoholism, other psychiatric diseases were seen in the 167 personally interviewed relatives. One relative had schizophrenia; four relatives had a chronic brain syndrome; one relative had a personality disorder; four relatives had mental deficiency; and one relative had an undiagnosed psychiatric illness. There were eight relatives who had a diagnosis of psychoneurosis. Four of these had anxiety neurosis, one had hysteria, and three had obsessive compulsive neurosis. Thus, no single psychiatric disease besides alcoholism and affective disorder was seen in any great frequency in these interviewed relatives.

INTEGRATING THE FINDINGS

The next step is to attempt an interpretation of the family findings in terms of some genetic hypotheses. This may be done by beginning with the various possible kinds of transmission.

An autosomal recessive transmission seems quite unlikely. In autosomal recessive transmission one expects few families with two generations of affected people. In our proband group, considerably over half the patients had an affected parent. In autosomal recessive transmission, one expects more affected sibs than parents. From Table 10-4 and Table 10-6, it is clear that parents and sibs are equally affected. In an autosomal recessive transmission one would expect the percentage of sibs with affected parents to be higher than the percentage of affected sibs of non-affected parents. From Table 10-8, this is clearly not true. It seems, then, that one can safely eliminate autosomal recessive transmission as a possibility in manic depressive disease.

Another possibility would be sex-linked recessive transmission. In this case there would be an increased number of males that were ill, and, in fact, exactly the opposite is true; i.e., affected female family members outnumber the males by a very significant factor.

Dominant gene transmission may be considered. The presence of affected members in two successive generations is the hallmark of dominant transmission, and this is certainly found in the present study. In dominant transmission the percent of affected parents should equal the percent of affected sibs, and this is certainly consistent with the data that have been presented in this chapter. In dominant transmission one would expect 50 % of the parents to be affected and 50 % of the sibs to be affected. From the all-sources data (Table 10-4), the figures are 34 % and 35 % respectively. In the family study data (Table 10-6) 41 % of all parents are affected and 42 % of all sibs are affected. Thus, there is about an 8 % to 16 % deficiency in the observed number of affected parents and sibs compared to the expected number. One would then have to invoke the concept of decreased penetrance of a dominant gene in order to explain the deficiency. The data concerning the percent of affected sibs who have one ill parent and the percent of affected sibs who have neither parent ill (Table 10-8) could be construed as being in favor of a dominant type of inheritance. Even though the gene did not manifest itself in a parent, the parent nevertheless would have to have had that gene. Whatever accounted for the decreased penetrance (psychologic, social, or other genetic factors) was present in the family grouping as proved by the fact that the child or proband had manic depressive disease. Consequently, one would expect an equal number of sibs to be affected whether or not a parent showed the illness; this was, of course, found. An autosomal dominant gene hypothesis, however, does not fit the data. It does not account for the increased number of females over males in the families of manic probands.

To deal with the sex differences the hypothesis of an X-linked dominant gene is quite reasonable. McKusick presents the characteristics of X-linked dominant traits.[1] An essential feature is the absence of father-to-son transmission. The absence of father-to-son transmission is seen from Table 10-7. This finding is highly significant in the present study. However, there have been cases reported by clinicians and also in the literature where ill fathers do in fact have manic sons. From our own data we would suspect that this is rare and might be explained on the basis of the fact that the mother of the manic proband in these cases herself carried the gene although she did not manifest it. An X-linked trait is also characterized by the fact that ill female relatives outnumber ill male relatives by a factor that approaches two. This is certainly true in the present study (see Tables 10-4 and 10-6). In X-linked dominant inheritance, affected males should always have an affected mother if penetrance were complete. From Table 10-4, it may be noted that 63% of the male manic probands had affected mothers. One must then continue to postulate incomplete penetrance in order to accept an X-linked dominant inheritance in manic depressive disease. One third of affected females in X-linked dominant inheritance should have an affected father, and two thirds an affected mother. This appears to be true (Table 10-4) in that female probands have 23% affected fathers and 50% affected mothers.

The data in Table 10-7 support this ratio also. One may note that there are only 12 ill father–ill daughter pairs but 29 ill mother–ill daughter pairs. If one accepts these data as being a representative population of manic depressives, the 12 ill father–ill daughter pairs account for one third the affected females who have an ill parent. In general, then, X-linked dominant inheritance with somewhat incomplete penetrance fits the present data rather well.

It would appear, then, that the increased frequency for manic depressive disease in females over males may simply be the result of the females' possessing two X-chromosomes. The risk would be additive for the female population, which would be expected to show twice as much of the illness as the male population. No recourse to endocrine, physiologic, or psychologic differences is necessary.

Ascertainment of ill relatives may be somewhat incomplete. This is certainly true of the all-sources data. However, the family study data, obtained by interviewing all first-degree family members at risk should be considerably more reliable. Nevertheless, because the method for picking up illness is solely dependent on a clinical interview and the possibility exists that ill family members may be more difficult to obtain for interview, incomplete ascertainment may account for the incomplete penetrance.

Although the population data support a dominant X-linked gene, it is quite possible that some contribution to the disease might be made by other genetic factors. From the all-sources data, it was noteworthy that 22 of the 61 manic probands, or greater than one third the cases, had alcoholism and/or affective disorder on both sides of the family, maternal and paternal. There is no obvious group with which to compare these 61 probands and the high frequency of illness on both maternal and paternal sides. However, simple inspection makes this frequency appear rather important. Such a finding might indicate that other genes are necessary in order to increase the probability of manifestation of the dominant X-linked gene.

Another finding may be of some importance in considering a second gene. In the previous chapter it was noted that almost all bipolar patients (those showing manias and depressions) had a premorbid cyclothymic or hypomanic personality. On the other hand, this premorbid personality was seen with much less frequency in the depression-only and the well family members of the manic probands. One might speculate whether a very common second genetic factor is necessary for a family member to specifically exhibit manias in addition to an X-linked dominant gene, which is necessary for the manifestation of the affective illness itself.

The possibility that other genes may influence the major gene in inheritance has some theoretical implications for the present study. The theory suggests that in the course of natural selection, each individual is the result of a delicate balance of genes. In the course of time the presence of modifying genes would decrease the deleterious effects of a dominant gene that produced the disease. In the long run, the effects of this would be to turn the disease gene into a recessive. Perhaps in the course of evolution such a situation would account for decreased penetrance and perhaps the presence of other types of modifiers would enhance the effect of a dominant gene. Suffice to say, however, from the data in the present study that the major contribution to manic depressive disease seems to be from an X-linked dominant kind of gene.

REFERENCES

1. McKusick, V. A.: On the X-chromosome of man, Washington, D. C., 1964, American Institute of Biological Sciences.
2. Perris, C., editor: A study of bipolar (manic-depressive) and unipolar recurrent depressive psychoses, Acta Psychiat. Scand. 42:(Supp. 194), 1966.
3. Winokur, G., and Clayton, P.: Family history studies: I. Two types of affective disorders separated according to genetic and clinical factors. In Wortis, J., editor: Recent advances in biological psychiatry, New York, 1967, Plenum Publishing Corp., vol. 9.
4. Winokur, G., and Pitts, F. N., Jr.: Affective disorder: VI. A family history study of prevalences, sex differences and possible genetic factors, J. Psychiat. Res. 3:113, 1965.

Chapter 11

Manic depressive disease and linkage with a genetic marker

The data presented in the previous chapter are quite suggestive of X-linkage in manic depressive disease. Interpretation of the material leads to consideration of an X-linked dominant gene's being a major contributor to the illness. As a consequence, a logical next step is a search for linkage with another and well-established X-linked marker.

Linkage occurs if two genes, each responsible for a separate trait, are on the same chromosome and are close enough together that they assort in a dependent fashion. Actually linkage occurs between loci for genes rather than specific genes themselves. Thus, two genes (which account for two specific traits) are considered linked in *coupling* if they are on the same chromosome and in *repulsion* if they are on homologous chromosomes. If there are two traits, A and B, and the loci for these two traits are linked in coupling, then A and B would be seen together in several members of a large family group. Likewise, in this case, the absence of A would be associated with the absence of B in the other members of the family group. If, on the other hand, the two traits A and B were linked in repulsion, most individuals in a large family group would have one or the other, but not both, of the two traits. Exceptions to these rules would occur in occasional family members because of crossing over between chromosomes, which would rearrange the location of specific genes but would not change the location of the gene system (locus).

In any single family the physical proximity of two genes on the same chromosome makes it likely that the characteristics of both genes will be found together in 50 % of the individuals in that family. In a population (not a family) association of a disease with a specific marker occurs fleetingly on the basis of linkage. However, this kind of association occurs only for a few generations. When enough generations have passed and enough crossing over has occurred between chromosomes, the association disappears. Therefore, linkage produces no permanent association in the population but may be found only within the family. The degree of concordance of traits in a family is a measure of the physical proximity of the two genes.

Finding the linkage of manic depressive disease with a genetic marker would provide information about the kind of genetic transmission, but even more importantly it would provide incontrovertible evidence of a genetic factor in the disease.

Some previous work on linkage in manic depressive disease has been reported. Tanna and Winokur investigated the possibility of linkage with the ABO blood locus in primary affective disorder.[3] No evidence for linkage was found. In this study the sib-pair method of Penrose was used.[2]

A subgroup of sib-pairs with a positive family history of mania in a first-degree relative was also studied in order to determine whether linkage existed between the ABO blood system locus and the locus for manic depressive disease. This was also negative.

Winokur and Tanna, in a subsequent work, found some suggestion of linkage between manic depressive disease and the Xg blood system locus, which locus appears on the X-chromosome. The data were few and the results were not statistically significant. However, the material was statistically significant as to X-linkage itself (but not for specific linkage with the Xg locus) in manic depressive disease.[4]

Reich, Clayton, and Winokur found two families who were assorting for color blindness and manic depressive disease.[1] In one family, five people had affective disorder, and in all cases these five people were either color blind or carriers of the color blindness gene. The probability of the association of these two events by chance was $1/2^5$. A second family was found in which six people had affective disorder. All six were either color blind or carriers of the color blindness gene, and the probability that this association was due to chance was $1/2^6$. When the two families were taken together, the evidence was highly reliable that the association was not due to chance itself (p = $1/2^{11}$ = 0.0005).

Further work has been done on this second family, which will be known as the Alger family. The material on this extended study of the Alger family will be presented here. All first-degree and available second- and third-degree relatives in the Alger family were personally interviewed. Color vision was tested in the males, using pseudoisochromic plates. The Munsell 100-hue test, which is able to discern female carriers at times, was administered to females. Male children of female members of the Alger family were tested. A color-blind son indicates that the mother possesses the gene for color blindness, for the son received his sole X-chromosome from the mother. Hospital records of living family members as well as dead family members were reviewed and color vision examinations that had been done elsewhere were obtained. The accompanying figure gives the pedigree for the Alger family.

Table 11-1 gives the clinical material that was accumulated on the various members of the Alger family who clearly had affective disorder.

Other family members of importance are III-4, affective disorder, depressed, not color blind; III-6, chronic alcoholism, not color blind; III-8, chronic alcoholism, not color blind. These family members not shown in the table are from the paternal side of the proband's family. On the maternal side significant family members are III-12, possible affective disorder with suicidal threats and depression, color blind; III-13, chronic brain syndrome associated with fluctuating depressive affect, daughter's son color blind; III-28, epilepsy, remitting psychosis, color blind; III-29, depressive and euphoric episodes by family history, color blind by family history; IV-30, affective disorder, depressed, color vision unknown; V-4, affective disorder, depressed, color vision unknown.

Table 11-1. Clinical factors in the Alger family (protan color blindness)

	III-9	III-14	IV-13	Proband IV-14	IV-15	IV-17	V-6	IV-20
Hospitalized	−	+	+	+	−	+	−	−
Saw M.D. for out-patient treatment	+	+	+	+	+	+	+	+
Electroshock treatment	−	−	+	−	−	−	−	−
Suicide attempt	−	+	−	−	−	−	−	−
Suicidal ideation	+	+	+	+	−	+	−	−
More than one episode	+	+	+	+	+	+	−	+
Remissions	+	+	+	+	+	+	+	+
Depression	+	+	+	+	+	+	+	+
Insomnia	+	+	+	+	+	+	+	+
Anorexia, weight loss	+	+	+	+	+	+	+	+
Delusions (self-condem-natory and nihilistic)	−	−	+	−	+	+	−	−
Mania	−	−	+	−	÷	−	−	−
Episodes more than 4 months' duration	+	+	+	+	+	+	+	+
Social incapacity	+	+	+	+	+	+	+	+
Color blind or carrier of gene	+	+	+	+	+	+	+	+
Diagnosis	AD, D*	AD, D	AD, M & D†	AD, D	AD, M & D	AD, D	AD, D	AD, D

*AD, D = Affective disorder with depression only.

†AD, M & D = Affective disorder with mania and depression.

Only one member of the Alger family, V-3, carries the gene for color blindness without manifesting affective disorder. He is cyclothymic and has had short-lived endogenous mood swings; he is 27 years old and only part way through the age of risk.

In the family of III-16, color blindness is found. One member has passed the age of risk without manifesting affective disorder, and this is probably an example of crossing over or uncoupling of the genes for affective disorder and color blindness. Further possibilities are that the disorder is polygenic and the second gene is absent, that the gene was not fully penetrant, or that color blindness was introduced by the husband of III-16.

Only definite cases of affective disorder were used in the statistical analysis. The probability that each of the family members with affective disorder would be color blind or carry the gene would be 1/2. Therefore, in this family alone the probability that this association is due to chance alone is $1/2^{7(p < 0.01)}$. All family members who had affective disorder except III-4, the paternal uncle of the proband, either manifested color blindness or carried the gene. The paternal side of the proband's family did not contain color blindness and consequently was not included in the calculations. One family member, V-4, the niece of the proband, had affective disorder. Her status as to color blindness is unknown. The Munsell 100-hue test indicated that she was probably color blind, but it was not conclusive.

Color blindness in the Alger family was of the protan type. In the calcu-

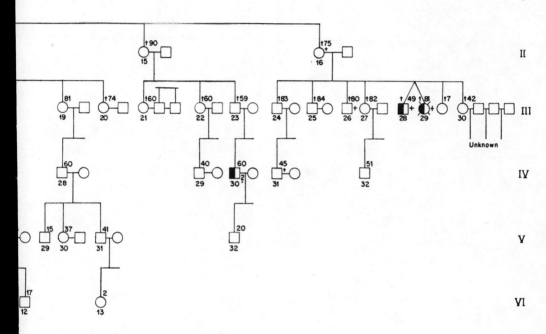

I

II

III

IV

V

VI

Unknown

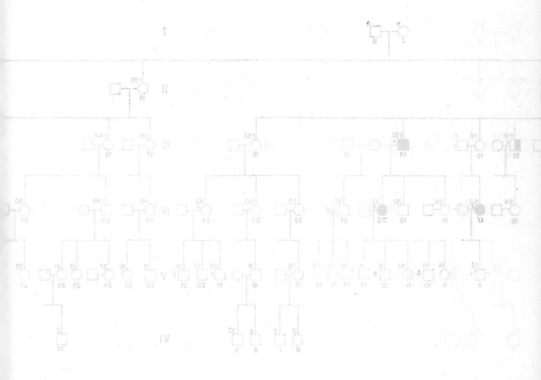

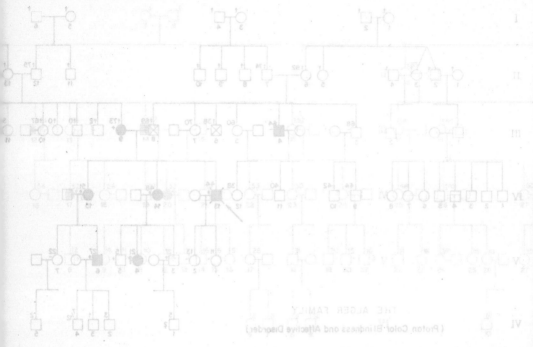

THE ALGER FAMILY
(Proton Color Blindness and Affective Disorder)

LEGEND:

- ■ – male with depression
- ● – female with depression
- ◙ – male with mania
- ◙ – female with mania
- † – dead

I,II,III,IV – generations, individuals',
numbers below symbols
Numbers at upper right of symbols are ages
(+) – color blind or carrier of color
blindness gene
? – color blind status unknown
(-) – not color blind or carrier

- □ – male with no depression or mania
- ○ – female with no depression or
mania
- ↗ – proband
- ⋀ – twins
- ◩ – alcoholic male
- ⊗ – alcoholic female
- ▣ – questionable affective disorder,
male
- ◐ – questionable affective disorder,
female

lations, the proband was not included. Only definite cases of affective disorder were used in the statistical analysis. Because the onset of manic depressive disease is variable and the age of risk is long, we chose not to analyze the data by starting with color blindness and determining the frequency of occurrence of manic depressive illness in those family members who were either color blind or carriers of the gene. This would have necessitated some correction for the amount of risk that had been traversed by a color blind person. Such an evaluation appears unnecessary, since the evidence for linkage is quite significant when just half the data are used.

Within the Alger family itself the evidence is highly reliable that manic depressive disease is very likely to be linked to the locus for color blindness (p < 0.01). In the previously published family the evidence for linkage between the color blindness locus and manic depressive illness was $1/2^5$. Altogether, the possibility that the concordance is the result of chance alone is $1/2^{12}$ or 1 in 4000.

Color blindness of the protan type is well known as an X-linked recessive gene. It occasionally shows up in heterozygotes, i.e., women who have the gene but do not manifest the full-blown trait. The locus for the color blindness gene is on the short arm of the X-chromosome, and presumably the locus for an X-linked dominant gene in manic depressive disease would be located in the same place.

Thus affective disorder in which mania occurs (manic depressive disease, bipolar psychosis) is quite probably linked on the X-chromosome with the locus for color blindness. This finding adds to the evidence in favor of X-linkage for manic depressive disease. Perhaps more important, it provides further proof of a genetic factor in manic depressive disease.

REFERENCES

1. Reich, T., Clayton, P., and Winokur, G.: Family history studies: V. The genetics of mania, Amer. J. Psychiat. **125**:1358, 1969.
2. Sutton, H. E.: An introduction to human genetics, New York, 1965, Holt, Reinhart & Winston, Inc.
3. Tanna, V. L., and Winokur, G.: A study of association of linkage of ABO blood types and primary affective disorder, Brit. J. Psychiat. **114**:1175, 1968.
4. Winokur, G., and Tanna, V. L.: Possible role of X-linked dominant factor in manic depressive disease, Dis. Nerv. Syst. **30**:89, 1969.

Chapter 12

The question of etiology: biologic approaches

At the present time, it seems clear that genetic factors play a significant role in the etiology of manic depressive disease. There are no data in any other field of research as strong and as predictive as those in the genetic area. These findings have been discussed in depth in previous chapters. Nevertheless, when one is dealing with an illness in which the clinical picture is one of remissions and exacerbations, as is the case in manic depressive disease, it is necessary to search for other etiologic factors that might explain why an individual has the manifestations of the illness at particular times in his life. Having found a viable genetic factor in the disease simply obligates the researcher to look in particular areas for contributions to the pathogenesis and the pathophysiology of the illness. One cannot go further into the etiology with a great deal of certainty at this time, but there are a number of findings that may either prove to be leads or provide reasonable hypotheses for further understanding of causation. These heuristic approaches are the contents of the present chapter. They will be reported under a number of subheadings.

VARIOUS RELEVANT OBSERVATIONS IN MANIC STATES

Clinicians have noted that the most common clinical picture in general paresis or syphilis of the brain includes euphoria, expansiveness, and grandiosity. These rather typical manic symptoms usually occur in the presence of memory changes, disturbances of consciousness, and deteriorating judgment and ethical control. Usually the infectious quality of the manic depressive's mood is lacking but, certainly in the patient with general paresis, his humor may be good. Mayer-Gross, Slater, and Roth quote figures which indicate that euphoria or expansiveness accompanies the dementia in about 40% of the cases of general paresis.[21] Of further importance is the fact that a typical depressive picture may also occur in syphilis of the brain. The pathology of general paresis is well known and is associated with atrophy in the frontal, temporal, parietal regions of the brain. The cortex is grossly disorganized, and the cells are in various stages of degeneration. *Treponema pallidum* may be found in the brain. Here, then, is a clear organic disease that manifests itself with both mania and depression. The fact that there is such generalized destruction of brain tissue probably makes it difficult to specify in which way or in which areas the production of the affective symptoms may have occurred.

An association between manic behavior and other types of known brain pathology has occasionally been reported. Oppler describes the case of a young man with a parasaggital meningioma who demonstrated clear manic behavior and who improved after operation.[24] The patient was a chronic alcoholic who started drinking at the age of 17 years and developed seizures for the first time at 23 years of age. He was discharged from the armed services with a diagnosis of a neurosis. At 29 years of age he was admitted to a veteran's hospital with hypomanic behavior and an occasional confused sensorium. A pneumoencephalogram showed a shifted third ventricle, and operation revealed a grayish white tumor in the right frontoparietal area. His manic behavior, which had worsened prior to the operation, disappeared after surgery. This patient had had considerable psychiatric problems prior to being admitted, and it is not possible to determine whether the manic behavior was a chance concomitant or whether it might have been caused by the tumor. Manic behavior is not a usual occurrence with brain tumors, but Oppler cites the work of Foerster, who described a case of suprasellar craniopharyngioma. When Foerster manipulated the tumor during surgery, he produced pressure of speech and flight of ideas. Foerster believed that the behavior was the result of the manipulation and its effects on the fourth and third ventricle. He claimed that he had made similar observations and they all led to the idea that any mechanical stimulation of the anterior section of the hypothalamus could precipitate a manic picture. Stern and Dancey reported a case of a patient with a glioma of the diencephalon who manifested a prolonged attack of mania.[31] In evaluating the available literature these authors concluded that episodes of manic behavior, when observed in association with circumscribed lesions, were associated with lesions located in the depths of the brain stem or at the base of the brain. Only rarely was this not true. Fulton and Bailey are cited by Stern and Dancey as saying that manic attacks were seen only in tumors in the vicinity of the base of the brain rather than in tumors affecting the hemispheres. All the above statements are made on the basis of relatively few observations, and, consequently, it is difficult to evaluate them. At this point no specific and consistent pathology has been found that produces a manic picture.

Dalén studied 35 patients under 40 years of age who were hospitalized for mania.[11] The foci of the investigation were family history and electroencephalography. The author believed that the data supported the idea that there might be two types of manic conditions: one caused by a specific genetic propensity, the other associated with brain damage that occurred during the perinatal period of life. This group of patients seemed to lack a hereditary predisposition to mania, showed greater frequency of perinatal situations (toxemia of pregnancy, breech presentation, etc.), which would involve a risk of brain damage, and had abnormal or borderline electroencephalograms.

Other factors besides gross anatomic lesions have been implicated in the production of manic behavior. Cooper reports a 35-year-old woman who had been undergoing intermittent hemodialysis for 13 months.[8] The patient had had chronic pyelonephritis and nonfunctioning kidneys as a result of the infection. After one of the dialyses she suffered a vein infection, had a high temperature, and was treated with erythromycin. Two days later her temperature was normal. Her blood urea was 188 mg. %. A dialysis was attempted but was unsuccessful because of thrombosed vessels. She went into a manic state with pressure of speech, ecstatic affect, and religious delusions. Intellectually there was no impairment nor was there any evidence of delirium.

She had several dialyses and ultimately over a 15-day period her blood urea was reduced from 188 to 135 mg.%. She was treated with chlorpromazine, and the manic psychosis decreased in intensity. Serum potassium varied between 3.8 and 4.9 mg.% during the 15-day period of disturbance. The patient was followed for 6 months after the episode and has remained mentally well. Dialysis is, of course, a complicated procedure with a potential for many changes in electrolyte levels. This patient had had no previous psychiatric history, nor did she have a positive family history for affective disorder. Once more it is conceivable that this was simply a chance association or that perhaps something in the hemodialysis did, in fact, precipitate the illness.

STEROID STUDIES

Many studies have been reported on the relationship of steroids to depression in particular. However, some of these findings are relevant to mania and to the illness, manic depressive disease. Quarton and co-workers, in an extensive review of the effects of steroid hormones on mental status, cite a frequent finding of euphoria in patients on cortisone and ACTH.[26] However, agitation and depression occur after administration of these hormones perhaps equally as frequently as euphoria. Fleminger studied a patient with psoriasis arthropathica. This patient was treated with both cortisone and ACTH.[15] There were significant mood changes with the administration of both the drugs, changes that Fleminger attributed to the drug rather than to the relief of symptoms. Cortisone produced mood elevation and euphoria, whereas ACTH produced depression.

Reports of clinical observations prompted a number of investigators to study endogeneous changes in steroid hormones in affective disorder. In Addison's disease there is a great deal of depression and apathy associated with the adrenal insufficiency. Cushing's syndrome is characterized by an increase in steroid secretion, and psychiatric symptoms are common in this syndrome. Most commonly, apathy, severe depression, delusions, and auditory hallucinations are found in Cushing's syndrome, but one also observes irritability and excitability with mood swings.[22] There have been a number of studies concerned with measuring adrenal cortical activity in various mental states. These have included evaluations of urinary excretion of 17-hydroxycorticosteroids, measurements of plasma 17-hydroxycorticosteroids, and measurements of cortisol secretion rates. Sachar has reviewed a good part of this literature and points out that there are conflicting reports on adrenocortical function. This seems to be a result of failure to control for the effect of hospitalization and medication, of questionable control groups, or of a lack of adequate diagnostic criteria.[28] Nevertheless, Gibbons studied 15 patients and noted that their depression was associated with elevated plasma cortisol secretion rates before treatment.[16] When depression cleared, there was a decrease in the secretion rate. Thus, there was a good correlation in the Gibbons study with severity and course of the illness. Gibbons also studied the secretion rate of corticosterone before and after successful treatment in six patients with endogenous depressions.[17] He noted a decrease in corticosterone from 3.5 to 2.4 mg./24 hours. There was a similar decrease in cortisol secretion rate and in urinary secretion of 17-hydroxycorticosteroids and 11-hydroxycorticosteroids. Gibbons believed that the concomitant changes in secretion of cortisol and corticosterone support the view that increased adrenocortical activity in depression is due to increased secretion of pituitary corticotropin. Kurland studied urinary 17-hydroxycorticosteroids and 17-ketoglucosteroids.[20] He found that the former showed no correlation with the severity or course of depression but that the latter did show a good correlation. Bunney and co-workers studied urinary 17-hydroxycorticosteroids and found high levels during psychotic turmoil but not otherwise.[5] Sachar studied 20 hospitalized patients before and after recovery from depressive illness. He found that a slight drop of 17-hydroxycorticosteroids in the urine occurred following recovery but this steroid change was not correlated with severity or course of the illness.[28] He found evidence that patients who were in states of organized psychotic behavior did not have elevated levels but those patients who were in acute turmoil states did have elevated levels.

There are some studies that deal more specifically with manic depressive disease and steroid metabolism. Bunney, Hartman, and Mason studied a patient with 48-hour manic depressive cycles by evaluating 17-hydroxycorticosteroid excretion levels during the manic periods and the depressive periods.[4] These levels were low on the days when the patient was manic and high on the days the patient was depressed. Bunney and Fawcett investigated three patients who committed suicide.[3] High urinary 17-hydroxycorticosteroid levels were found just prior to the self-destructive behavior. Rubin investigated two rapidly cycling manic depressive patients in the same fashion. During the course of hospitalization the mean urinary 17-hydroxycorticosteroid excretions became lower as time lapsed.[27] In one patient the mean 17-hydroxycorticosteroid excretions were not significantly different between the phases of the cycle; in the other patient there was a significantly lowered excretion of urinary 17-hydroxycorticosteroids during the second manic phase. Plasma 17-hydroxycorticosteroids for both patients were high during the depressive phases, but this was not reflected in increases in urinary steroid excretion. Coppen reports examining eight manic patients before treatment and finding an average concentration of plasma 11-hydroxycorticosteroids that was entirely within normal range.[10] No change occurred with clinical recovery. Platman and Fieve studied newly admitted patients and found increased levels in plasma cortisol in both newly admitted manic and depressive patients.[25] The levels fell on recovery. There were diurnal patterns that were altered in the manic phase but these also returned to normal on recovery. The manic patients who were treated with lithium carbonate were also studied, and lithium carbonate seemed to raise the plasma cortisol levels.

Butler and Blesser studied three patients who were diagnosed as having severe depressive illness.[6] Before pretreatment studies all medication was stopped for two or more days. Each patient was treated with electroconvulsive therapy and antidepressant drugs. In all three patients the pretreatment studies revealed elevated plasma and urinary corticosteroid levels, disturbed diurnal rhythm of plasma cortisol, and adrenocortical resistance to dexamethasone suppression. These pituitary-adrenal abnormalities are similar to those seen in Cushing's syndrome. All abnormal findings disappeared with the successful treatment of the depressions. The authors believe that because of these findings, considerable diagnostic confusion might arise in a patient with depression and suspected Cushing's syndrome.

The references cited in this section constitute only a sample of the voluminous bibliography on steroid metabolism, stress, and depression. In general, some of the reports are in conflict and many are suspect because of methodologic problems such as concomitant drug intake and length of time in hospital prior to testing. Some of the findings may simply be responses to stress. The field remains of interest, however. Positive findings may be considered as leads to etiology or perhaps only as manifestations of the illness.

SLEEP STUDIES IN MANIC DEPRESSIVE DISEASE

Sleep patterns in manic depressive patients are frequently rather typical. Patients classically complain of disturbed sleep when depressed. More specifically they say they have no difficulty getting to sleep but wake up in the early part of the morning and cannot get back to sleep. This pattern is referred to as terminal insomnia. There have been only a few systematic studies of sleep in depressive patients. These may or may not be relevant to manic depressive disease, since the clinical criteria for the studies did not demand that the depressed subjects have had a mania as part of their clinical picture.

Hawkins and Mendels studied 21 depressed patients and 15 controls by monitoring their sleep in the laboratory.[19] These investigators found that patients with depression took longer to get to sleep than did controls (increased sleep latency) and also showed more wakefulness. Depressives showed a lower percentage than controls (p < 0.05) of the stage of sleep in which dreaming occurs (stage I REM). Deep sleep (stage IV) was lower in amount in the depressives when compared to the controls (p < 0.01). Stage IV sleep remained low in depressives even after clinical improvement. Further systematic work on sleep in rigorously defined manic depressives might be of value in the study of the cause and pathophysiology of the illness.

ELECTROLYTE STUDIES IN MANIC DEPRESSIVE DISEASE

One set of findings may be of great importance in manic depressive disease. These concern electrolytes. Using isotope dilution techniques, Coppen found an increase in residual sodium of about 50% during the depressive illness, which returned to normal after recovery.[9,10] Residual sodium is not extracellular space sodium but consists mainly of intracellular sodium and exchangeable bone sodium. Of possible significance in the electrolyte studies is the fact that Coppen and co-workers, measuring the distribution of sodium in water by isotope dilution techniques, found that residual sodium showed a 200% increase over normal in manic patients. On recovery, the residual sodium returned to normal, but when some of the manic patients became depressed, they showed a 50% increase in residual sodium. Thus patients who had mania showed an increase in the same direction as those patients who had depression, but the increase was considerably greater. The lithium ion that has been used with success in the treatment of mania causes changes in electrolyte metabolism. Coppen showed that lithium carbonate in doses of 1 Gm. daily produced a decrease in exchangeable sodium by an average of about 620 mEq. He interpreted this decrease as a change in the distribution of sodium since the loss could not be accounted for by increased urinary losses of sodium. According to Coppen, it was probable that the decrease in exchangeable sodium occurred at the expense of residual sodium.

Calcium has been studied by Flach.[13,14] He maintained depressed patients on a constant intake of calcium and phosphorus and studied urinary excretion of calcium prior to and during recovery. Recovered patients showed a decrease in urinary calcium excretion when compared to neurotic patients, who did not show such a change. In further work, Flach used radioisotopes as well as balance studies on depressed patients and found a decrease in bone resorption rate and an increased retention of calcium on recovery.

The findings on electrolytes may turn out to be of great importance, but, as in the other leads that concern etiology, considerably more research is necessary. Apropos of this, the relationship of steroid metabolism to electrolyte changes may be of some importance.

BIOCHEMICAL THEORIES

Recent observations have led to potentially profitable hypotheses regarding the etiology and pathophysiology of affective illness. In the mid-1950's data became available on patients who were treated for hypertension with reserpine. Achor studied 58 patients who were treated with reserpine or *Rauwolfia* for a 6-month period and found that of these, 10 had a significant emotional upset and three had major depressions.[1] He studied a further series of 70; 15 had significant depressive states. All of these occurred within 2 months of the start of the reserpine treatment for hypertension. Muller and co-workers studied 93 patients receiving *Rauwolfia* and reserpine and found that in 2 to 12 months after beginning treatment seven, or 7.5%, had developed significant psychiatric illnesses.[23] Of these seven patients, five needed electroshock therapy for depression; two of the patients had what were considered to be anxiety states. The data suggest that the treatment with reserpine is associated with a significant number of people falling ill with depressive illnesses. Whether the depression produced by reserpine is the same as a depression that is seen in manic depressive disease is, of course, still an open question, but this kind of observation has led to potentially fruitful hypotheses about manic depressive disease.

The finding of reserpine-induced depressions was of importance in stimulating the formulation of two theories concerning the production of affective disorder. One of these is the "catecholamine hypothesis" of depression and the other involves the indoleamines. Thorough reviews of these hypotheses as well as other aspects of the biochemistry of affective states have been written by Coppen and also by Schildkraut and Kety.[10,29] Schematically the various degradation pathways involved in these theories are as follows:

Tyrosine → 3, 4-Dihydroxyphenylalanine →
Dopamine → Norepinephrine → Normetanephine ⟶ Vanillylmandelic
                      ↘   ↗ acid

                3, 4-Dihydroxymandelic
                      acid

Tryptophan → 5-Hydroxytryptophan →
5-Hydroxytryptamine → 5-Hydroxyindoleacetic acid
   (serotonin)

Typtophan → Tryptamine → Indol-3-acetic acid

Reserpine appears to interfere with the intraneuronal binding of the catecholamines and serotonin. Because of this interference in the binding, the catecholamines and serotonin freely circulate and may be inactivated by deamination on mitochondrial monoamine oxidase. Thus, by this breakdown, there is a depletion of amine stores in the tissue. Two groups of drugs have had some success in the treatment of depression. The first group is composed of the monoamine oxidase inhibitors (MAOI), and the second of the tricyclic antidepressants. In animals the MAOI's produce excitement and reverse reserpine-induced sedation. This reversal correlates better with brain levels of norepinephrine than with changes in levels of serotonin. A MAOI increases the levels of catecholamines in the brain, presumably by preventing their breakdown due to the enzymatic action of the monoamine oxidase. The tricyclic drugs also prevent reserpine-induced sedation and probably inhibit cellular uptake, and thus inactivation, of norepinephrine.

In the catecholamine hypothesis the biosynthesis of norepinephrine starts with tyrosine, which is, in turn, converted to 3, 4-dihydroxyphenylalanine, then to dopamine, and finally to norepinephrine, which may be broken down via a monoamine oxidase to vanillylmandelic acid or 3, 4-dihydroxymandelic acid. This last, in turn, is converted to vanillylmandelic acid. The hypothesis states that depression is caused by a decrease in brain norepinephrine and that mania may well be caused by an increase of the same substance. Schildkraut and Kety have shown a rise in normetanephrine excretion during the period of clinical improvement in depressed patients with tricyclic antidepressants.[29] Normetanephrine is an intermediate step in the pathway from norepinephrine to vanillylmandelic acid. Most normetanephrine in urine is of peripheral origin, but peripheral changes in catechol metabolism may reflect central nervous system changes. MAOI's have been associated with decreased urinary excretion of vanillylmandelic acid as well as 5-hydroxyindoleacetic acid (the end point of serotonin metabolism) in man. Even though there seems to be a consistent relationship between the influence of effective antidepressant drugs on norepinephrine metabolism, the proof of the theory remains dependent on the finding of naturally occurring changes in the illness and particularly on naturally occurring changes within the brain.

The theory involving indoleamines is related to the biosynthesis of serotonin. Tryptophan is converted to 5-hydroxytryptophan, then to 5-hydroxytryptamine (serotonin), and finally to 5-hydroxyindolacetic acid. MAOI's produce an increase in brain 5-hydroxytryptamine.

There has been little to suggest a relationship between mania and reserpine, though it might be postulated that the brain monoamines could be be increased in mania. Reserpine, however, is known to interfere with the binding of serotonin. Of relevance to both the catecholamine and indoleamine theories is the work of Haškovec and Ryšánek, who gave large doses of reserpine plus imipramine to depressed patients who were resistant to imipramine (a tricyclic antidepressant drug).[18] Improvement occurred in the majority of patients after a short manic phase. Observations were made on urinary excretion of vanillylmandelic acid, the product of norepinephrine, and 5-hydroxyindoleacetic acid, the product of serotonin. There was an increase in the latter but no change in the former. Thus, reserpine seems to have a paradoxical chemical effect when combined with imipramine, and this effect appears to be associated with indoleamine metabolism.

In a group of 13 depressed patients Coppen reports loading patients with large doses of L-tryptophan and measuring urinary excretion of tryptamine and indole-3-acetic acid.[10] During depression there was an abnormally low excretion of tryptamine. After recovery from the depression, tryptamine excretion rose by an average of 70%. No significant changes were found in the excretion rates for indole-3-acetic acid. The findings were interpreted as a demonstration of abnormal tryptophan metabolism in depression, for tryptamine, like serotonin (5-hydroxytryptamine), is a product of tryptophan. However, tryptamine and serotonin are produced in two different metabolic pathways. Coppen also studied urinary excretion of tryptamine in a small group of patients suffering from mania, but there the results were not as clear as they were in depression. About half the patients had normal or raised excretion of tryptamine, and half had decreased rates, very similar to those of depressed patients. In favor of the indoleamine hypothesis is the finding that when tryptophan is added to a MAOI the decrease in depressive symptoms is significantly enhanced when compared to a group of patients who received a MAOI alone.[10]

The studies concerning the catecholamine hypothesis and the theory involving indoleamines are at a very early stage of development, and, consequently, it is not possible to evaluate them definitely at this point. One finding of some importance, however, may be that of Shaw, Camps, and Eccleston, who measured 5-hydroxytryptamine in the hind brains obtained from depressed, probably depressed, and other individuals who had died by suicide.[30] These were compared with control individuals. The latter had died by other means. The levels of 5-hydroxytryptamine were significantly lower in the depressed and probably depressed groups than in the control subjects.

In a series of researches Dewhurst concluded that there are two major types of cerebral amines.[2,12] One kind (type A) is excitant in action and fat soluble. These type A amines are indoleamines or phenylethylamines. They produce physiologic and behavioral alerting. The other kind of amine, type C, is water soluble and has a depressant effect. Type C amines are catecholamines. The most potent type A amine is tryptamine; the most potent type C amine is epinephrine, which occurs only in small amounts in the brain. A third kind of amine, type B, has biphasic qualities. Evidence was found which indicated that type A amines act through a specific receptor in the brain; likewise type C amines are mediated by a receptor. The biphasic amines, type B, act on both kinds of receptors. Dewhurst found that the alerting effect of the catecholamines was due to their influence on peripheral rather than central receptors.

Type A amines in man produce mood elevation. Further, a specific antagonist to type A receptors, methysergide, showed benefit in manic patients. Two trials of methysergide in manic patients and controls have been positive. Thirteen out of 15 manics responded in 24 hours. Thus, the first clinical trial, using a rationale derived from the Dewhurst theory, has been favorable.

Dewhurst has criticized both the catecholamine hypothesis and the indoleamine theory. He studied eight carcinoid patients who secreted a large amount of 5-hydroxytryptophan, which reached the brain. It was decarboxylated in the brain to 5-hydroxytryptamine. Six of these patients had no psychiatric illness and two had psychiatric illnesses that could adequately be accounted for without recourse to 5-hydroxytryptamine. As regards MAOI's, Dewhurst measured the main substrates that occur in the brain—normetanephrine, metanephrine, 5-hydroxytryptamine, and tryptamine. Tryptamine is a product of tryptophan by a different pathway from the one that produces serotonin. Tryptamine was increased fourfold by the enzyme inhibitors. The other three substrates also increased, but significantly less so. Thus, the metabolic products of the catecholamines and serotonin were affected least in comparison with tryptamine.

CONTRIBUTION OF CLINICAL FINDINGS TO THE BIOLOGIC APPROACH

Biologic approaches to the problems in etiology of affective disorders have produced a number of imaginative theories and findings. At this point, it seems possible that one or the other or even an amalgamation of the theories may be pursued with potential profit. However, even the most carefully designed chemical study may founder on the shoals of imprecise diagnosis. It is necessary to work with as homogeneous a clinical group as is possible to find. For this reason, the following statement is offered concerning a number of logical clinical entities that should be investigated. All these groups may be considered under the major rubric *affective disorders:*

To study the *reactive depression,* the investigator would be well advised to find a model containing both depressive symptoms and a clear association with psychologic factors that might precipitate the depression. A model for this would be the grief reaction.[7] In the grief reaction, persons who are bereaved after the death of a family member or a close friend develop some of the symptoms that are seen in depression. The clinical course of bereavement is very clear and the symptoms dissipate themselves within the course of 6 to 10 weeks.

A second group that might be profitable to study would be one composed of those patients who suffer from *secondary affective disorders.* In this case, depressive symptomotology occurs in the context of a long-standing psychiatric illness such as anxiety neurosis, obsessive compulsive neurosis, hysteria, or alcoholism. The symptoms are often those seen in primary affective disorder.[32]

A third logical and homogeneous group would be one composed of patients with *manic depressive disease.* In order to fulfill the requirements for this, the subject should have had a history of a mania in the past, even though at the time that he is investigated he may be suffering from a depressive illness.

A fourth group would be that of *depressive disease* (unipolar psychosis), in which case the individual should have had one or more depressions but no evidence of any mania. It would be well that, if he had a family history of affective disorder, no mania should have been seen in the family.

To study *mania,* one may consider at least two groups. The first of these is composed of patients who are suffering from manias with or without a previous history of a depression. The second type of reasonable mania is the patient who has manic symptoms with general paresis.

Finally, if the investigator has an unlimited clinical supply of patients, he might be wise to take manics and depressives with specific kinds of family histories. An example of this would be a manic patient who has a family history of alcoholism but nothing else in his family. Another example might be a patient with a depression but no history of mania who has a parent who has exhibited both manias and depressions. The more refined one attempts to be in obtaining groups that are homogeneous both for family members and for their own clinical pictures, the more difficult it is to find a sizable group to study. As a consequence, it seems that the four types of depression described above and the two types of mania might be a logical point of departure.

It is only with relative diagnostic precision that one can hope to obtain viable results. Of course, it is quite conceivable that the pathophysiology of all depressions regardless of their genetic etiology is the same. But it is also just as reasonable to assume that the pathophysiology of different kinds of depressions would be different. Further studies involving biologic factors must seriously take into account the problem of homogeneity of groups.

REFERENCES

1. Achor, R., Hanson, N., and Gifford, R. W., Jr.: Hypertension treatment with rauwolfia serpentina (whole root) and with reserpine, J.A.M.A. **159**:841, 1955.
2. Amines, alerting and affect, Lancet **1**:1237, 1968.
3. Bunney, W. E., and Fawcett, J. A.: Possibility of a biochemical test for suicide potential: an analysis of endocrine findings prior to three suicides, Arch. Gen. Psychiat. **13**:232, 1965.
4. Bunney, W. E., Hartmann, E. L., and Mason, J. W.: Study of a patient with 48-hour manic depressive cycles: II. Strong positive correlation between endocrine factors and manic depressive patterns, Arch. Gen. Psychiat. **12**:619, 1965.
5. Bunney, W. E., Mason, J. D., Roatch, J. F., and Hamburg, D. A.: A psychoendocrine study of severe psychotic depressive crises, Amer. J. Psychiat. **122**:72, 1965.
6. Butler, P. W. P., and Blesser, G. M.: Pituitary-adrenal function in severe depressive illness, Lancet **1**:1234, 1968.
7. Clayton, P. J., Desmarais, L., and Winokur, G.: A study of normal bereavement, Amer. J. Psychiat. **125**:168, 1968.
8. Cooper, A.: Hypomanic psychosis precipitated by hemodialysis, Compr. Psychiat. **8**:168, 1967.
9. Coppen, A.: Mineral metabolism in affective disorder, Brit. J. Psychiat. **111**:1133, 1965.
10. Coppen, A.: The biochemistry of affective disorders, Brit. J. Psychiat. **113**:1237, 1967.
11. Dalén, P.: Family history, the electroencephalogram, and perinatal factors in manic conditions, Acta Psychiat. Scand. **41**:527, 1965.
12. Dewhurst, W. G.: New theory of cerebral amine function and its clinical application, Nature **218**:1130, 1968.
13. Flach, F.: Calcium metabolism in states of depression, Brit. J. Psychiat. **110**:588, 1964.
14. Flach, F.: Psychopharmacologic and metabolic studies on states of depression. In Lopez Ibor, J. J., editor: Proceedings of the Fourth World Congress of Psychiatry, Amsterdam, 1966, Excerpta Medica Foundation.

15. Fleminger, J. J.: The differential effect of cortisone and of ACTH on mood, J. Ment. Sci. **101**:123, 1955.
16. Gibbons, J. L.: Cortisol secretion rate in depressive illness, Arch. Gen. Psychiat. **10**:572, 1964.
17. Gibbons, J. L.: The secretion rate of corticosterone in depressive illness, J. Psychosom. Res. **10**:263, 1966.
18. Haškovec, L., and Ryšánek, K.: The action of reserpine in imipramine-resistant depressive patients, Psychopharmacologia **11**:18, 1967.
19. Hawkins, D. R., and Mendels, J.: Sleep disturbance in depressive syndromes, Amer. J. Psychiat. **123**:682, 1966.
20. Kurland, H.: Steroid excretion in depressive disorders, Arch. Gen. Psychiat. **10**:554, 1964.
21. Mayer-Gross, W., Slater, E., and Roth, M.: Clinical psychiatry, ed. 2, Baltimore, 1960, The Williams & Wilkins Co.
22. Michael, R., and Gibbons, J.: Interrelationships between the endocrine system and neuropsychiatry, Int. Rev. Neurobiol. **5**:243, 1963.
23. Muller, J., Pryor, W., Gibbons, J., and Orgain, E.: Depression and anxiety occurring during rauwolfia therapy, J.A.M.A. **159**:836, 1955.
24. Oppler, W.: Manic psychosis in a case of parasagittal meningioma, Arch. Gen. Psychiat. **64**:417, 1950.
25. Platman, S. R., and Fieve, R. R.: Lithium carbonate and plasma cortisol response in the affective disorders, Arch. Gen. Psychiat. **18**:591, 1968.
26. Quarton, G., Clark, L., Cobb, S., and Bauer, W.: Mental disturbance associated with ACTH and cortisone: a review of explanatory hypotheses, Medicine **34**:13, 1955.
27. Rubin, R. T.: Adrenal cortical activity changes in manic depressive illness, Arch. Gen. Psychiat. **17**:671, 1967.
28. Sachar, E. J.: Corticosteroids in depressive illness: I. A re-evaluation of control issues and the literature. II. A longitudinal psychoendocrine study, Arch. Gen. Psychiat. **17**:544, 1967.
29. Schildkraut, J., and Kety, S.: Biogenic amines and emotion, Science **156**:21, 1967.
30. Shaw, D. M., Camps, F. E., and Eccleston, E. G.: 5-hydroxytryptamine in the hind-brain of depressive suicides, Brit. J. Psychiat. **113**:1407, 1967.
31. Stern, K., and Dancey, T.: Glioma of the diencephalon in a manic patient, Amer. J. Psychiat. **98**:716, 1942.
32. Woodruff, R., Murphy, G., and Herjanic, M.: The natural history of affective disorders: I. Symptoms of 72 patients at the time of index hospital admission, J. Psychiat. Res. **5**:255, 1967.

Chapter 13

The question of etiology: psychologic and social approaches

PSYCHODYNAMIC INTERPRETATIONS OF DEPRESSION AND MANIA

No book on manic depressive disease would be complete without mention of the psychodynamic and psychologic factors believed to be important in this illness. It is reassuring to note that several authors in recent major works have approached this aspect of depression with open and critical minds.

Abraham, in 1911, was first impressed with the likeness of the manic depressive to the obsessional neurotic, specifically the ambivalence of the patient with an attitude of hate that paralyzed his capacity to love.[1] Later, ambivalence came to occupy an important place in explaining the hate turned inward against oneself which the depressed patient was said to exhibit. Abraham also felt that in depression there was regression of the libido to the oral and anal sadistic levels of psychosexual development.

Freud, in the monograph *Mourning and Melancholia,* originally published in 1917, postulated the dynamics of depression as follows: The melancholic person suffers an object loss. This loss is not displaced onto another object but is incorporated by the ego into itself. The ego then identifies with the lost, now incorporated, object. Identification is a narcissistic mechanism and along with it usually goes ambivalence.[10]

> In this way an object loss was transformed into an ego loss, and the conflict between the ego and the loved person into a cleavage between the critical activity [this later in Freud's thinking becomes the ego ideal and still later the superego] of the ego and the ego as altered by identification.*

Since incorporation is done in accordance with the oral or cannibalistic phase of libidinal development by devouring, the depressive's refusal of nourishment is understandable. Suicide and self-incriminations are understandable. Since the ego can treat itself as the object, it is able to direct against itself the hostilities which relate to an object and which represent the ego's original reaction to the object in the external world. The work involved in such an ego conflict accounts for the sleeplessness of the patient. There were some symptoms that, Freud felt, could not be explained psychologically. For instance, he felt a somatic factor needed to be invoked to explain the symptom of diurnal

---

*From Strachey, J., editor: The standard edition of the complete psychological works of Sigmund Freud, London, 1957, Hogarth Press, Ltd., vol. 14, p. 249.

variation with the amelioration of the condition toward evening. This led him to question whether an impoverishment of ego libido directly by toxins could not also produce certain forms of the disease.

In 1924, Abraham confirmed Freud's analysis of mourning and of depression, reemphasizing certain points from personal experience and experience with patients.[1] An interesting sidelight was Abraham's admission that on first reading Freud's *Mourning and Melancholia* he found it difficult to follow the train of thought. Abraham stated that after the death of his own father his hair had turned gray for a time. His father had developed gray hair during his terminal illness. On reflection, Abraham realized that he had incorporated his dead father. Abraham also wrote that what he felt was inherited and constitutional in the depressed patient was an overaccentuation of oral eroticism with a subsequent fixation of the libido at an oral level. This left the patient vulnerable to injury through infantile narcissism brought about by successive disappointments in love especially since they occurred before the oedipal wishes had been overcome. Finally, in later life, there was a repetition of the primary disappointment.

Melanie Klein theorized a complex series of events occurring during infancy.[15,16] She introduced the concept of the "infantile depressive position", i.e., depressive feelings that the baby experiences during weaning. What the baby mourns is the mother's breast and what it stands for—love, goodness, and security. Later depressions are repetitions of this infantile depressive position.

Mabel Blake Cohen and her associates studied in depth 12 cases of manic depressive psychosis treated from 1 to 5 years with psychoanalytic psychotherapy.[7] There are no diagnostic criteria mentioned, but from the excerpts it seems that the cases were truly manic depressive although one patient is said to have had a schizophrenic mother. The idea is also presented that many manic depressives evolve into chronic schizophrenia chiefly of the paranoid type in the course of time. If this is seriously felt to be the case, one could suppose that in the successful treatment of manic depressive patients schizophrenia is being prevented. There was no mention of how the data were gathered, but formulations about the manic depressive character were made in three areas: (1) the patterns of interactions between the parents and the child and between the family and the community, (2) the ways in which these patterns influenced the character structure of the child and affected his relationships with other people in his subsequent life, and (3) the way in which these patterns were repeated in therapy and could be altered by therapy. It was felt that each family of the 12 manic depressives studied was set apart from the surrounding milieu by some factor which singled that family out as different. These factors differed widely; examples given included being a member of a minority group, economic differences, and alcoholism in the father. In each case, the patient's family felt the social difference keenly and reacted to it with intense concern and with an effort, first, to improve its acceptability in the community and, second, to improve its social prestige by raising the economic level of the family or by winning some position of honor or accomplishment. This duty frequently fell on the patient. A few paragraphs after these statements the authors continue: "In a few cases the family's isolation seemed to stem from the fact that they were 'too good' for the neighboring families due to the fact that they had more money or greater prestige." These statements are somewhat contradictory. The study is a well-written impressionistic work with a good survey of the psychoanalytic literature as an introduction. Caution should be exercised in accepting generalizations about the manic depressive, his family, and his environment on the basis of 12 cases. On the same grounds, it is equally hard to justify a treatment program based on these formulations. In addition, since it is well-known that affective illness and alcoholism are common among families of manic depressives, these facts surely should be included in the considerations if environmental factors are to be studied.

There are many others who have contributed to the development of theories explaining the origins of depressions in manic depressive disease. For a more complex analysis the reader is referred to Mendelson's *Psychoanalytic Concepts of Depression.*[21]

Turning to circular insanity, Freud stated that it would be tempting to regard these cases as nonpsychogenic except for the fact that the psychoanalytic method has succeeded in arriving at a solution and effecting a therapeutic improvement in several cases of this kind.[9] He felt that in both depression and mania the same "complex" was responsible, the difference being that in depression the ego had succumbed to it whereas in mania the ego had either mastered it or pushed it aside. He later states that probably the conflict with the ego in melancholia calls forth an extraordinary high anticathexis, which explains mania. He wrote as if he felt all manias followed a depressive phase.

Abraham, in his 1924 writings, considers that in mania the superego, instead of being excessively critical of the ego as it is in depression, becomes merged with the ego, allowing narcissism to enter upon a positive pleasurable stage.[1]

> Now that his ego is no longer being consumed by the introjected object the individual turns his libido to the outer world with an excess of eagerness. This change of attitude gives rise to many symptoms, all of them based on an increase in the person's oral desires. The patient devours everything that comes his way. We are all familiar with the strength of the erotic cravings of the manic patient. But he shows the same greed in seizing on new impressions from which, in his melancholic state, he had cut himself off. Whereas in his depressive phase he had felt that he was dispossessed and cast out from the world of external objects, in his manic phase he as it were proclaims his power of assimilating all his objects into himself. But it is characteristic that this pleasurable act of taking in new impressions is correlated to an equally pleasurable act of ejecting them almost as soon as they have been received. Anyone who has listened to the associations of a manic patient will recognize that his flight of ideas, expressed in a stream of words, represents a swift and agitated process of receiving and expelling fresh impressions. In melancholia we saw that there was some particular introjected object which was treated as a piece of food that had been incorporated and which was eventually got rid of. In mania, all objects are regarded as material to be passed through the patient's 'psychosexual metabolism' at a rapid rate. And it is not difficult to see from the

associations of the manic patient that he identifies his uttered thoughts with excrement.*

Lewin reviews the psychoanalysis of elation.[18] He points out that it was Helene Deutsch, in 1933, who was impressed by the importance of denial as the basic defense mechanism in mania and hypomania. Others, of course, have carried this even further to state that mania is the denial of depression. Lewin develops his own theory of oral eroticism, namely a triad of oral activity, i.e., a wish to devour, a wish to be devoured, and a wish to go to sleep. Lewin shows how this is applicable to various illnesses, including claustrophobia, other phobias, and mania.

It is difficult to summarize these theories. It must be said that the writings of Freud and Abraham contain colorful clinical descriptions of manic depressive patients as well as admissions of uncertainty about the extent of the constitutional or somatic components of the illness. Later writings dealing with this same subject lack both these distinctions. Suffice to say that how one might subject these theories to the null hypothesis poses an important problem.

The number of patients treated by psychoanalysis is probably small. Only 14 manic depressive patients among 592 (2%) were treated in 10 years at the Berlin Psychoanalytic Clinic, according to Fenichel.[9] Knight later added 360 cases from other institutes, among which 30 (8%) were manic depressive.[17] It is quite possible, since this is the only affective disorder listed as a psychosis, that, rather than being only *manic* depressives, the group includes psychotic depressives without mania. In his composite results of treatment, 37 of the 44 (84%) stayed in treatment more than 6 months— a very high figure compared to other diagnoses reported. Of the 37, 11 (30%) were apparently cured or much improved, 14 were improved, and 12 (32%) showed no change or were worse. With the advent of drugs and electroshock therapy, 32% showing "no change or worse" seems like an unnecessarily high figure. The capricious, episodic nature of the illness would leave the claim of 14% (6/44) "apparently cured" open to some doubt. However, the use of the word "apparently" denotes a cautious attitude in the author.

CHILDHOOD BEREAVEMENT AND ADULT DEPRESSION

The loss of a parent during childhood has frequently been linked to adult psychiatric depression. It has also been associated with various other psychiatric illnesses, including schizophrenia, sociopathy, alcoholism, and drug addiction.

The literature on the subject is voluminous. Gregory, in 1958, critically reviewed the data published up to that time and demonstrated that most of the studies suffered from one or more of the following[13]:

(1) Comparisons between unlike samples
(2) Samples not representative due to selection (not systematically obtained)
(3) Chance errors in sampling

---

*From Abraham, K.: Selected papers on psychoanalysis, London, 1950, Hogarth Press, Ltd.

(4) Fallacies in deduction (analysis)
  (a) Unjustified generalizations
  (b) Unjustified specificity
  (c) Association does not imply causation
  (d) Absence of association does not imply alternative causation

Since that time, other studies have been published. In 1965, Pitts and co-workers reported no significant differences in parental deprivation (not restricted to bereavement) between various psychiatric diagnoses and a medically ill control group matched for age, sex, and socioeconomic status.[25] Beck found that there was a significantly greater incidence of loss of a parent in childhood in highly depressed patients (determined by a depressive inventory score and by clinical judgment of the depth of the depression) compared to nondepressed patients.[2] However, when these same patients were grouped according to psychiatric diagnoses no significant differences were noted; i.e., highly depressed schizophrenics and psychotic depressives had a similar incidence of childhood bereavement. In 1966, Dennehy reviewed factors affecting the incidence of orphanhood in order to point out the difficulties in choosing an adequate control group for a study of childhood bereavement.[8] She attempted to select a random population of psychiatric normals for an estimate of the incidence of orphanhood. However, her three control-group samples gave estimates of orphanhood that varied widely, and all showed figures of orphanhood considerably higher than the 1921 census, a fact that was difficult to explain. From life tables, the expected incidence of loss of parents was calculated, and this corresponded closely with the observed values in the 1921 census and the 1959 claims for widows' pensions. Consequently, these last two were used as controls. Comparing, then, 1020 psychiatric patients to these controls she found an excess of male depressives who had lost their mothers and of female depressives who had lost their fathers. For both sexes, depressives suffered loss of either parent to excess between the ages of 10 years and before reaching their fifteenth birthdays. There was an excess of both male and female schizophrenics who had lost their mother before age 5 years, and the male schizophrenics demonstrated an excess of father loss between the age of 5 years and before reaching their tenth birthday. Male alcoholics showed a significant increase of loss of both parents, whereas female alcoholics showed an excess of those who lost mother only. Male drug addicts showed an excess of father loss, and female drug addicts an excess of mother loss. All groups except drug addicts showed a proportion who were born to slightly older mothers and fathers, the mean age of both mother and father being higher than the general population figure. The mean age of both parents of drug addicts was lower than the general population figure. However, the increase in the bereavement rate of psychiatric patients did not refer only to patients born of older parents; thus, bereavement was not considered to be solely the result of the increased average age of parents of psychiatric patients. Brown and Epps, using the 1921 census data as controls, found both male and female prisoners had a significant increase in paternal and maternal deaths before the age of 15 years.[5] A study by Granville-Grossman, using non-ill sibs as controls, showed that the ages of schizophrenics did not differ significantly from their non-ill sibs at the time of the death of a parent.[12] Hill and Price, using nondepressed psychiatric patients as controls (a large number of organic and epileptics and no schizophrenics), found that depressed patients had lost more fathers by death before their fifteenth birthday.[14] This difference was most marked in women and for bereavement at the ages between 10 and 14 years. This last finding had been noted earlier by Brown[3,4] and is in agreement with the Dennehy findings of depression.

It seems obvious that the data in the field are conflicting. Bereavement is a universal phenomenon at any age, and why some are affected and others are not needs explanation. Conversely, although the rate at which it occurs may be higher in depressed patients than in controls according to some studies (but not all studies), it still occurs in a relatively small number (usually less than 15%) of patients. Also, its nonspecificity in producing psychiatric illness reduces its importance as an etiologic factor. Brown has pointed out (as did Michael Rutter in his recent book[27]) that it may not be bereavement at all which affects some psychiatric patients but rather the disruption of the home, financial problems, etc., which follow the bereavement. Finally, there are no studies that deal specifically with rigorously defined manic depressive patients; thus, its effect on this illness is totally unknown.

ADULT BEREAVEMENT AND ADULT DEPRESSION

Object loss (real or fantasied, conscious or unconscious) is an important concept in the psychodynamics of depression. Because of object loss, Abraham and Freud drew analogies between mourning and melancholia. The reaction to death, a noncontroversial object loss, should provide a good model for studying a reactive depression.

Lindemann first wrote on normal grief from observations on 101 subjects.[19] Unfortunately a large but unknown number of his subjects were psychotherapy patients in treatment. Another part of his group, the most carefully observed, were hospitalized victims of an acute disaster—the Coconut Grove fire in Boston. The use of these two groups casts some doubt on the nornormality of the reaction he describes.

Marris interviewed 72 young London widows an average of 2 years (range 10 to 46 months) after the deaths of their husbands.[20] Although the interviews were not systematic, he recorded five reactions frequently mentioned by the widows: lasting deterioration in health (31), difficulty in sleeping (57), loss of contact with reality (47), withdrawal (54), and hostility (25). Nine widows mentioned reactions from all five groups, and the majority, reactions from at least three groups. No inquiry into how long these reactions persisted was made, although only 14 considered themselves recovered at interview. Perhaps it is because these were young widows or perhaps it is because after 2 years of widowhood there is some distortion in remembering symptoms that these reactions seem unusually severe. The book in which these data are published is a thoughtful and pertinent account of the problems of widowhood in Great Britain.

Recently Clayton, Desmarais, and Winokur interviewed 40 relatives of patients who died at a large general hospital.[6] These people were seen between 2 and 26 days after the deaths and were interviewed using a systematic symptom inventory, dealing mostly with depressive symptoms. Only three symp-toms—depressed mood, sleep disturbance, and crying—occurred in more than half the subjects. Three other symptoms—difficulty concentrating, loss of interest in TV and news, and anorexia and/or weight loss—occurred fre-quently but still in less than half the subjects. Symptoms such as ideas of self-condemnation, guilt, and suicidal thoughts were infrequent; and although not systematically inquired about, symptoms of hostility were also unusual. These symptoms began either during the terminal illness or after the death. Symptoms such as taking medicines or increasing the alcoholic intake oc-curred almost exclusively in those who had used drugs or drunk heavily before. When bereavement symptoms were analyzed in relation to sex, age, length of the deceased's illness, and relation to the deceased, no striking differences were noted. Twenty-seven of the 40 patients were followed up 1 to 4 months later. At follow-up, 81% of the patients were improved and only 4% were worse. The others, although subjectively they felt improved, were not im-proved objectively, by symptom inventory. Those who were improved dated their improvement to 6 to 10 weeks after the death. Subjects did not develop numerous somatic symptoms at follow-up. Twenty-five percent of the subjects had serious medical illnesses. Forty-four percent of the subjects had consulted a physician, but only half (22%) felt their symptoms to be related to grief. Ninety-eight percent of the subjects did not seek psychiatric assistance during the bereavement period, and the conclusion was drawn that this was a psy-chologic reaction rarely handled by the psychiatrist.

A few other interesting points from this study should be mentioned. First, a girl described a symptom similar to one experienced by her father at his death on the first interview, but on the follow-up interview several months later she had forgotten this symptom and remembered only that she had been "hysterical" at the time. At times of intense emotion, individual symp-toms are probably not well remembered. Second, hostility was an uncommon symptom, and when it occurred, it seemed to be a pattern of reacting for the person involved. This is similar to the finding of Friedman and co-workers, who reported on behavioral observations of parents anticipating the death of a child.[11] These authors had three fathers who were openly hostile on learning the diagnoses of their children. All three of these fathers had a his-tory of significant psychiatric problems, two in the form of overt paranoid behavior. Last, from this study and one currently underway, we have had the opportunity to interview within days after the loss of a spouse two well, relatively young women with previous histories of clear-cut affective disorder. Both these women felt there was no comparison between normal bereavement and primary depression. They said the suffering and mental anguish expe-rienced during an affective episode were beyond description and not com-parable to any other emotion experienced during a well period, including during bereavement.

Another way of approaching this subject is to start with hospitalized psychiatric patients. Parkes has written extensively on bereavement with emphasis on this latter approach.[22] He reviewed case histories of 3245 patients admitted to Bethlehem Royal Hospital and Maudsley Hospital during the years 1949 to 1951. Of these, 94 had presenting illnesses that had come on either during the last illness or within 6 months following the death of a parent, spouse, sibling, or child (presumably this does not mean that they were necessarily admitted to the hospital within 6 months but dated the onset of their symptoms to within 6 months of the death). Thus only 2.9% of the hospital admissions dated the onset of their illness to a bereavement. Assuming that the bereavement rate of the population from which the hospital admissions were drawn was the same as that of the general population, he calculated the expected bereavement rates and found that the bereavement rates following the death of a spouse (31 in number) were six times greater than expected whereas the number admitted after the death of a parent (47) did not differ greatly from expectation. There were more women than men in these 94, and this could not be explained by the population at risk nor the population of patients admitted to the hospital. The diagnoses of the patients were 28% reactive depression, 20% manic depressive disease, and the remaining 52% divided between organic disease, schizophrenia, anxiety reaction, and other diagnoses. There is some suggestion in the work that the amount of social interaction between individuals is an important factor in determining how one will react to the death of the other. As a conclusion he states that bereavement can cause a variety of clinical conditions and that the traditional modes of psychiatric diagnosis are not adequate to characterize appropriately the loss reaction. It seems more reasonable to say, in view of the variety of diagnoses, that bereavement may be a precipitating event in a small number of people requiring mental hospitalization. In a record study like this without accurate history of preexisting illness and the onset of symptoms, caution should be employed before bereavement is labeled as a cause of mental illness. It would also be misleading to characterize a schizophrenic or a manic depressive as a loss reaction in hospital records rather than give him an ordinary primary diagnosis. In two later papers Parkes gave a good critical review of the published literature on reactions to bereavement, including normal bereavement, pathologic bereavement, and psychosomatic and psychoneurotic reactions to loss.[23,24] He then compared a sample of 21 personally interviewed patients (3 outpatients and 18 inpatients) with widows described by Marris. Actually, since all his patients were not widows, he used a subsample of 14 patients from the interview study to match with widows studied by Marris. His patients were those brought to his notice by the staff during the years 1958 to 1960. Six other patients were not included because they refused to be interviewed or were too ill to give a detailed account of their reaction. Parkes points out that all but one of his 21 patients had a reaction that was in some way distorted or exaggerated and it was this distortion or exaggeration which caused the patient to be regarded as mentally ill. The ways in which his patients differed significantly from Marris' subjects were in "difficulty in accepting the fact that the lost person was dead" and in "expressing ideas of guilt or self-blame." Parkes' patients were not selected because of recent bereavement but by the fact that the presenting illness had begun within 6 months of a bereavement. He found, then, that at least 15 of the 21 had reaction which had lasted longer than 6 months after the death, the longest being 6 years. In the second part of this paper he gives a classification of bereavement reactions: (1) the stress-specific grief response and its variants, i.e., (a) typical grief, (b) chronic grief, (c) inhibited grief, (d) delayed grief; and (2) nonspecific responses. He mentions that in his series of 21 personally interviewed patients he found no case of retarded or psychotic depression but did find three cases in his earlier record study. It is conceivable that at least one of the six patients who were not interviewed could have been a retarded or psychotic depression. Freud and Abraham had never seen a case of mania following bereavement. Parkes from the literature found 13 cases of mania following closely the death of a loved one and added one case of his own. In our present series, out of 100 episodes of mania, four had illnesses coming on immediately following a bereavement, although they all had had previous or subsequent attacks or both without such a precipitant.

In the study of psychiatric patients, it seems essential to include in the considerations the patient's prior psychiatric history, preexisting illness, and family history of psychiatric disorders. Since the patients whom Parkes personally interviewed and carefully described resembled primary depressions in many respects, it would be imperative to show that they had a different family history and long-term course from those of primary depressives or manic depressives before they could be accepted as "grief reactions." It would also be important to show that the clinical picture differed significantly from that of primary depressives or manic depressives. Parkes himself points out, in discussing nonspecific responses to bereavement, that this is a reaction which probably can be precipitated by a number of stresses and situations of which bereavement is but one. The same could be said for those he classifies as stress-specific grief responses.

In the consideration of object loss and life stress, a recent study by Hudgens and associates should be mentioned.[26] They studied a group of 40 affective disorder patients and a group of 40 matched nonpsychiatric medical controls for life stress preceding hospitalization. They found that in 10 affective disorder patients the current episode followed within 6 months an objective stress; yet in the same patients a similar temporal association between stress and previous episodes of psychiatric illness was rare. They calculated the expected rate by chance of a coincidental occurrence of a life stress and an episode of affective disorder and found that it did not differ from the observed rate. Furthermore, in comparing the affective disorder patients with the controls in regard to a large number of recent and remote stressful events, they noted significant differences only in a higher incidence of interpersonal discord during the present illness of the affective disorder patients as compared to the nonpsychiatric patients. This difference is understandable and not surprising when one considers that being depressed or manic usually results in interpersonal difficulties. The psychiatric patients also had a higher incidence of psychiatric disorder among their relatives and a lower incidence of nonpsychiatric hospitalization in the year prior to admission.

In conclusion, psychologic and social approaches have seemed plausible because of the fact that people respond to life situations with happiness and unhappiness. Whether these effects bear any relation to clinically observed manias and depressions remains highly questionable. Certainly, at the present time, it is not possible to cite hard evidence in favor of the psychologic and social approaches having contributed important insights into the etiology of manic depressive disease.

REFERENCES

1. Abraham, K.: Selected papers on psychoanalysis, London, 1950, Hogarth Press, Ltd.
2. Beck, T.: Depression, New York, 1967, Harper & Row, Publishers (Hoeber Medical Division).
3. Brown, F.: Depression and childhood bereavement, J. Ment. Sci. **107:**754, 1961.
4. Brown, F.: Childhood bereavement and subsequent psychiatric disorder, Brit. J. Psychiat. **113:**1035, 1967.
5. Brown, F., and Epps, P.: Childhood bereavement and subsequent crime, Brit. J. Psychiat. **112:**1043, 1966.
6. Clayton, P., Desmarais, L., and Winokur, G.: A study of normal bereavement, Amer. J. Psychiat. **125:**170, 1968.
7. Cohen, M. B., Baker, G., Cohen, R. A., Fromm-Reichmann, F., and Weigert, E. V.: An intensive study of twelve cases of manic depressive psychosis, Psychiatry **17:**103, 1954.
8. Dennehy, E.: Childhood bereavement and psychiatric illness, Brit. J. Psychiat. **112:**1049, 1966.
9. Fenichel, O.: Die therapeutischen Resultate in 10 Jahre, Berliner Psychoanalytisches Institut, Int. Z. Psychoanal., 1930.
10. Strachey, J., editor: The standard edition of the complete psychological works of Sigmund Freud, London, 1957, Hogarth Press, Ltd., vol. 14.
11. Friedman, S., Chodoff, P., Mason, J., and Hamburg, D.: Behavioral observations on parents anticipating the death of a child, Pediatrics **32:**610, 1963.
12. Granville-Grossman, K. L.: Early bereavement and schizophrenia, Brit. J. Psychiat. **112:**1027, 1966.
13. Gregory, I.: Studies of parental deprivation in psychiatric patients, Amer. J. Psychiat. **115:**432, 1958.
14. Hill, O. W., and Price, J. S.: Childhood bereavement and adult depression, Brit. J. Psychiat. **113:**743, 1967.
15. Klein, M.: Mourning and its relationship to manic depressive states, Int. J. Psychoanal. **21:**125, 1940.
16. Klein, M.: Contributions to psychoanalysis 1921-1945, London, 1950, Hogarth Press, Ltd.
17. Knight, R. P.: Evaluation of the results of psychoanalytic therapy, Amer. J. Psychiat. **98:**434, 1941.
18. Lewin, B.: The psychoanalysis of elation, New York, 1950, W. W. Norton & Co., Inc.
19. Lindemann, E.: Symptomatology and management of acute grief, Amer. J. Psychiat. **101:**141, 1944.
20. Marris, P.: Widows and their families, London, 1958, Routledge & Kegan Paul, Ltd.
21. Mendelson, M.: Psychoanalytic concepts of depression, Springfield, Ill., 1960, Charles C Thomas, Publisher.
22. Parkes, C. M.: Recent bereavement as a cause of mental illness, Brit. J. Psychiat. **110:**198, 1964.
23. Parkes, C. M.: Bereavement and mental illness: I. A clinical study of the grief of bereaved psychiatric patients, Brit. J. Med. Psychol. **38:**1, 1965.
24. Parkes, C. M.: Bereavement and mental illness: II. A classification of bereavement reactions, Brit. J. Med. Psychol. **38:**13, 1965.
25. Pitts, F. N., Jr., Meyer, J., Brooks, M., and Winokur, G.: Adult psychiatric

illness assessed for childhood parental loss and psychiatric illness in family members—a study of 748 patients and 250 controls, Amer. J. Psychiat. **121**:1, 1965.

26. Morrison, J., Hudgens, R. W., and Barchha, R.: Life events and psychiatric illness, Brit. J. Psychiat. **114**:423, 1968.
27. Rutter, M.: Children of sick parents: an environmental and psychiatric study, London, 1966, Oxford University Press.

Chapter 14

Therapy in manic depressive disease

Manic depressive disease is an episodic illness with spontaneous remissions that is characterized by mood swings and capacity for complete recovery from an attack. The discussion of its treatment will deal separately with the treatment of depression and of mania and finally with current suggestions for prophylactic therapy.

TREATMENT OF DEPRESSION

The treatment of depression can be considered under four headings—general aspects of treatment, antidepressant drug therapy, electroshock therapy, and treatment of the prolonged unremitting depression.

General aspects of treatment in depression

As Mayer-Gross points out, the first duties of a physician are to guard his patients against the dangers of the illness and to provide them with relief from the worst symptoms.[45] The purposes of these aspects of management then are (1) to prevent serious social and medical consequences of the depression, (2) to temper depressive affect and to alleviate unnecessary guilt feelings, and (3) to help the family understand the patient and his illness.

The most serious consequence of depression is suicide. In several follow-up studies the findings have indicated that about 15% of patients with manic depressive disease who have died have committed suicide.[60] The specific risk for suicide for each episode of depression is not known. On some occasions depressed patients commit murder. This is seen in murder-suicide cases such as depressed mothers who may kill their children and themselves or despondent middle-aged men who murder their families and themselves, both types believing there is no hope and that their families cannot survive without them. If the problem of suicide arises, the patient should be immediately hospitalized in a closed ward of a psychiatric hospital if this is at all possible. The simplest method of finding out whether suicide is a problem is by asking the patient. If the answer to this question is positive, the safest way to deal with the problem is by immediate hospitalization. On some occasions, because of varying factors, it is impossible to get the patient into a hospital. Sometimes under these circumstances the patient who has a good relationship with his physician will agree to keep him informed about any serious changes in his thinking. This is second best to hospitalization but at least is another way of handling the concern over suicide.

If the patient is socially incapacitated and creating difficulties within the

148

family environment, it is of value to consider hospitalization, even if he is not suicidal. This would break up serious and ongoing deterioration in family relationships.

It is necessary to emphasize to the depressed patient that he should not embark on any great psychologic or social changes in his life during the depression. Thus, he should be encouraged to retain his job. If he is in school and cannot keep up because of his symptoms, he should be encouraged to take a medical leave of absence rather than quit entirely. He should not consider such major changes as divorce during the period of time that he is suffering from the illness. He should be cautioned that an increase in his drinking could make symptoms worse rather than improve them. After he is well, the patient is, of course, once more on his own and may make decisions about major changes.

Depressed patients present themselves with a mood change and a set of physical and psychologic symptoms. Simple reassurance from the doctor that he is familiar with this type of illness, that it is usually limited in terms of duration, and that after recovery no particular mental defect will remain is often quite comforting to the patient. This reiteration is of value in the immediate care but does not have any effect on the natural course of the illness. Because the depressed patient is frequently beset with doubts about himself and feelings of guilt, it should be pointed out that these are nothing more or less than the symptoms of the illness and have no basis in reality. These kinds of reassurance often make the patient feel better for short periods of time, but it is necessary to repeat them at frequent intervals.

In the midst of a depression, no depth therapy ought to be attempted. The patient often already feels very guilty, and examination of his motivation only increases this kind of feeling. Exploration into his motivation and the way he deals with important people may only increase his feelings of self-derogation and possibly make him suicidal. Besides, depressed patients often describe relationships incorrectly when depressed and view them in a different light when well. Falsification, in keeping with their self-depreciated image, occurs during the depression and causes relationships to be seen in a less favorable fashion. After the depression has remitted, some physicians advocate intensive psychotherapy to determine the cause of the depression. There is no evidence that this intensive therapy prevents subsequent depressions; consequently, it seems of questionable value. Further, there is no reason to believe that the cause of primary affective illness is psychologic. Most patients after recovering from a depression have little interest in pursuing an exploration of their psychologic problems.

If the patient in the midst of a depression develops marked dependency on the physician, it is wise to meet his demands for the duration of the illness. Ordinarily this dependency is a symptom of the illness and will dissipate itself when the patient has improved. One way in which a physician might do this is to see the patient for relatively short periods of time on a more frequent basis than is ordinarily done. Thus, rather than see the patient for an hour once a week the physician might find it valuable to see him for two half-hour periods in the course of the week.

Frequently a problem arises about how much activity should be recommended to and for the depressed patient. If the patient is experiencing marked difficulties in concentration, it is unwise to force him into a situation in which there will be many intellectual demands. This kind of situation would tend only to make him feel more incapacitated and worthless. On the other hand, it is often of value to attempt to get the patient to participate in other activities, both social and physical. Overcoming the anergia that is seen in a depressed patient sometimes improves his mood and alleviates depressive affect for short periods of time.

Sometimes, the physician recommends a vacation for the "tired overworked" businessman or housewife who may be suffering from a depression. Although a vacation may rest a mild depression, the joyless depressed patient gets little out of the holiday and returns feeling no better and perhaps worse.

Because sleep difficulties are frequently seen in depression, nightly sedation is recommended. One gram of chloral hydrate is frequently of value. Usually the sleep difficulty is of such a nature that the person has no trouble falling asleep but awakens in the early part of the morning. Therefore, a combination of a fast-acting barbiturate with a slow-acting barbiturate might be of some value to keep the patient asleep for the entire night. Such a combination might be 90 mg. of secobarbital sodium and 150 to 300 mg. of barbital. A disadvantage of this combination is that the patient may feel somewhat groggy in the morning. Another way of dealing with nighttime sedation is by the use of the antidepressant drugs in large doses at bedtime.

Some depressed patients benefit from the administration of amobarbital in doses of 60 mg. three times a day. This relieves some of the feelings of anxiety or agitation, enabling the patient to get through the day in an acceptable fashion. Amytal may be used in the same dosage together with the specific antidepressant medication.

In a few patients the use of methamphetamine hydrochloride, 5 to 10 mg., or methylphenidate hydrochloride, 10 to 20 mg. in the morning, is of value. This usually helps the patient who feels rather depressed in the early morning and improves as the day continues (diurnal variation). In a patient who is reliable as far as taking medication is concerned, the use of either of these drugs might make some difference in his ability to function with the symptoms. In addition, either drug can be used in the same dosage together with specific antidepressant medication.

Some females report an increase in their depressive symptoms premenstrually. In these cases, salt restriction and/or a diuretic may help alleviate the symptoms. Dalton recommends daily *intramuscular* progesterone (approximately 25 mg.) from the fourteenth to the twenty-eighth day of the cycle in those women with severe premenstrual tension.[15] The dosage can be increased or decreased if necessary and later, after improvement, can be changed to oral progesterone.

Dealing with the family is necessary for the sake of the patient. Families often find depressed patients different and difficult to understand. A family will ascribe this change to something in the environment and, because of this, will urge the patient to make changes in the environment. If the family can be helped to understand that the patient is suffering from an illness whose cause is unknown, but whose course is known, the family will find relief also.

Families should understand that many of the things they see in the patients are simply symptoms of this illness. The family tends to exert pressure on the patient ("go to church, get out more, friends are coming in, read more," etc.) in obvious and subtle ways. If, however, this pressure increases the patient's guilt or feeling of inadequacy, an effort should be made to relieve the patient of this pressure, by talking to the family if necessary. The family should also understand the risk of suicide in the depressed patient (especially middle-aged men). Often the patient communicates suicidal thoughts to the family openly or through preoccupation with death—wills, funeral arrangements, and cemetery plots. The family should feel free to call the physician should it feel the patient is suicidal or in any way worse.

Specific antidepressant drug therapy

The two large categories of antidepressant drugs used are the tricyclic iminodibenzine derivatives and the monoamine oxidase inhibitors (MAOI).

In 1965, Davis published a comprehensive review of the efficacy of tranquilizing and antidepressant drugs and electroshock therapy (410 references).[16] After examining the data he felt there was relatively consistent evidence for the effectiveness of three antidepressants—imipramine, amitriptyline, and phenelzine. He found that the rare studies with inconsistent results were generally done either with insufficient dosage or with a very small and/or chronic sample of patients. He pointed out that discrepancies in results may also reflect differences in patient populations or inadequate length of treatment. With this in mind, he concludes that dosage may be particularly important and definitive dose-response studies have not been done. Best results seem to be obtained with doses of imipramine or amitriptyline of 150 to 250 mg. per day for at least 3 weeks. Giving up to 100 mg. of the antidepressant at night helps induce sleep and is preferable to large daytime doses. It has been observed that, if a patient does not manifest improvement by the third or fourth week of medication, the chances are poor that he will respond. This suggests, then, a reasonable time period for a trial of chemotherapy. Many physicians continue patients who show improvement on chemotherapy up to 1 year.

In a recent book, Beck also reviews the many conflicting studies on antidepressants through 1965 and summarizes the various methodologic problems involved in studies of the pharmacotherapy of depression.[4] Overall and associates also discuss methodology in psychiatric drug research, as do Sargant and many other thoughtful researchers confronted with evaluating the incongruity in results.[50,61]

Lehmann discusses various treatment modalities of importance to the physician dealing with the depressed patient.[40] He reiterates the findings of Hollister and Overall that different drugs are therapeutic in different kinds of depression and that the anxious depression responds more favorably to thioridazine than to imipramine.[29] He also feels that the antidepressant effect of the newer demethylated imipramine-like drugs—desipramine, nortriptyline, protriptyline—is somewhat lower than that of the parent substance.

More recent studies tend to compare one iminodibenzine derivative with another without the use of a control group given placebo. In one such study,

McConaghy and co-workers found in treating 100 outpatients suffering from depressive states that 55% of those receiving amitriptyline responded well compared to 33% receiving protriptyline.[47] This last figure is close to the percent of patients in other studies who responded to placebo. The percent of patients responding to placebo (approximately 23%) should be kept in mind when one evaluates all drug studies.[66]

There are very few recent studies concerned with the efficacy of MAOI in treating depression. Bucci reviewed the studies dealing with tranylcypromine and found the results so varying that he felt its usefulness and limitations still remained to be clarified.[9] A good review of MAOI is contained in the Davis paper. Davis found 11 studies of various MAOI's where the drug was more effective than placebo and six studies where the placebo was equally effective.[16] He reported on no study where MAOI's were superior to imipramine in the treatment of depression, although there were studies where the reverse was true. In the United States the most commonly used MAOI's are probably phenelzine and tranylcypromine. The starting dose of phenelzine is 15 mg. three times a day, and of tranylcypromine 10 mg. two times a day. Dietary restrictions are necessary with all MAOI's. A time period of 2 weeks, if possible, should elapse between changing from a tricyclic amine to a MAOI or vice versa. In a short lead article on treatment of depression, it is inferred that MAOI's are particularly useful in treating depressions with anxiety and tension symptoms.[8]

In treating ill members of the same family, several authors have presented evidence that these members respond preferentially to a tricyclic amine or alternately to a MAOI.[33] Further evidence is needed to verify this fact, but it should be kept in mind in selecting a drug for therapy.

It would seem safe to say, then, that there are a number of studies showing that the two early iminodibenzine derivatives (imipramine, amitriptyline) are superior to placebo in treating depressed patients. More recent iminodibenzine derivatives and the MAOI's should probably be reserved for patients who fail to respond to the first two drugs.

Electroconvulsive therapy

The development of the somatic therapies has been a milestone in the history of psychiatry, resting on the assumption that psychiatric conditions can be influenced therapeutically by nonpsychologic methods.

In 1917, Wagner-Juaregg introduced fever therapy in general paralysis of the insane and used malaria parasites to induce fever. In 1933, Sakel began using injections of subcoma doses of insulin in treating symptoms arising from abstinence in morphine addicts. When symptoms of the newly abstinent morphine addicts decreased, Sakel decided to give the same treatment to other forms of excitement. Quite accidentally, when he attempted to determine optimal dosage, some of the schizophrenic patients being treated fell into coma. When they emerged from coma, Sakel found that not only had the excitement abated but the psychotic symptoms themselves had lessened. Thus, insulin coma treatment was born. The rationale other than the one based on its empiric value was then, and still is, to a large extent, obscure.

In 1935, Meduna introduced a method of inducing convulsions by the injection of Metrazol. This rationale was based on the erroneous belief that epilepsy and schizophrenia do not coexist in the same person and might, in fact, be antagonistic to each other.

In Italy, in 1938, Ugo Cerletti and Lucio Bini induced therapeutic convulsions in a man with electricity. In the United States, electroconvulsive therapy was first used in 1940, at the Pennsylvania Hospital.

Many of the papers and books mentioned in the discussion of antidepressant drugs deal with the efficacy of electroconvulsive therapy (ECT) in the treatment of depression. It hardly seems worthwhile to dwell on the subject, but it is reasonable to say that ECT is now a well-accepted method for the treatment of depression. Earlier studies, such as Huston and Locher's, showed a more rapid recovery rate in manic depressives treated with ECT than before its introduction.[30]

More current studies accept its efficacy and compare drug treatment with it. Zung, in a retrospective study, found that hospitalized patients receiving ECT were more depressed than those receiving antidepressant drugs (the possibility that those given ECT had been unsuccessfully treated with antidepressant drugs prior to admission was not discussed), that they improved more on completion of treatment, and that they were more improved on discharge (not statistically significant although the other two statements were).[70] Unfortunately, the dosage of some of the antidepressant drugs used was far from maximal. There was no difference in the time spent in the hospital between the two groups. In the discussion he reviews more recent papers comparing drugs with ECT.

The method of giving ECT is thoroughly discussed by Kalinowsky and Hoch.[32] The standard procedure consists of passage of a small, measured amount of electricity through two electrodes placed on the temporal areas of the patient. The voltage varies between 70 and 130, the time of passage between 0.1 and 0.5 seconds, the amount varying between 200 and 1600 ma. This induces in the patient a brief tonic phase (10 seconds) followed by a clonic phase (30 to 40 seconds). The tonic phase is generally preceded by a brief flexion throughout the whole body, attributed to a direct stimulation of the motor area. The convulsion is accompanied by apnea. Very few patients become incontinent of urine or feces.

Recently Pitts, Woodruff, and associates have published a series of papers dealing with drug modifications of ECT—the anesthetics used, preoxygenation, and succinylcholine.[52,53,67,68] Their work indicates that methohexital is superior to thiopental, preoxygenation is not necessary if post convulsive respiratory resuscitation is used, and the optimal dose of succinylcholine is 0.5 mg./kg. They recommend the following method of treatment: Thirty to 60 minutes after he has been premedicated with 1 mg. subcutaneous atropine, the patient is anesthetized with 50 mg. intravenous 5% methohexital given in a 5-second period. *Immediately* thereafter, through the same intravenous needle, succinylcholine (0.5 mg./kg.) is given during a period of 1 to 2 seconds. After an interval of 50 seconds the ECT current is passed. Immediately after the clonic seizure phase, respiration is induced for three full excursions of the thorax by means of a bellows and mask. Subsequent artificial respiration may be continued if and when blood oxygen drops below 90% or at 20-second intervals until the time of spontaneous breathing. If the physician wants to measure oxygenation, ear lobe oximetry is a simple procedure.

Recently nondominant unilateral ECT has been recommended. Although not all studies confine the use of unilateral ECT to depressed patients, no study to date has found unilateral ECT less effective in alleviating symptoms than bilateral ECT.[5,10,31,36,44,69] Most studies agree that there is a significant lessening of memory loss from unilateral ECT. One study that shows no difference in memory function after unilateral and bilateral ECT is less extensive and less well controlled than subsequent studies.[22] McAndrew and associates failed to show fewer or less severe organic side effects in dominant and nondominant unilateral ECT as compared to bilateral ECT.[46] However, despite a battery of 22 psychologic tests used to demonstrate this finding, there were no tests given assessing immediate memory and memory for recent events—the two factors shown by Cannicott and by Levy to be significantly impaired by bilateral ECT, and less impaired, unimpaired or improved with unilateral ECT.[11,43]

Variations in the administration of unilateral ECT have been dealt with only briefly. In most of the studies five to 20 treatments are given (average 6 to 8) without mention of how often they are given, but presumably three times a week. Abrams, giving nondominant unilateral ECT, compared pre- and post-ECT Wechsler memory scores in six acute schizophrenics given ECT five times a week with four acute schizophrenics given ECT three times a week.[1] There were no statistical differences in the memory impairment after 20 ECT's of these two groups. This may be a method for giving the same number of treatments in a shorter period, thus shortening the hospital stay.

Therapy of the chronic depression

Despite adequate treatments of the kind already reviewed, a certain number of patients fail to respond. Kraines recently wrote a provocative paper dealing with the therapy of chronic depressions.[35] He feels, rightly so, that in dealing with this type of patient, drug combinations are indicated despite published warnings of danger, provided the physician is aware of the dangers and is on guard. He recommended various combinations, including the judicious simultaneous use of a MAOI and a tricyclic drug.

There are other treatments that, because they are new and reports of success are limited, should probably be reserved, at this point, for this type patient.

Coppen and associates showed that a combination of the amino acid tryptophan and a MAOI was a more effective antidepressant than MAOI alone.[12] More recently, when the antidepressant effect of tryptophan (41 patients), with and without the addition of MAOI, was compared with the antidepressant effect of ECT (36 patients), they were found equally effective.[13] The dose of DL-tryptophan in suspension was 5 to 7 Gm. given once daily for 28 days. The tryptophan-treated patients were divided into smaller groups, and some were given additional medications. Those patients treated with tryptophan and MAOI showed greater improvement than did those treated with tryptophan alone. Those patients treated with tryptophan, MAOI, K+, and carbohydrate supplements seemed to be most improved. However, the groups are small and improvement ratings are not significantly different.

Persson and Roos report a case of recurrent depressive illness treated successfully with 5-hydroxytryptophan, and Hertz and Sulman report a patient with recurrent depressive illness in whom prophylactic tryptophan prevented the patient from having a characteristic annual depression.[51,27]

Recent attention has been drawn to the treatment of imipramine-resistant depressive patients with reserpine. Pöldinger has reported two series of patients on imipramine or desipramine (11 in 1959 and 7 in 1963) who were treated for 1 to 2 days with reserpine or tetrabenazine intramuscular (IM) or intravenously (IV).[54,55] Patients were given either a single dose of 2.5 to 7.5 mg. reserpine or a single dose of 50 to 100 mg. tetrabenazine IM or IV, daily, for 1 or 2 days. Of these 18 patients, 11 responded favorably, usually with rapid and marked improvement. Haškovec and Ryšánek gave 15 patients with endogenous depressions reserpine in addition to their imipramine and found that, although 14 responded favorably, at follow-up 6 months later only six had maintained their improvement.[23]

Another enhancement to imipramine in the treatment of depression was recently advanced by Prange and associates.[57] Twenty patients receiving 150 mg. daily of imipramine were divided in two matched groups. Ten were given 25 mg. of triiodothyronine (T_3) and 10 patients were given placebo. Ignorant of treatment, a psychiatrist rated the patients. Those given T_3 significantly improved more rapidly than those given placebo; and, in 5 weeks, when four of the imipramine-placebo patients failed to respond, three received T_3. All three obtained remissions in 1 week.

In 1964, Costain, Redfearn, and Lippold reported a series of depressed patients treated with polarization—the passage of small polarizing currents through the brain.[14,42,58] Their results were encouraging. In a nonsystematic, uncontrolled way, we have tried this technique with disappointing results. Herjanic and Herjanic used this procedure in Canada and reported on 20 patients, nine of whom were manic depressive, depressed.[26] Two of the nine needed hospitalization for ECT shortly after termination of the treatment. The other seven did well and continued to at a 6- to 9-month follow-up.

Although it is true, with the exception of the T_3 study, that the authors of these papers may have been biased (i.e., there were no "blind" aspects to the studies), this hardly seems a reasonable criticism in light of the fact that, when usual treatments fail, new and imaginative methods may bring relief to the chronically depressed patient.

As others before him, Lehmann reemphasized the consideration of prefrontal lobotomy in the chronically depressed patient who has failed to respond for 2 to 3 years to every possible therapy.[40] Post and associates recently published an evaluation of patients who underwent bimedial leucotomy.[56] The progress of these patients before and for 3 years after the operation was recorded. It is a comprehensive study, dealing with all aspects of evaluation of such a procedure. Members of all diagnostic groups were benefited by the operation, but the greatest benefit was for those who showed a pure psychotic depression picture over the age of 60 years.

TREATMENT OF MANIA

Although it is possible to discuss the psychologic management of a patient who is depressed, this kind of management cannot be accomplished with the truly manic patient. In a manic state, the patient feels great and is talkative, irritable, irritating, sexually aroused, confident, expansive, and completely lacking in insight or good judgment. Because of his uplifted mood, he feels in no need of treatment and refuses, with vehemence, offers of assistance. Hospitalization is frequently necessary. When the manic is hospitalized, his excessive energy is easier to handle if he is given room to roam and is not confined to a locked room. This does not mean that he should be on an open, unlocked floor.

The treatment of mania will be divided into two parts—electroconvulsive therapy and chemotherapy.

Electroconvulsive therapy

Most of the literature dealing with the effectiveness of ECT discusses its use in specific illnesses—manic depressive disease, schizophrenia, reactive depression, etc. It is difficult to find literature dealing specifically with the treatment of mania with ECT. Boman-Barany reported on three patients with mania treated with ECT who had complete recovery from the episodes.[7] Geoghegan published a case report of a woman with recurring manic attacks treated for 20 years with hydrotherapy, bromides, morphine, paraldehyde, wet packs, rectal narcosis, nembutal, other drugs, and petit mal electrotherapy, with very little or no effect on ameliorating the symptoms or ending the episodes.[20] The patient had experienced 25 manic episodes lasting an average duration of 3.8 months. At 71 years of age, in her twenty-sixth attack, she was given "intensive" ECT and was practically recovered within 4 days, although further treatments were given in the next 3 weeks. Holbrook found that 100 manic patients treated with psychotherapy, sedation, etc. had an average hospital stay of 127 days whereas 100 manic patients treated with ECT had an average hospital stay of only 41 days.[28] All the ECT-treated patients left the hospital before 5 months, whereas 27 of the others remained longer, one for over 2 years. Schiele and Schneider reviewed publications dealing with the use of ECT in manic patients.[62] From 16 reports, they collected 466 manic patients. The "recovery" rate averaged 62% for the series (26% being the lowest recovery rate and 100% being the highest) and an average of 18% were considered "improved" (range 0% to 33%). Thus, 80% were recovered or improved and an average of 20% showed "no improvement" (range 0% to 25%). To this series they added their own findings, comparing manic patients treated with ECT or nothing. Their own findings were strikingly inconclusive. They summarize from their own findings and those of the other authors by stating the following conclusions:

1. The course is shortened by ECT in favorable cases.
2. ECT is particularly helpful in controlling the acute excitement, aggressiveness, and exhaustion.
3. More frequent treatment (up to 3 a day) and a greater total number of treatments are necessary than in the depressed patient.
4. The danger of relapse is greater than in the depressed patient.

Oltman and Friedman gave a clear analysis of temporal factors in manic depressive psychosis with particular reference to ECT.[49] They found, in examining the records of 262 manic depressives and reporting on the attacks separately as manic or depressive, that ECT was less effective in the manic phase than in the depressive phase. In the depressed patients, 70% treated with ECT were released from the hospital in 2 months (higher if the patient was in the first episode) as compared to only 18% of the untreated group. In the manic patients, 60% treated with ECT left the hospital in 4 months, compared to 35% of the untreated group. In the treated group of manics, 24% remained in the hospital more than 6 months as compared to 46% of the untreated group. These authors felt that part of the poorer results in the manics could be explained by the fact that the patients were treated with the standard method of shock. They believed that manics required an accelerated program of treatment. Langsley and associates compared ECT and chlor-promazine in the treatment of 106 acute schizophrenics and manics (all ill less than 3 months or, if ill before that, in remission for at least 6 months before the onset of the present illness) and found that the two forms of treatment seemed to produce essentially equivalent degrees of improvement.[38] However, in comparing the length of hospitalization in the two groups, they found that the median hospital stay for the 52 ECT-treated patients was 105.5 days and for the 54 chlorpromazine-treated patients, 89.5 days (statistically different at the 1% level of significance). Thirteen ECT-treated patients stayed longer than 6 months compared to four of the chlorpromazine-treated patients. Thus, although ECT can be considered an efficacious treatment of mania, there are a large number of patients who do not respond or who do so only partially and slowly.

Chemotherapy

In May 1954, chlorpromazine became available to American physicians. Since it has been marketed longest of all the phenothiazines, reports dealing with its usefulness in treating mania are most numerous, although other phenothiazines, particularly thioridazine, are also acknowledged as valuable therapeutically. Lehmann reported on 71 psychiatric patients treated with chlorpromazine and stated that the most gratifying results were obtained in the group of patients in the manic or hypomanic states.[41] He later concluded that acute manics responded quickly and chronic manics, hospitalized more than 1 year, responded more slowly. In a larger study, Lehmann reported complete recovery in 37 of 77 manics (48%) within 40 days.[39] None of the remaining 40 were unimproved. Doses in this study were low, only occasionally reaching 800 mg. per day. It is difficult to compare studies, for doses of the drugs vary, as do the rating scales for improvement. In the study of Langsley and associates just mentioned, comparing ECT and chlorpromazine treatment in acute schizophrenics and manics, there are a number of different factors rated on a "simple improvement, no change, or worse" scale.[38] In "response to treatment" 20% of the 54 patients treated with chlorpromazine improved and 23% of the 52 ECT-treated patients improved. It must be said that, despite the initial enthusiasm related to phenothiazines, the percent of patients who respond is far from maximal.

Haloperidol (butyrophenone) has been widely used in Europe for a number of years. It was not available to American physicians until 1967, so the bulk of the papers dealing with its efficacy in treating mania are European in origin. It is an antipsychotic drug that is chemically distinct from the phenothiazine derivatives, yet its most common side effect—extrapyramidal reactions—is similar. Entwistle and associates treated 10 manic patients with large doses, initially IM, of haloperidol with rapid initial results.[19] One patient relapsed during the maintenance period and needed ECT. In examining the records of these patients and comparing, in six patients, treatment of manic episodes before with ECT or phenothiazines, the authors concluded that there were probably quicker responses to haloperidol. There were no prolonged hospitalizations as there were in three of the six treated previously by these other means. Rees and Davies gave 42 manics haloperidol orally in smaller doses beginning with 0.5 mg. twice a day and building up in 1 week to 3.0 mg. twice a day. Thirty-five (83%) improved.[59] The authors felt its rapid action was usually striking.

Probably the most exciting drug available for the treatment of mania is lithium carbonate. Since its introduction, by Cade, into the psychiatric world in 1949, numerous reports with encouraging results from Australia, Denmark, England, Russia, and finally the United States have appeared in the literature.

Original usage of lithium chloride as a salt substitute, and subsequent deaths, led to its disrepute as a safe drug in the treatment of anything. It now becomes clear that the drug can be used with safety. Blood levels should be monitored frequently when patients are beginning on it and less frequently when they are being maintained on it. Usually patients are hospitalized to begin treatment. A fine tremor of the hands is extremely frequent and can be seen in patients who receive even very small doses. If the tremor is pronounced or if other toxic symptoms such as diarrhea, vomiting, ataxia, tinnitus, or blurred vision are present, the dosage should be reduced. Signs of dangerous intoxication include a thirst and an output of dilute urine, confusion, fasciculations, nystagmus, seizures, and coma. The usual starting dose of lithium carbonate is 300 mg. three times a day. This is increased until the blood level, taken in the morning, reaches between 1 and 2 mEq. per liter. With this treatment the mania is said to abate in 6 to 10 days. After the improvement is attained, the dosage is decreased to maintain the blood level at 0.4 to 0.8 mEq. per liter. Patients with cardiovascular, renal, or central nervous system pathology or disease should not be given lithium carbonate. Manic patients taking lithium may be given ECT, phenothiazines, barbiturates or antidepressants if needed.

Schou accumulated the results with lithium treatment in mania of various authors up to 1959 and found that out of 370 patients, 304 (82%) could be listed as improved.[64] This is not too different from the percent of patients recovered and improved (80% total) with ECT; however, the length of hospitalization is probably much less when lithium is used (no study comments on this, but studies evaluating ECT vs. no treatment use the number of patients discharged in less than 4 months as an end point) and the probability of maintaining recovery much greater when lithium is used. Unfortunately there are no comparison studies using lithium, phenothiazines, haloperidol, and ECT, and there are almost no double blind studies using lithium. The Veterans Administration and National Institute of Mental Health are currently conducting a joint study of lithium treatment in mania and depression, and hopefully this will enhance our knowledge of its usefulness and answer the questions posed by lithium skeptics. As of this writing, lithium is generally not available in the United States and is still considered an experimental drug by the Food and Drug Administration; therefore, permission for its use should be obtained. Schlagenhauf and associates added 72 more manic patients treated with lithium carbonate (10 of their own—all responded well— and 62 from 2 other authors) and arrived at the same conclusion; i.e., 58 of 72 (81%) responded favorably to the drug.[63] Their description of the method and of the clinical response is recommended to anyone using lithium carbonate for the first time. Kline, in a paper for the American Psychiatric Association, reviewed the history of lithium usage in psychiatry and reported that in 979 accumulated manic patients, 88% were improved or recovered and 12% unimproved.[34] Surely, if carefully monitored, this may prove the best treatment available for the manic patient.

Blackwell and Shepherd state that "lithium is modestly effective in the treatment of mania."[6] The overwhelming impression derived from a review of the literature is that lithium is highly effective in the treatment of mania. Double blind studies are infrequent in evaluating any somatic therapy of mania. Surely, it will be good to have some, but because of the lack of them, the bulk of papers lauding lithium for the treatment of mania cannot be ignored.

Dewhurst, after human and animal studies, proposed a new theory of the relationship of cerebral amines to mood.[17] Type A amines are fat soluble and are excitant. They produce the phenomena of the alert state. An example of this type amine is tryptamine. Type C amines are water soluble and are depressant. They produce the phenomenon of drowsiness or sleep. An example of this type amine is adrenaline. Methysergide is a specific antagonist of the type A receptor.[37] Based on the physiologic assumption that some forms of mania are caused by an excess of type A amines or increased sensitivity of the type A receptors, Dewhurst has used small doses of methysergide (1 mg. 3 times a day) in the treatment of mania.[18] Cases of reversible retroperitoneal fibrosis in long-term use of methysergide have been reported, so in mania the drug should be used with caution. The preliminary experience indicates that, if methysergide is not effective within 48 hours, prolongation of treatment or increase of dosage is not likely to be beneficial. Haškovec and Souček treated 10 manic patients with low doses of methysergide, starting with the intramuscular route and converting to oral administration by the fifth day.[24] Seven patients showed very good improvement, and one good improvement. One remained stationary and one deteriorated. In six of the improved, methysergide was replaced with a placebo after 8 to 14 days (mean 10.8); and five relapsed and one remained well. In the two others who had improved, methysergide was replaced with routine neuroleptic and did less well.

PROPHYLACTIC TREATMENT OF MANIC DEPRESSIVE DISEASE

Up to this point, there are two prophylactic treatments recommended for the manic depressive patient. Geoghegan and Stevenson reported on a group of patients given ECT once a month for 5 years.[21] These patients had

had two or more attacks of mental illness in the preceding 5 years. Thirteen patients accepted the treatment and 11 patients refused. At the end of 3 years the 13 patients who received treatments were free of attacks, and all the 11 who refused had had one or more attacks. At the end of 5 years, Stevenson and Geoghegan found that two of the 13 experimental patients had been readmitted compared to all 11 of the control group.[65] In a case history truly worth reading, Hastings presented a circular manic depressive whose course was modified by "prophylactic electroshock."[25] This man, treated for two 5-year periods with ECT once a month or once every 2 months, considered these two periods his only "relatively well" periods. During them he was hospitalized only one time compared to numerous hospitalizations (always yearly) when not receiving ECT. The second 5-year period was ended in 1959 and drug therapy was used but proved to be unsuccessful. Prophylactic ECT was reinstituted. The great drawback to this kind of treatment, Hastings felt, was the extreme, illogical fear of ECT present in most patients. It is difficult enough to maintain patients on drugs when they feel better, so it would probably be impossible to maintain large numbers of patients on ECT. Since the illness is episodic and unpredictable in most cases, ECT seems to be an overzealous treatment for the majority of patients. However, there may be an occasional patient with frequently occurring attacks, whose life is thoroughly disrupted by the illness, where such treatment is warranted.

Lithium carbonate is heralded by some as an effective prophylactic agent. Baastrup and Schou (1967) reported on 88 female patients given lithium continuously for at least 12 months.[2] These patients, to be included in the study, had to have had at least two manic depressive episodes during 1 year or one or more episodes per year during at least 2 years. The patients belonged to three diagnostic groups—manic depressives, recurrent depressives, and atypical cases. The authors calculated the relapse frequency (the number of episode starts per year) and the psychosis rate (the average number of months per year the patient was sick—either with supervision at home or in the hospital) of each patient during lithium treatment and prior to it. Without lithium the patients had relapses, on the average, every 8 months and with lithium, every 60 months. Without lithium, the patients were sick 13 weeks a year and with lithium, 1.5 weeks a year. Both of these are significant at the 0.001 level. If two patients who responded poorly were excluded from the average, the results were even more striking. Atypical cases responded least well to lithium maintenance.

In the 18 patients who had relapses during lithium therapy, the relapses lasted an average of 1.2 months compared to an average of 2.2 months without lithium (significant at the 0.01 level). Therefore, lithium treatment not only produced a decrease in the frequency of relapses but also shortened the relapses if they did occur. The authors comment that calculating episodes of sickness does not tell the whole picture. Many patients, although not sick enough to be hospitalized or cared for, experienced slight to moderate depressive and hypomanic symptoms during their free periods. With lithium, these symptoms no longer occurred.

Blackwell and Shepherd critically evaluated the data accumulated on lithium as a prophylactic drug.[6] Among other things, they reexamined the data of Baastrup and Schou. They pointed out that the selection criteria did not necessarily include a population of patients with a high risk of recurrence of the illness. By choosing patients who had to have had at least two episodes in 1 year or one or more episodes per year during at least 2 years, they included patients who had had a single continuous episode, interrupted by periods of treatment. In reevaluating the data of Baastrup and Schou, Blackwell and Shepherd then excluded 22 (of 88) patients who appeared to have had one continuous episode, without knowledge of previous episodes, before beginning treatment with lithium. In addition, some patients remained ill while being on lithium or relapsed, and in others the remission produced by lithium was less than the patients had experienced without lithium. All in all, Blackwell and Shepherd concluded that in 55 cases the prophylactic effect of lithium was doubtful. They then presented data on 13 patients (out of 308 admissions), who met the Baastrup and Schou criteria, treated with a heterogenous group of psychotropic drugs. These patients, too, had impressive records of improvement. Thus, it must be said that the question of the prophylactic action of lithium is unanswered.

In a letter to the editor, Melia reported on a double blind study of a small number of patients treated with lithium prophylactically.[48] His diagnostic criteria are not well clarified: "Most were manic depressives, there were also recurrent depressives, recurrent manias and recurrent schizoaffective illnesses." He took 18 such patients who had been on lithium at least 9 months; and to nine of them he gave placebo and to nine he continued the lithium. For 2 years these patients were followed, chiefly as outpatients. Relapses were reserved for those mood swings severe enough to necessitate hospitalization. Six patients, four on lithium and two on placebo, had no relapses. The number of days from the start of the trial to the date of the relapse was calculated in all others, and those six without relapse were considered to have relapsed the day after the trial ended—thus counting the number of days as 2 years. The mean length of remission achieved by patients on lithium was 433 days, compared to 224 days by patients on placebo. This barely failed to be significant at the 5% level. The feeling was that lithium has a striking effect on some patients whereas, on the other extreme, there is also a group of patients who derive no benefit from it given prophylactically.

In another letter to the editor, Baastrup and Schou refer to a paper of Angst, who studied the effect of prophylactically administered imipramine and lithium.[3] The results showed that lithium administration led to a significant decrease ($p < 0.005$) whereas the imipramine-treated group did not differ significantly from the untreated group.

In summary, it is probably fair to say, as did Melia, that some patients derive great benefit from lithium prophylactically. The same is probably true of other drugs and EST also. A great deal more needs to be learned about manic depressive disease before predictions for favorable prophylactic response to lithium can be made. Until that time, it is not unreasonable to try this treatment in patients who are severely disabled by their disease.

REFERENCES

1. Abrams, R.: Daily administration of unilateral ECT, Amer. J. Psychiat. 124:384, 1967.

2. Baastrup, P. C., and Schou, M.: Lithium as a prophylactic agent, Arch. Gen. Psychiat. **16:**162, 1967.
3. Baastrup, P. C., and Schou, M.: Prophylactic lithium? Lancet **2:**349, 1968.
4. Beck, A. T.: Depression, New York, 1967, Harper & Row, Publishers (Hoeber Medical Division).
5. Bidder, T. G., Duffy, J. P., Brunschwig, L., and Strain, J. J.: Memory function following unilateral and bilateral electroconvulsive therapy. In Scientific proceedings, summary of the one-hundred twenty-third meeting of American Psychiatric Association, Detroit, 1967, The Association.
6. Blackwell, B., and Shepherd, M.: Prophylactic lithium: another therapeutic myth? Lancet **1:**968, 1968.
7. Boman-Barany, K.: Electroshock therapy of manic states, Nord. Med. (Hygiea) **15:**2535, 1942.
8. Treatment of depression, Brit. Med. J. **2:**164, 1968.
9. Bucci, L.: The psychiatrist and MAO inhibitors, Dis. Nerv. Syst. **29:**127 (Feb.) 1968.
10. Cannicott, S. M.: Unilateral electroconvulsive therapy, Postgrad. Med. J. **38:**451, 1962.
11. Cannicott, S. M., and Waggoner, R. W.: Unilateral and bilateral electroconvulsive therapy, Arch. Gen. Psychiat. **16:**229, 1967.
12. Coppen, A., Shaw, D., and Farrell, J. P.: Potentiation of the antidepressive effect of a monoamine-oxidase inhibitor by tryptophan, Lancet **1:**79, 1963.
13. Coppen, A., Shaw, D., Herzberg, B., and Moggs, R.: Tryptophan in the treatment of depression, Lancet **2:**1178, 1967.
14. Costain, R., Redfearn, J. W. T., and Lippold, O. C. F.: A controlled trial of the therapeutic effects of polarization of the brain in depressive illness, Brit. J. Psychiat. **110:**786, 1964.
15. Dalton, K.: The premenstrual syndrome, Springfield, Ill., 1964, Charles C Thomas, Publisher.
16. Davis, J.: Efficacy of tranquilizing drugs and antidepressant drugs, Arch. Gen. Psychiat. **13:**552, 1965.
17. Dewhurst, W. G.: New theory of cerebral amine function and its clinical application, Nature **218:**1130, 1968.
18. Dewhurst, W. G.: Methysergide in the treatment of mania, Lancet **1:**1369, 1968.
19. Entwistle, C., Taylor, R. M., and MacDonald, I. A.: The treatment of mania with Haloperidol ("Serenace"), J. Ment. Sci. **108:**373, 1962.
20. Geoghegan, J. J.: Manic depressive psychosis (manic phase) and electroshock, Canad. Med. Ass. J. **55:**54, 1946.
21. Geoghegan, J. J., and Stevenson, G. H.: Prophylactic electroshock, Amer. J. Psychiat. **105:**494, 1949.
22. Gottlieb, G., and Wilson, I.: Cerebral dominance: temporary disruption of verbal memory by unilateral electroconvulsive shock treatment, J. Comp Physiol. Psychol. **60:**368, 1965.
23. Haškovec, L., and Ryšánek, K.: The action of reserpine in imipramine-resistant depressive patients, Psychopharmacologia **11:**18, 1967.
24. Haškovec, L., and Souček, K.: Trial of methysergide in mania, Nature **219:**507, 1968.
25. Hastings, D. W.: Circular manic-depressive reaction modified by "prophylactic electroshock," Amer. J. Psychiat. **118:**258, 1961.
26. Herjanic, M., and Herjanic, B. M.: Clinical report on a new therapeutic technique: polarization, Canad. Psychiat. Ass. J. **12:**423, 1967.

27. Hertz, D., and Sulman, F. G.: Preventing depression with tryptophan, Lancet **1:**531, 1968.
28. Holbrook, C. S.: What can we expect from electro-sleep (electroshock) treatment? Southern Med. J. **41:**444, 1948.
29. Hollister, L. E., and Overall, J. E.: Reflections on the specificity of action of anti-depressants, Psychosomatics **6:**361 (Sept.-Oct.), 1965.
30. Huston, P. E., and Locher, L. M.: Manic-depressive psychosis: course when treated and untreated with electric shock, Arch. Neurol. Psychiat. **60:**37, 1948.
31. Impastato, D. J., and Pacella, B. L.: Electrically produced unilateral convulsions (a new method of electrocerebrotherapy), Dis. Nerv. Syst. **13:**368, 1952.
32. Kalinowsky, L. B., and Hoch, P. H.: Somatic treatments in psychiatry, New York, 1961, Grune & Stratton, Inc.
33. Kline, N. S.: Selective response of twins to an antidepressant drug, Dis. Nerv. Syst. **29:**333 (May) 1968.
34. Kline, N. S.: The history of lithium usage in psychiatry. (To be published as part of monograph series, "Modern Problems of Pharmacopsychiatry," by S. Karger, AG., Basel, Switzerland.)
35. Kraines, S. H.: Therapy of the chronic depressions, Dis. Nerv. Syst. **28:**577, 1967.
36. Lancaster, N. P., Steinert, R. R., and Frost, I.: Unilateral electroconvulsive therapy, J. Ment. Sci. **104:**221, 1958.
37. Amines, alerting and affect, Lancet **1:**1237, 1968.
38. Langsley, D. G., Enterline, J. D., and Hickerson, G. X., Jr.: A comparison of chlorpromazine and EST in treatment of acute schizophrenic and manic reactions, Arch. Neurol. Psychiat. **81:**384, 1959.
39. Lehmann, H. E.: Therapeutic results with chlorpromazine (Largactil), in psychiatric conditions, Canad. Med. Ass. J. **72:**91, 1955.
40. Lehmann, H. E.: Clinical perspectives on antidepressant therapy, Amer. J. Psychiat. **124:**12 (Supp.), 1968.
41. Lehmann, H. E., and Hanrahan, G. E.: Chlorpromazine, Arch. Neurol. Psychiat. **71:**227, 1954.
42. Lippold, O. C. F., and Redfearn, J. W. T.: Mental changes resulting from the passage of small direct currents through the human brain, Brit. J. Psychiat. **110:**768, 1964.
43. Levy, R.: The clinical evaluation of unilateral electroconvulsive therapy, Brit. J. Psychiat. **114:**459, 1968.
44. Martin, W. L., Ford, H. F., McDanald, E. C., Jr., and Towler, M. L.: Clinical evaluation of unilateral EST, Amer. J. Psychiat. **121:**1087, 1965.
45. Mayer-Gross, W., Slater, E., and Roth, M.: Clinical psychiatry, Baltimore, 1954, The Williams & Wilkins Co.
46. McAndrew, J., Berkey, B., and Matthews, C.: The effects of dominant and nondominant unilateral ECT as compared to bilateral ECT, Amer. J. Psychiat. **124:**483, 1967.
47. McConaghy, N., Joffe, A. D., Kingston, W. R., Stevenson, H. G., Atkinson, I., Cole, E., and Fennessy, L. A.: Correlation of clinical features of depressed outpatients with response to amitriptyline and protriptyline, Brit. J. Psychiat. **114:**103, 1968.
48. Melia, P. I.: Prophylactic lithium, Lancet **2:**519, 1968.
49. Oltman, J. E., and Friedman, S.: Analysis of temporal factors in manic depressive psychosis with particular reference to the effect of shock therapy, Amer. J. Psychiat. **107:**57, 1950.
50. Overall, J., Hollister, L., and Dalal, S.: Psychiatric drug research, Arch. Gen. Psychiat. **16:**152, 1967.

51. Persson, T., and Roos, B. E.: 5-Hydroxytryptophan for depression, Lancet **2**:987, 1967.
52. Pitts, F. N., Jr., Desmarais, G. M., Stewart, W., and Schaberg, K.: Induction of anesthesia with methohexital and thiopental in electroconvulsive therapy, New Eng. J. Med. **273**:353, 1965.
53. Pitts, F. N., Jr., Woodruff, R. A., Jr., Craig, A. G., and Rich, C. L.: The drug modification of ECT: II. Succinylcholine dosage, Arch. Gen. Psychiat. **19**:595, 1968.
54. Pöldinger, W.: Diskussionsbemerkung an der 129. Versammlung der Schweiz Gesellschaft für Psychiatrie, Schweiz. Arch. Neurol. Psychiat. **84**:327, 1959.
55. Pöldinger, W.: Combined administration of desipramine and reserpine or tetra-benazine in depressive patients, Psychopharmacologia **4**:308, 1963.
56. Post, F., Rees, W. L., and Schurr, P. H.: An evaluation of bimedial leucotomy, Brit. J. Psychiat. **114**:1223, 1968.
57. Prange, A. J., Jr., Wilson, I. C., Rabon, A. M., and Lipton, M. A.: Enhancement of imipramine antidepressant activity by thyroid hormone. Presented at the A.P.A. meeting, Boston, May, 1968.
58. Redfearn, J. W. T., Lippold, O. C. F., and Costain, R.: A preliminary account of the clinical effects of polarizing the brain in certain psychiatric disorders, Brit. J. Psychiat. **110**:773, 1964.
59. Rees, L., and Davies, B.: A study of the value of Haloperidol in the management and treatment of schizophrenic and manic patients, Int. J. Neuropsychiat. **1**:263, 1965.
60. Robins, E., Murphy, G., Wilkinson, R., Gassner, S., and Kayes, J.: Some clinical considerations in the prevention of suicide based on a study of 134 successful suicides, Amer. J. Public Health **49**:888, 1959.
61. Sargant, W.: Psychotropic drugs, Brit. Med. J. **1**:249, 1968.
62. Schiele, B. C., and Schneider, R. A.: The selective use of electroconvulsive therapy in manic patients, Dis. Nerv. Syst. **10**:291, 1949.
63. Schlagenhauf, G., Tupin, J., and White, R. B.: The use of lithium carbonate in the treatment of manic psychoses, Amer. J. Psychiat. **123**:201, 1966.
64. Schou, M.: Lithium in psychiatric therapy: stock-taking after 10 years, Psychopharmacologia **1**:65, 1959.
65. Stevenson, G. H., and Geoghegan, J. J.: Prophylactic electroshock: a five-year study, Amer. J. Psychiat. **107**:743, 1951.
66. Wechsler, H., Grosser, G. H., and Greenblatt, M.: Research evaluating antidepressant medications on hospitalized mental patients: a survey of published reports during a five-year period, J. Nerv. Ment. Dis. **141**:231, 1965.
67. Woodruff, R. A., Jr., Pitts, F. N., Jr., and McClure, J. N., Jr.: The drug modification of ECT: I. Methohexital, thiopental and preoxygenation, Arch. Gen. Psychiat. **18**:605, 1968.
68. Woodruff, R. A., Jr., Pitts, F. N., Jr., and Craig, A. G.: Electrotherapy: the effects of barbiturate anesthesia, succinylcholine and pre-oxygenation on EKG, Dis. Nerv. Syst. **30**:180, 1969.
69. Zamora, E. N., and Kaelbling, R.: Memory and electroconvulsive therapy, Amer. J. Psychiat. **122**:546, 1965.
70. Zung, W. W. K.: Evaluating treatment methods for depressive disorders, Amer. J. Psychiat. **124**:40 (Supp.), 1968.

The structured interview

Following is the structured interview that was used to examine the manic probands and their available first-degree relatives. During the interview, a positive response led to expansion of the examination in that area.

Name_____ Age____ Sex: M___F___ Race: C___N___Other____

Religion: C_____ P_____ J_____ O_____ Hospital and Dx: _____

Occupation_____ Father's occupation_____

Related to index case No. _____
F.H.: Father
      Mother
      Sibs
      Children

Clinical course of psychosis

Age first ill_____ Length first illness_____or chronic_____

    Hospitalized: No_____ Yes_____ Where_____

Second illness_____ Length_____or chronic_____

    Hospitalized: No_____ Yes_____ Where_____

Third illness_____ Length_____or chronic_____

    Hospitalized: No_____ Yes_____ Where_____

Fourth illness_____ Length_____or chronic_____

    Hospitalized: No_____ Yes_____ Where_____

Fifth illness_____ Length_____or chronic_____

    Hospitalized: No_____ Yes_____ Where_____

Sixth or more_____ No._____ Ever chronic: Yes_____ No_____

Symptoms	Present illness	Previous illness

Manic depressive disease

1. Depressed mood (blue, worried, discouraged)
2. Slow thinking (retardation)
3. Poor appetite and weight loss

Symptoms	Present illness	Previous illness

Manic depressive disease—cont'd

    4. Constipation
    5. Terminal insomnia
    6. Initial insomnia
    7. Tiredness
    8. Loss of concentration
    9. Diurnal variation
  10. Suicidal ideas
  11. Suicide attempts
  12. Decreased sex interest
  13. Agitation (hand wringing, pacing, etc.)
  14. Many somatic complaints
  15. Guilt feelings and delusions
  16. Tearfulness
  17. Euphoria
  18. Flight of ideas and overtalkativeness
  19. Overactivity
  20. Increased sex interest

Schizophrenia

  21. Passivity feelings
  22. Delusions of depersonalization
  23. Disturbance of symbolization
  24. Auditory hallucinations
  25. Bodily hallucinations
  26. Delusions
  27. Blunting of affect
  28. Giggling or inappropriate affect
  29. Apathetic
  30. Querulous
  31. Mannerisms
  32. Restless
  33. Jerkiness
  34. Abnormal spontaneous moments
  35. Abnormal induced moments
  36. Abnormal posture
  37. Rigidity
  38. Marked complaints
  39. Marked aversion
  40. Mute
  41. Speech abnormality

Chronic brain syndrome

  42. Disorientation
  43. Impaired memory

Anxiety neurosis

  44. Breathlessness
  45. Palpitation
  46. Chest pain

Symptoms	Present illness	Previous illness

Anxiety neurosis—cont'd

47. Attacks or spells
48. Apprehension
49. Trembling
50. Phobias

Hysteria

51. Amnesia
52. Fits
53. Aphonia
54. Deafness
55. Blindness
56. Paralysis

Miscellaneous

57. Mental retardation
58. Peptic ulcer
59. Hypertension
60. Asthma
61. Migraine
62. Diabetes
63. Heart disease, CVA
64. Cancer
65. Epilepsy
66. Tuberculosis
67. Kidney disease
68. Social incapacity
69. Alcohol intake
70. Interfere with
    A. Marriage
    B. Work
71. Trouble with law

Clinical data and diagnosis in family members

This appendix gives a summary of the diagnoses on the family members of the 61 manic probands. It reflects information received from a systematic family history from the proband and family members, records, and diagnoses from hospitals and physicians and systematic personal diagnostic interviews with 167 first-degree relatives of the probands.

Columns 1, 2, and 3 give the sex, age at index admission, and age of onset of the illness in the 61 probands. The remaining columns are devoted to the diagnoses in the family members of the probands. Age of onset in the relatives who were psychiatrically ill is denoted by parentheses. A question mark in the parentheses indicates that the age of onset in the ill relative is unknown.

Under the column for siblings, S refers to sisters, B refers to brothers; under the column for children, s refers to sons, d refers to daughters.

The symbol + indicates that the relative was deceased at the time of the study. The letters (Tw) in parentheses indicate subject is a twin; (IT) indicates the subject is an identical twin; (FT) indicates the subject is a fraternal twin.

Following are the symbols for the various psychiatric illnesses:

A	= Alcoholism		Hy	= Probable hysteria
AN	= Anxiety neurosis		M	= Manias only
CBS	= Chronic brain syndrome		MD	= Manias and depressions
C-G	= Compulsive gambler		O-C	= Obsessive compulsive
D	= Depression only		PrDem	= Presenile dementia
Enur	= Enuresis		R	= Mental deficiency
Ep	= Epilepsy		Soc	= Sociopath
GPI	= General paresis		Su	= Suicide
Hebe	= Hebephrenic schizophrenia		Undx	= Undiagnosed psychiatric illness

In the column concerned with extended family the symbols are:

P	= Paternal		GrM	= Grandmother
M	= Maternal		GrUn	= Great uncle
Au	= Aunt		GtGrF	= Great grandfather
Csn	= Cousin		Neph	= Nephew
GrAu	= Great aunt		Nie	= Niece
GrF	= Grandfather		Un	= Uncle

(All-sources data)

No.	Sex	Age on admission	Age of onset	Father	Mother	Siblings	Children	Extended family
1	M	21	19	55 O–C(10)	48 D(34)	S4 S13 B19 B16 R	0	0
2	F	18	18	Unknown	45	0	0	M Un–Su
3	F	24	20	56	52 D(40)	S19	0	P GrM–D P Un–D, Su P Au–D
4	F	32	17	65	58	B33	0	0
5	M	39	18	64+	46+	S4+	s18 s16 s14 d9	M Csn–A M Csn–A
6	M	54	54	73+	80	B60 S64 M(18) B45	s16 d20	0
7	F	57	48	74+ CBS	77 D(74)	S55 B42 B50 MD(25)	d24 D(23)	P Csn–D P Au–D P Au–D P Un–D M GrUn–D
8	F	52	19	77	88+ D(?)	S66 D(?) S60 MD S62	s24 D(?) d27 (1st Marr.) d13 Enur d13 (2nd Marr.)	M Csn–D, Su M Csn–D, Su M Csn–MD Neph–D Nie–D
9	F	46	42	78 D(70)	76 D(?)	S45	s24 MD(24) s19	0
10	M	46	23	68+	48+ M(?)	S54 A S50	d12 d6	M Un–A

Continued.

(All-sources data)—cont'd

No.	Sex	Age on admission	Age of onset	Father	Mother	Siblings	Children	Extended family
11	M	47	44	36+	60+ D(?)	B21+ B49 M(45)	s16 d13 d13 (IT)	M Un–Su M Un–A M Au–M P Un–A
12	F	31	30	68	66 D(18)	S37 D(37)	0	M Au–D M GrM–PrDem
13	M	58	57	75+	94+ D(50)	S75 S70 D(55) B+, 2 days (Tw)	s20	0
14	F	44	36	67+ MD(?)	73	0	s21 s14	0
15	F	60	30	92	?+	B+ S+ S+ S+ S+ S? S?	0	0
16	M	31	31	Unknown	30 D, Su(?)	0	0	M GrF–Hebe M GrUn–Su M GrAu–Su
17	F	32	17	67	62	B42 B39 S38	s9 s1 d8 d6	P GrUn–Su
18	M	24	18	56	50 D(32)	S26 B21 B18 S16 O–C	0	0
19	M	48	26	75+	75+ D(?)	B50 M(60) B54 B52 S59 S57 S45 D S45 D (IT)	s16 d12	0
20	F	42	30	64 A	65 D(30)	0	d24 MD(24)	P GrUn–Undx M Au–D M Un–D

21	F	34	31	46+	58	S35 D(25)	s5	P GrUn–D P GrUn–D P GrAu–D P GrAu–D P Au–D
22	F	50	18	81+	83 CBS	S58 MD* S57 A S53 D(31)	d22 M(17) d19 MD(15) d15 d10	Neph–MD, Su M Csn–Su
23	F	46	23	Unknown+	76 D(?)	B30+ S42+ A	d14 s16 s17	M Csn–D
24	F	58	58	83+ D(60)	62+	S28+	s33 d27	P Au–D
25	M	26	25	65	68	0	0	0
26	F	32	16	62 R	52 M(?)	S32 B31 A	0	M Un–Su
27	F	18	18	42	35 A, D(34)	B19	s2 s6/12	M GrM–A M Au–D
28	F	39	24	67 C–G	61	S43 AN S39 S37 B35 B34 C–G	d11 d7	P Un–R P GrF–A M Csn–Soc
29	M	32	23	56	60 M(50)	B35 (FT) B31 D(30)	d3	M GrUn–D M GrUn–A P Csn–D
30	F	21	19	61 C–G	59 D(40)	B23 (FT) S25 S24	0	P Un–CBS
31	F	58	23	81	73+	0	s25	M GrF–Su

*Patient originally diagnosed as possible manic depressive; had lobotomy for persistent illness; now appears schizophrenic. Onset of illness at approximately age 20 years.

Continued.

(All-sources data)—cont'd

No.	Sex	Age on admission	Age of onset	Father	Mother	Siblings	Children	Extended family
32	M	52	20	79+ A	74 CBS	B50 D(40) S43	s16 d20 D(15)	P Un–A P Un–A P Csn–Su P Csn–Undx M Un–A M Un–A
33	M	58	48	56+	75+	S61 B49 B42 B54 MD(30)	s33 d31 D(18)	M Un–A
34	F	22	17	57 C–G	52 D(27)	S32 R	s1	M GrM–D M Csn–Su M Csn–D M GrUn–D P Au–D P Un–C–G P Csn–D M Csn ⎤ M Csn ⎬–R M Csn ⎦
35	M	40	18	67 O–C	61 Hy	B29 O–C	s13 s11 s7	P Csn–Aff. Su P Csn–D
36	M	24	16	52	50 D(25)	B24 (FT) B27 D(18)	0	M GrM–D M Csn–D M Csn–A M Csn–D P Au–D M Csn–R
37	F	25	23	Unknown	21+	B27	s7 d2 d <1	M Au–A M Au–D

38	M	40	25	67 A(20)	63 D(30)	B43 A(30)	0	M Un–Soc M Un–A
39	F	50	47	82 CBS	65+	S50 MD(40) (IT) B54 B30 D(29) B39 MD(37) S55	0	P Csn–Su P GrF–Pos. Su M GrAu–Undx
40	F	18	17	53	49	S24 D(20) S28 B20 AN S12 S9	0	P Un–R
41	M	16	16	40 A	39 D(25)	S13	0	M GrF–D
42	F	27	21	45 A	43 A	B25 A S23 S21 D(20) S20 1/2 Sibs: B18 R, Soc B16 S15 B14 B13 S12 B10 B9 B5	d8 s5 s3 d3/12	M Csn–MD M Au–MD M GrF–A M Un–A
43	F	44	40	65 A, D(60)	62 D(40)	B37 D(36)	s21 d17	M Un–MD M Un–A P GrM–A P Csn–D P Csn–A
44	F	21	18	59 M(45)	49	S32 MD(17) B20 B1	0	M GrF–A P Un–A P Un–A P Csn–A
45	F	31	23	50+	54	B37 B32 B27 B23 B22 S25	0	P GrM–D P Un–A P Un–Soc M Au–D

Continued.

(All-sources data)—cont'd

No.	Sex	Age on admission	Age of onset	Father	Mother	Siblings	Children	Extended family
46	F	73	66	61+	78+	S71 D(65) B70	d45	P Au–MD P GrF–C–G
47	M	67	53	48+ A, Su	84+ D(60)	S61 B25 S58 Undx B55 Pos. AN	s41 AN	M Un–MD M Un–A M Csn–MD M Csn–D P Csn–A
48	F	63	33	65+	85 MD(20)	B60	s38+ A d43 s1+ R	M Csn–MD
49	M	45	44	72	72	S42	d15	M GrF–D
50	F	39	28	77	64 D(41)	B37 AN	0	M GrM–D M Un–R
51	M	19	16	43	42 M(?)	B12	0	M GrF–MD M Un–Su? M GrUn–A P Un–A P GrF–A P GtGrF–A P Csn–A P Csn–A
52	F	17	17	43+ D	40	B20 S16 S15 S14 S13 S11 S19	0	M GrF–A M GrUn–D M Un–A P GrM–A P GrUn–Undx
53	M	39	28	74+	77 D(67)	S53 B43 B48 B46 D(?) S2+ S4+ (FT)	s16 Enur s12 Enur s7	M GrM–D M GrF–A M GtGrF–A M Csn–R

No.	Sex	Age	Age			Codes		Diagnoses
54	F	37	29	65	38+	B44 B31 B28 B30 B35 D(31) S47 MD(35) S44 MD(43) S33 D(28) S40 Ep	s14 d12 d10 s8 d4	M Csn-R M Csn-R M Csn-R P GrF-Encephalitis 0
55	M	21	21	50+ A, Su	52	B17 S14	0	P Csn-R
56	M	34	25	59	60 D(59)	B30 B35	d11	M Au-Ep M GrUn-MD M GrUn-A P GrF-Su P GrUn-Su P GrUn-Undx P Au-D
57	M	54	53	61+ A	36+	1/2S45	s31 s30 s16 s12	M GrF-D M Csn-Su
58	F	56	35	57+	79 D(54)	S54 S49 B43 B42 A	0	0
59	M	54	36	72+ A	78 CBS	S58 D(39) S55 MD(19) S51 D(30)	d20	P Un-A P GrM-D, Undx
60	M	69	39	77+	95+	S67	0	P Un-GPI M Csn-D M Au-D M Au-D
61	F	25	16	55 D, Drug Abuse (50)	47+	B24 Soc S20 B12	0	M Un-A

Appendix **C**

Two case abstracts of manic probands

Following are two case abstracts of manic probands that serve to illustrate the quality of the illness and course. The case numbers refer to those in Appendix B.

No. 30 is a 25-year-old single white secretary who first became ill at 19 years of age. Her illness at that time was dominated by depressive features and she responded well to 20 insulin subcoma treatments. She remained well during the subsequent 12 months and was then readmitted to the hospital in such an agitated state that cold sheet packs were necessary to calm her down. She received a second course of insulin subcoma therapy and this was followed with ECT because her symptoms failed to remit.

The patient was discharged as improved following the episode; however, since that time she has never been completely well. Her symptoms have varied from a mild persistent depression, with anergy, insomnia, appetite loss, and difficulty concentrating, to shorter periods of hypomania, with manifest overactivity, extravagance, push of speech, and promiscuity. Her affect during these episodes is euphoric or irritable. Whereas she is passive and dependent while depressed, she becomes aggressive and commanding when hypomanic.

During the past 5 years this patient has had an additional six hospitalizations, the longest being 6 months (index admission was fourth admission). On two occasions, depression has been the major problem and the remaining four admissions have been for primarily manic behavior, although she frequently has depressed days or even weeks during her manias. On at least three occasions her manic episodes were preceded by depressive episodes or by a worsening of her chronically depressed state. Most frequently she has been managed on a combination of phenothiazines, antidepressants, and supportive psychotherapy for her unstable moods, both high and low.

One interesting feature of this case is a change in sexual orientation, which occurs when this patient is manic or hypomanic. Whereas she is usually a staid heterosexual single girl who eschews any interest in promiscuous sexuality, when hypomanic or manic, she becomes promiscuous with both men and women. Indeed one of the early signs of a developing hypomania is a love letter to her social worker.

As a consequence of her persistent illness and frequent hospitalizations, this patient has not been able to return to college and has held a great number of jobs, usually secretarial. Her performance when she is able to work is adequate.

176

PREMORBID PERSONALITY

The adolescent years prior to the onset of the illness were ones of "normal activity" and effort. The patient was a mediocre student and had boyfriends but no sexual intercourse. Her homelife was described as harmonious, in spite of her mother's depressive illness. The patient recalls rather severe premenstrual tension as part of her adolescence. Her family describes her as always having high and low moods.

FAMILY HISTORY

The patient's father is 63 years old and has been a compulsive gambler all his life. The early life of the patient was marked by marital strife as a consequence of the father's gambling; when the patient was 5 years old, her parents were divorced. Her father left the family a reasonable economic settlement.

The patient has a fraternal twin brother who has never been ill. He is an energetic and successful student who is working toward a graduate degree.

There are two older sisters, who are described as placid and stable.

The patient's mother, now 61 years old, had the onset of an episodic affective psychosis at the age of 48 years and has had approximately five episodes treated in a hospital with EST. Her recovery is "complete"; however, it appears that some symptoms do persist: insomnia, anxiety, pessimism. The mother has never had a mania. She is described by the family as a "rock" and appears rigid and unyielding as regards the patient's illness.

MENTAL STATUS

This patient's appearance and demeanor vary markedly according to her mood. She appears as a shy, withdrawn, quiet, very proper "young lady" when depressed; and as an aggressive, seductive, rather brightly attired, urbane girl-about-town when hypomanic. She has some insight into the variation of her life style according to mood, and even though she has had a long period without complete remission, she has not developed the autism, thought disorder, and social withdrawal characteristic of schizophrenia.

No. 41 is an 18-year-old white male student who has admitted to a neuropsychiatric facility for the first time in June 1966 (index episode). At that time he was hyperactive, euphoric, and grandiose and had a flight of ideas. His family described a 2-week period of intense "writing" of a musical comedy during which he ate little and slept 3 to 4 hours per night. He was expansive and expressed fleeting delusions of being a famous writer of musical comedies.

His hospitalization lasted 6 weeks, and on discharge he was calm and rational. No symptoms of either mania or depression were noted. Treatment in the hospital had consisted of varying doses of phenothiazines in response to fluctuating symptoms, and he was discharged on medication. During several days in the hospital he was also noted to be "severely depressed" although these periods did not last more than 1 day.

The patient's mood was unstable at home, and for the next 12 months he was admitted to the hospital five times. The duration of these hospitalizations varied from 2 weeks to 3 months. For his manias the patient has been given drug therapy, usually with a good response. However, on one occasion he was treated with adequate doses of lithium carbonate (blood level was over 1 mEq. per liter for several days) and obtained no relief of the symptoms. During the short periods of time between hospitalizations the patient was noted to be "high" or "low" but never "normal." Since his last hospitalization (March 1967) the patient has had one period of 6 months during which he was considered by himself, his family, and his physician to be normal. However, on at least three occasions he has had brief (2- to 4-week) periods of hypomanic behavior marked by hyperactivity, grandiosity, extravagance, and increased sexuality. The "theme" of all his manic or hypomanic episodes has been similar; each time he has the intention to become or the idea that he has become a famous composer of musical comedy.

During most of the 24 months following his hospitalization he has suffered a low-grade "depression" marked by insomnia, feelings of inadequacy, and difficulty concentrating.

Currently he is attending college and takes phenothiazines when necessary for initial insomnia. He has missed the first semester of this academic year as a consequence of a brief hypomanic episode.

PREMORBID PERSONALITY

The patient was born of a normal pregnancy and delivery. His development and early years were considered normal. He was an extremely energetic and successful student, and his energy was remarked upon by his family and teachers. His parents describe his premorbid personality as moody with both "highs" and "lows." A list of his activities prior to the onset of his illness reveals a very successful and active student, i.e., "Most likely to succeed." In addition to being in an accelerated academic program 1 year ahead of his peers, the patient was vice president of the student council, editor of the school newspaper and literary magazine, chairman of the student scholarship fund and cultural committee, and writer of the school musical comedy. His grades were generally A's, and he was on the honor roll during the five semesters prior to the onset of his illness. Following his final hospitalization the patient was class valedictorian.

FAMILY HISTORY

The patient's father is now 41 years old and a pathologically heavy drinker. He is a most successful businessman whose problems with alcohol are medical and marital. The patient's mother is now 41 and has suffered an episodic depressive syndrome (age 25 and 30 years). She was hospitalized for psychiatric treatment on one occasion. There is a sister 2 years younger than the patient who is cyclothymic, although not as much as the patient.

MENTAL STATUS

During interviews with this patient it becomes apparent that the style and content of his personality vary according to his mood. When depressed, he is quiet, cynical, and insecure; when hypomanic he is aggressive, flamboyant, garrulous, and ambitious. There is no evidence of a formal thought disorder. The patient presents a warm affect and has good empathy with the interviewer.

Glossary

All-sources material Material obtained by studying records, obtaining family histories, and interviewing family members about themselves.

Association When two genetically separate traits have a nonrandom occurrence in a population; this is probably most likely explained by pleiotropic effects of a single gene.

Bipolar psychosis Illness in which both manias and depressions occur.

Depressive disease Primary affective disorder in which only depressive episodes are seen.

Family history material Material gleaned by talking to a family member about various other family members.

Family-study material Material obtained by interviewing a specific family member about himself.

Incidence Number of new cases in a particular population during a specific period of time.

Linkage (of two genes or two gene loci) When two genes, each responsible for a separate trait, are close enough on the chromosome that they assort in a dependent fashion.

Manic depressive disease Primary affective disorder in which mania is seen; usually, but not always, depression is also seen in this kind of patient.

Monopolar psychosis Essentially synonymous with unipolar psychosis, it refers to affective illnesses that are primary in nature and in which only depressions occur.

Morbidity risk (or disease expectancy) Estimate of the probability that an individual will develop an illness at some time or another during his life if he survives the period of risk (manifestation period) for the illness.

Prevalence Number of cases alive in the population at a certain point in time (point prevalence) or during a period of time (period prevalence).

Primary affective disorder Illness characterized by depressions or manias, or both, seen in an individual who lacks a history of preexisting psychiatric illness exclusive of uncomplicated episodes of depression or mania.

Proband (index case) Subject with whom the research has started; in the present study manic probands were found, and this led to their families being investigated.

Risk period Time in the life of a patient during which a specific illness may manifest itself; varies in different diseases.

Secondary affective disorder Depression seen in patients in whom another psychiatric illness (hysteria, anxiety neurosis, alcoholism, etc.) has existed prior to the affective symptoms.

Unipolar psychosis Illness that is primarily affective in its manifestation and exhibits only depression; more specifically, as defined by Perris, it refers to an illness in which three or more depressions occur without any evidence of mania.

Index